T0015559

PRAISE FOR *THE ANSWER IS YOU*

"At a time when we could not be in greater need of systems that prioritize our shared humanity, Alex makes the difficult work of social change accessible to all. An important read for those on the journey of making this world better and wondering where to start."

—**Jacqueline Novogratz,** founder and CEO of Acumen, author of *New York Times* bestsellers *The Blue Sweater: Bridging the Gap between Rich and Poor* and *Manifesto for a Moral Revolution: Practices to Build a Better World*

"*The Answer Is You* is a powerful reminder we all have a superpower that can catalyze beautiful and needful change on this planet. Whether it's through one's career, volunteering in one's community, or joining a giving circle, it's our responsibility to identify our unique superpower and use it to heal ourselves, our communities, and our Mother Earth."

—**Edgar Villanueva,** author of *Decolonizing Wealth: Indigenous Wisdom to Heal Divides and Restore Balance*, activist, and philanthropist

"In *The Answer is You*, Alex Amouyel asks each of us to get in the game and stay the course in addressing some of the world's biggest challenges, such as climate change and rising inequality. This inspiring read will help you on your journey to find the problem you care about and just start solving for it."

—**Linda Pizzuti Henry,** CEO of the *Boston Globe*

"With *The Answer Is You*, Alex Amouyel brings her fifteen years of experience working in social impact to help everyone reflect on the problems that really matter, their own superpowers, and the actions they can take to create a life full of impact. Read this book—and learn from her as well as an impressive and diverse array of social entrepreneurs, innovators, and activists whose stories will wow and inspire you. Everyone has a role to play in improving the world, and Alex shows us that the time to start living your purpose is now."

—**Jeremy Heimans,** cofounder and CEO of Purpose, as well as coauthor of *New Power: How Power Works in Our Hyperconnected World—and How to Make It Work for You*

THE ANSWER IS

THE ANSWER IS

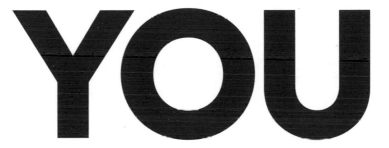

YOU

A GUIDEBOOK TO CREATING
A LIFE FULL OF IMPACT

ALEX AMOUYEL

mango
PUBLISHING GROUP

CORAL GABLES

Cover Design: Morgane Leoni
Art Direction: Morgane Leoni
Layout & Design: Megan Werner
Author Photo: Tony Luong

For permission requests, please contact the publisher at:
Mango Publishing Group
2850 S Douglas Road, 4th Floor
Coral Gables, FL 33134 USA
info@mango.bz

For special orders, quantity sales, course adoptions and corporate sales, please email the publisher at sales@mango.bz. For trade and wholesale sales, please contact Ingram Publisher Services at customer.service@ingramcontent.com or +1.800.509.4887.

The Answer Is You: A Guidebook to Creating a Life Full of Impact

Library of Congress Cataloging-in-Publication number: 2021951872
ISBN: (p) 978-1-64250-721-8, (e) 978-1-64250-722-5
BISAC category code: SOC033000, SOCIAL SCIENCE / Philanthropy & Charity

Printed in the United States of America

DEDICATION & DONATION

For my nephew, Alistair Galileo Pierre Amouyel, born on November 24, 2020, during a pandemic—like this book. You are our future.

Good news! By buying this book, you are already giving back. Fifty percent of the net profits I make from the sales of this book will be donated to Solve Innovation Future, the philanthropic venture arm of Solve which invests in our Solver teams, and to other great organizations solving world challenges such as the ones you will read about in this book. See more info here: solve.mit.edu/drive-investments-to-solver-teams

"How wonderful it is that nobody need wait a single moment before starting to improve the world."

—*Anne Frank, age thirteen, hiding from the Nazis, in* The Diary of Anne Frank, *1947*

"The only way you're going to stay the course is to make sure the problem you're trying to solve brings you alive. And to solve that problem, you owe it to yourself just to start. Everything you need to know you will learn on the job. It's really critical to do important work in the world."

—*Temie Giwa-Tubosun of LifeBank, Lagos, Nigeria, 2020*

TABLE OF CONTENTS

PROLOGUE

The geeks among you will fondly remember *The Hitchhiker's Guide to the Galaxy* and the supercomputer that takes millions of years to come up with the Answer to the Ultimate Question of Life, the Universe, and Everything. After all that time, the supercomputer's answer is...

42.

What does that mean?!

Then, humans realize there was a fatal flaw in the whole endeavor: What was the Question to begin with?

Full disclosure, I am not a supercomputer—though soon enough, artificial intelligence may be able to write books, if it does not already possess that ability. Nor do I have access to one. While my workplace, MIT, has a whole bunch of the most advanced supercomputers, they are otherwise occupied on genomics, COVID-19 research, and other pressing matters.

However, if I may be so bold, I do have *an* Answer to *a* Question I think is one of the Ultimate Questions of Life, the Universe, and Everything (if not *the one*).

The Question is: *How can we solve the big, intractable challenges of our time, such as pandemics, climate change, and inequity and injustice?*

The Answer is *You.*

You may not always know it, but you have the power to do good and change the unfair systems this world is built upon.

In fact, you have the duty and obligation to do so. If the pandemic has convinced me of one thing, it's that the world cannot wait.

Now more than ever, we need you, and everyone else, to take action to solve world challenges. Whoever you are, wherever you come from, we need your skills, your time, and your money. We need your talent, creativity, ingenuity, superpowers, and hard work.

At this time, more than ever before, we are forced to consider how we've built this world; how we want to spend our waking hours when we have the privilege to have that choice; and what our purpose truly is, both at an individual and collective level.

Whether we intended to or not, we have built a world that may be better than it was a century ago for a lucky few, but that still does not work for billions of people. It is a world still rife with exploitation, extraction, oppression, inequality, and injustice. There are more slaves today than at any other point in history (one in every two hundred people), and we still seem to be doing our worst to ensure we heat this planet up past the point of no return as quickly as possible.

In addition to the current global pandemic, jobs and small businesses are disappearing, financial insecurity and income inequality keep increasing, millions of children are out of school, and we have centuries of racial injustice to continue to contend with. Though these challenges all predate the pandemic, they have been exacerbated at both global and community levels, and it is of greatest urgency that we deal with them today.

To tackle these challenges, we need everyone. As Megan Smith, the United States Chief Technology Officer under President Obama, likes to say: "If we include everyone, we can solve everything."

In the midst of all of this mess, many of you are already stepping up and getting in the game to help change its unfair rules. People young and old, especially Millennials and Gen Zers, already want to do a great deal more than continuing to accumulate travel photos on Instagram. They want to lead lives of purpose.

When I first had the idea to write this book, I thought I would need to make the case for why you need to get into the social impact game. But in the interim, the pandemic and the renewed Black Lives Matter movement have shown me that most of you already know that. From all walks of life, you are yearning to do something: You are joining protests, donating dollars, boycotting brands, bringing food to frontline health workers, and more. But that alone is not enough, and you want to do more, even though the enormity and complexity of the challenges we face can feel frustrating and confusing.

As we struggle to come to terms with how profoundly this pandemic has changed our lives and our futures, it can be hard to find the energy to fight back against inequity and oppression. Some days, it can be hard just to get out of bed. But everyone can do something with the skills and resources they already have; it just takes a blueprint to get started on creating and living a life full of impact.

In this book, I will tell the stories of "ordinary people doing extraordinary things" (a line President Biden used on the day of his inauguration during the "Celebrating America" evening event). You've likely heard about Malala and Greta, but there are so many more impact innovators and changemakers whose stories you may never have encountered. Those are the ones whose lives you will read about here.

Perhaps these changemakers are the future Mandelas and Gandhis. Above all, they are people who by and large did not start out any differently than you or me. In fact, many started with far less. But they decided to get started anyway—to solve a problem—and did so slowly but surely, working day in, day out, with their blood, sweat, and tears to improve their community, their country, and the world.

I hope the stories of these problem-solvers will serve as a guide for how *you* can use your unique skills and resources—your own superpowers—to enact change. Throughout, I will overlay advice and frameworks I have found helpful in thinking about my own impact journey. You'll also get the inside track on the social impact space and learn how to carve out your own spot in it.

I hope to inspire you to start thinking critically about the problems we face and the solutions you might be able to offer. After reading this book, I hope you come away with a sense of optimism about how you might take action in ways both big and small. This isn't to say that creating a life full of impact will be an easy journey; yet it will be a rewarding and most necessary one.

Now more than ever, this is an invitation to begin (or continue) the hard work of repairing the world and to forge a path for hope and action. There is not a moment to spare.

Throughout the book and to illustrate each chapter, you will be introduced to many incredible problem-solvers. I start with Amanda's story; unlike the others, you will follow her story in between each chapter as a through-line to the book.

AMANDA'S INJUSTICE

When she left the hospital that day, Amanda Nguyen recalls, "I'd never fully understood the definition of lonely until that moment."

Amanda didn't start out wanting to be an activist. Far from it: she calls herself a "super nerd" and studied government and astrophysics in college. But the life and future prospects of this daughter of two Vietnamese refugees changed dramatically when she was raped in her final semester at Harvard—a trauma inflicted each year on 1.3 billion people worldwide (mostly on women and transgender people).

Today, the organization Amanda founded, Rise Justice Labs, promotes access to democracy and equal rights under the law for everyone. She observes, "I cared about these issues before, but I had no idea what survivors actually have to go through until I had to walk the Kafkaesque labyrinth myself. That's really how I got started—when I realized my story was not only my own."

In the wake of the attack, Amanda spent six hours at the hospital for medical staff to perform her rape kit exam. The crime scene was her body: "Most people don't know it takes three to seven hours, because it's both lifesaving medical attention and forensic evidence for the case."

After the hospital, she made her way to the local rape crisis center, where there weren't enough seats in the waiting room.

Amanda dreamt of one day becoming an astronaut and had already lined up a great first step after graduation, a position at NASA in the Obama administration's final years in DC. But when she spoke with a pro bono legal service for survivors of sexual assault, they told her that rape trials take up to three years on average. If she wanted to go forward, they advised that the case would take over her life for at least the next two years.

She had to make an agonizing choice between starting her career and seeking justice. While she wanted both, she chose her career for the short term with the knowledge that she had fifteen years in Massachusetts before the statute of limitations ran out for reporting the crime and filing charges against the perpetrator.

However, Amanda was shocked to discover that her rape kit would be destroyed after six months unless she petitioned the state for an extension. It would not even be tested, despite the fifteen-year statute of limitations! When she asked to be able to hold onto her rape kit for the length of the statutory limit, she was told there was no procedure in place for this.

Double standards abounded. For example, a convicted rapist had the right to hold on to the evidence for the duration of his conviction, but the survivor of the crime did not. This routine destruction of untested evidence was unique to the crime of rape—something Amanda found absurd, given the number of cold cases, including murders, that are solved each year because the police held onto evidence for decades that later yielded DNA.

Petitioning for an extension was a costly affair she had to undertake every six months, and it only served to remind her of the trauma. The unfairness of all this struck her as a bureaucratic loophole with "a massive, massive impact on someone's life."

"The Massachusetts criminal justice system was a game that was not set up for survivors." When Amanda considered the fact that she had many more resources than a great number of other survivors of sexual assault, she decided she had no choice but to rewrite the law. And with help from other survivors and allies, that is what she ended up doing. You will find out more as her story unfolds throughout this book.

Build Your Seat at the Problem-Solving Table

> "Everybody should have a place at
> the problem-solving table."
>
> —Rafael Reif, President of the Massachusetts Institute
> of Technology, speaking at Solve at MIT in 2017.

Thousands of applicants, hundreds of reviewers and judges, sixty finalists, and thirty-plus Solver teams selected every year, with over fifty million dollars in funding to date for social innovators across the globe—that is MIT Solve!

In 2016, I got an irresistible offer from the Massachusetts Institute of Technology (MIT), perhaps the leading tech and innovation engine in the world; I was asked to be the founding executive director of their new initiative. Solve's mission is to drive innovation to solve world challenges. It does so with the belief that anyone can be a problem-solver, and that in fact, everyone should be—each in their own way.

Solve focuses specifically on impact innovators: We find, fund, and support early-stage tech-based social entrepreneurs who are tackling the world's most pressing challenges, ranging from how we can extract carbon from the atmosphere to how we can educate refugees, reduce maternal mortality, dismantle systems of oppression that create and exacerbate racial inequities, and prepare for infectious outbreaks to keep them from becoming pandemics.

It's through Solve that I first met Amanda, albeit virtually, given that she was selected as an Elevate Prize winner in the fall of 2020. In addition to seeing more of her story, you will also hear from many other everyday innovators and problem-solvers within each chapter. My hope is that their stories, together with my advice interspersed throughout, will help and inspire you to get started or continue on your own impact journey.

How do you live a life full of genuinely positive social and environmental impact?

How do you play your part to bend the arc of humanity toward justice?

How do you move the needle at least a little to change systems that have created a world still rife with exploitation, extraction, and oppression for too many?

The Answer is *You*. We need you to claim your seat at the problem-solving table. Actually, we need you to build your own seat; and really, to build a more open, equitable, and just table, too. As Edgar Villanueva says in his book *Decolonizing Wealth*, "It's about building ourselves a whole new table—one where we truly belong."

This book will help you do this, whoever you are, whether you are just starting out your career, halfway through it, or even in retirement. It's never too early or too late to get started doing good in the world.

But before we begin, let me tell you a little bit about who I am and how I built my seat at the problem-solving table. It's important to be clear from the outset about the genesis of my purpose, superpowers, and shortcomings.

But First, a Little Bit About Me

From a very young age, I wanted to devote my life to doing good in the world. I recognize that this is partly because of privilege. I grew up in Paris, a millennial in an upper-middle class family of people with lots of graduate degrees, and I attended an international school with classmates from all around the world—there were students from Syria, Lebanon, Korea, Senegal, and more.

My basic needs were always met, yet money was conversely not so plentiful as to corrupt my ideals. As a result, I've never felt the need to accumulate as many dollars as I could, nor have I felt this was a good measure of success in life.

At the same time, I am the daughter and the granddaughter of refugees. My father is French; born in Algeria, he never saw the land of his birth after the war of decolonization ended in 1962. My maternal grandmother, who is Russian of Jewish origin, was born in 1920 just after the Russian Revolution and left the Soviet Union as an infant to escape both Communism and anti-Semitism, only to settle in Berlin a few years before the Nazis took power.

Unlike many, her family managed to escape Berlin and Europe; they fled to Palestine, where she met a British army officer who was to become my grandfather. When I hear of a young Syrian woman crossing the Mediterranean to escape war and ISIS in her country, it reminds me of my grandmother seventy-five years ago, though she was traveling in the other direction.

In a sense, both my privilege and my heritage have shaped my desire—and even presented me with an unavoidable obligation—to devote my full potential to making a positive impact on the world, given that unlike so many, I have a choice as to how I spend my waking hours.

At ten, I wanted to be a prosecutor and put bad people in prison. I watched quite a bit of TV at the time (cue the soundtrack of *Law & Order*, but imagine it dubbed in French). But that idea did not stick for too long. At twelve, I wanted to be a scientific researcher to rid the world of cancer, an ambition that carried me through college and on to start a PhD at age twenty at the Laboratory of Molecular Biology in Cambridge, UK—the lab where James Watson and Francis Crick had characterized DNA some fifty years prior.

But I didn't have the temperament for bench lab work, pipetting small quantities of antibodies into tiny test tubes and waiting for gels to run in the hope that after twenty years, the research might produce an insight into the childhood cancer I was studying. Even if it ever did, given that the cancer was so rare, pharmaceutical companies would likely never have an interest in developing a cure. Unable to clearly see the impact of my work on a faster timeframe, or even to know if my work would in fact have any impact at all, I was miserable.

To the dismay of my parents and my lab director, I quit. My father was especially disappointed. I could have won a Nobel Prize in Medicine, he said, betraying his own unfulfilled ambitions.

I was not ready to give up on the idea that I should devote my life to doing good in the world, so I retorted, "Don't worry, they have a Nobel Prize in Peace, too." Yes, I had big ideas and grand ambitions, although at the time, I said it more in defiance than anything else.

After quitting my PhD program, I went to teach English in China for a few months. Still unsure of my next step other than wanting to do good, I applied for a master's program in International Affairs and started a two-year program, splitting my time between France and the UK. Along with my studies, after several stints at student charities, I interned at Amnesty International.

The work was important but soul-crushing. Tasks included filling out a Microsoft Access database of all the people killed during the Sri Lankan conflict, for example. I could not see myself in this role, either, and regardless, there was no paying job available.

I applied to Human Rights Watch, Save the Children, and countless other organizations I admired in the social impact space. None even granted me an interview.

Unable to find a full-time paying job in social impact, I joined a management consulting firm, the Boston Consulting Group, like so many of my ambitious peers who lacked a clear sense of purpose. As a colleague loved saying, no one grows up wanting to be a management consultant. After eighteen months learning a great many business concepts and how to move boxes around on PowerPoint (which did turn out to be pretty useful), I was lucky enough to be assigned a pro bono project with none other than Save the Children, one of my favorite nonprofits!

A few months after that, no doubt thanks to my beguiling PowerPoint box-moving skills, I was offered a chance to join Save the Children full-time. There, I got to work as an internal consultant and travel from my home in London to various "Country Offices" around the world in Pakistan, North Korea, Haiti, Lebanon, Jordan, and Cambodia, among many others.

After a few years there, feeling a little downtrodden from living out of suitcases in countries marked "red" on Save the Children's security map, I relocated to New York to work at the Clinton Global Initiative (CGI). After some time there, I became the Director of Programs and had the opportunity to interact with some of the foremost social impact leaders of our time.

At CGI, the people who intrigued me the most were not necessarily the myriad heads of state, CEOs, philanthropists, and celebrities who graced our stage and greenroom. They were of course impressive, and there were both fun and absurd moments (ones I doubt I'll ever experience again). I once cried my eyes out while curled up hiding under a table backstage during President Obama's speech in 2015 because a senior production crew member had yelled at me for not forcibly removing Matt Damon from the stage in time, with the result that President Obama had to wait backstage for a total of two minutes—an eternity for a sitting US president!

Overall, though, I was most fascinated by the less well-known entrepreneurs, activists, and artists from Pakistan, Sudan, Somalia, and Vanuatu—those without fame, fortune, or power who had devoted their lives to doing good in their communities, and slowly but surely, making a difference in the world.

Dr. Raj Panjabi of Last Mile Health trained community healthcare workers in rural Liberia at the height of the Ebola crisis; Khalida Brohi fought to empower women and stop honor killings in Pakistan; and Sonita Alizadeh, an Afghan teenage girl, rapped about forced marriage in a musical expression of the lived reality of girls and women.

I would tell my team that a plenary would be successful if the audience turned up to see Jon Bon Jovi perform but left remembering only what someone like Yazidi activist Nadia Murad said on CGI's stage in 2016—someone likely unknown to the audience before they had come in an hour earlier. (Nadia went on to become the Nobel Peace Prize winner in 2018, advocating for survivors of sexual violence.)

Though my time at CGI deeply formed my impression of the key challenges facing the world today and introduced me to inspiring people working tirelessly to confront global issues, it also came with paradoxes. While we were helping big corporations, governments, and foundations move millions and billions of dollars into social impact programs, during our climate plenary, the executives of large fossil fuel corporations were seated in our front row as sponsors. And while I strongly believe CGI pioneered public-private partnerships and impact investing, there was still something missing.

While CGI focused on big cross-sector partnerships between existing institutions, MIT's goal in launching Solve was to focus on social entrepreneurs and impact innovators—the very people I was most interested in. Although everyone at MIT who interviewed me presented a slightly different version of what Solve could or should be, MIT had enough resources, ambition, intelligence, and commitment to do something meaningful to support these impact innovators.

Perhaps most importantly, my vision of what was missing in today's world was fully aligned with MIT's vision. Their faculty members had helped put a man on the moon and create the internet, and they had won countless Nobel Prizes.

This felt like a place to pull off the biggest of ambitions: to harness the talent and ingenuity of incredible innovators all around the planet, and to help them solve the world's great challenges. I was in.

And through all of this, I discovered something quite simple: The Answer is *You*. We need all of you.

Let's Start with the Many Contradictions of the Social Impact Space

The social impact sphere I have been part of for over fifteen years is a messy conglomerate of organizations and people who portray themselves as the do-gooders who have all the answers if you give them the money. It's also full of unintelligible jargon, buzzwords, acronyms, confusion, and hypocrisy.

First, there are the well-known players: international NGOs with a savior complex who fly in after a disaster and fly out almost as fast as they came; then, the governments of rich countries or the so-called "Global North," who care more about short-term reelection cycles and lobbyists than investing in long-term solutions that would support real equity and opportunity for all, and who dole out international aid as a continued form of colonialism. You also have bureaucratic and shambolic multilateral institutions that never seem to have funding to deploy actual programs on the ground, but host colloquiums and write white papers, as though these make a difference.

Corporations have also stepped into the fray: they understand that their customers and employees care about social and environmental impact, but they put their corporate social responsibility department under marketing in their hierarchies, because fundamentally, to them, it's all about brand perception. Lest we forget, there are the foundations named after oil tycoons, who have greenwashed their reputation by funding museums in the most expensive zip codes and who do not accept unsolicited applications—meaning you have to play polo with someone in their organization before you can even apply for a grant.

The most recent additions to these do-gooders are the techno-utopian Silicon Valley entrepreneurs who made their money after getting us addicted to "likes" and therefore think they are smarter than we are. They believe they can hack the problems of this world with an app or two, or perhaps with their newest holy grail: a crypto fund.

These are caricatures, of course, but despite these, there are many good groups and individuals doing really critical work. But these caricatures also have some elements of truth, especially when it comes to the slacktivists, cause adopters, and optical allies who co-opt the language of impact until it is reduced to token gestures.

All of these people, good, bad, and in between, would come together at big conferences prior to the pandemic. And let's be clear, I orchestrated a goodly number of those myself, where everyone drinks champagne in ballrooms while talking about the plight of refugees, without anyone with the lived experience of a refugee in sight.

It's no wonder we're not making good enough or fast enough progress on climate change, inequality, and injustice, with this gigantic soup of muddled interests focused mainly on short-term thinking, much of which actually aligns with maintaining existing power structures and the oppressive status quo.

What Gives Me Hope in the Face of All of This?

The Answer is *You.*

Sydney Gressel, a pediatric nurse at the University of California medical center in San Francisco, was asked by her friends how they could help her and her colleagues on the frontlines of the COVID-19 crisis back in March 2020.

She answered, "Pizza."

Initially, the idea was to boost morale, but when shelter-in-place orders were enacted and restaurants throughout the city closed, medical staff could no longer step out to grab food nearby. Sydney's friends realized that two problems brought about by COVID-19 could be tackled through a single program: if restaurants could prepare meals for healthcare workers using money given to them through donations from the community, this would put them back in business and keep their kitchens open while also providing workers on the frontlines with the fuel they needed.

That idea became Frontline Foods, and chapters quickly sprang up all over the US. Even with a global pandemic and its permeating feeling of hopelessness, you don't always need a lot of money or tech like AI, VR, and robots to do good in the world. Pizza can be a tool for good, even if it's obviously not the whole answer.

Sydney and Amanda are not alone in wanting to make a difference. In fact, among Millennials and Gen Zers—the generations born from 1982 onwards—they are the majority, sometimes perhaps the silent ones. I call them the problem-solving generation. Survey after survey shows that members of these generations care about social and environmental causes; what many of them want is to lead lives of purpose, work for employers who reflect their values, and devote their studies and careers to being of service.

In increasing numbers, both Millennials and Gen Zers lack trust in traditional institutions. For example, the 2020 Edelman Trust Barometer reported that "despite a strong global economy and near full employment, none of the four societal institutions that the study measures—government, business, NGOs, and media—is trusted. The cause of this paradox can be found in people's fears about the future and their role in it."

According to the Deloitte 2019 Global Millennial Survey, this creates "a generation disrupted," with 41 percent lacking trust in political leaders and 49 percent lacking trust in religious leaders. With a widespread sense that traditional institutions and organizations are not able to respond and solve the challenges of the twenty-first century, we need new players to rise up.

It's up to all of us—up to you!—to change the world for the better. It's about building your own seat, not to mention a new problem-solving table, and using all the powers you have available to improve our collective situation. You have more power than you think to enact change.

The good news is that the problem-solving generation is not bound by profession or age, but by a desire to devote one's life to doing good. Perhaps every generation has had these people in their midst, but my hope is that we can now shift and enshrine problem solving and positive impact as the norm for everyone.

Consider Roya Mahboob, who has been educating Afghan women to become entrepreneurs through digital literacy and community building. Miranda Wang is using bacteria and biochemistry to recycle previously unrecyclable plastics. Rajesh Anandan is employing people on the autism spectrum as quality engineers to create a fairer workplace for all.

These impact innovators are on the front lines of the big issues facing humanity today. Sometimes we don't look deeply enough to see them, and often they have to do their work with far fewer resources than they need, but they persevere and work tirelessly to solve problems facing their community and the world.

Dispelling Some Myths

Let's be clear—there is no easy answer or magic wand I can wave to show you how to become the next Greta Thunberg, or the next social entrepreneur hero with their own TED talk. In fact, I would not advise you to see that as an outcome to be desired. My aim with this book is not to create more "heroes," but rather to help you chart your own impact journey and work with others to effect change.

There are many myths I hope to dispel here, including these:

- The problems are too big, and I am but one person; what I do does not matter.
- I have to work for a nonprofit to have an impact, and all for-profit organizations are bad.

- I can only have an impact through my job.

- If I do take a social impact job, I will barely earn any money, certainly not enough to take care of my family and live a comfortable life.

Instead, what you will hear from me and everyday problem-solvers is that what you do matters. You can have an impact working at a for-profit company or a nonprofit, and you can have an impact outside your job, too—in fact, that's where most people start.

Let's begin by busting the first myth: "But I am just one person, how can I change the world? How are my actions not just token gestures to make me feel better, an insignificant drop in a leaky bucket?"

"Yes, there are incredible people like Mahatma Gandhi, Rosa Parks, or Nelson Mandela, but I am not them."

So why does your contribution matter? Why even get started?

First, you need to get started, because you really have no choice anymore. You, your (future) kids, and the rest of the world cannot wait. The global challenges we face, exacerbated by the coronavirus pandemic, are too urgent and acute. You cannot leave them to the next generation, as earlier generations so conveniently did.

In many parts of the world, the idea that your children would be better off than you were has seemed like a given. But in the US today, wages for the middle class have stagnated for decades, and even before the pandemic, life expectancy for American men was actually going down. Additionally, it seems clear that our world's oceans, air, forests, and biodiversity are all in imminent danger.

While billions of people have escaped extreme poverty in recent decades (using the United Nations and World Bank's definition of extreme poverty as living on less than two dollars a day), the large majority of people in the world still have little choice when it comes to what they do with their waking hours. When you yourself have that choice with at least some of your time, you have the opportunity to do good, and you therefore have an obligation to step up.

Climate activist Greta Thunberg articulates the gravity of our collective situation: "We need everyone to push from every possible angle in the right direction... You don't really have a choice if you understand the urgency."

The second reason to take action as if you will be able to make a difference is this hard truth: as per 1960s civil rights activist Eldrige Cleaver: "You either have to be part of the solution, or you're going to be part of the problem."

You are not a passive bystander. The people you elect, the brands you buy, the companies who benefit from your labor, or the companies you invest in (through your pension, 401K, or brokerage account) are not doing enough; in many cases, they're also causing the problems. The good news is that as an individual, you have agency and power every day in both large and small ways, whether it's through your day job, your side gig, or your purchasing and investment decisions.

The oft-quoted Margaret Mead remains relevant today: "Never doubt that a small group of thoughtful, committed citizens can change the world; indeed, it's the only thing that ever has."

And you are in fact not alone. You, too, can join the generation of people committed to solving world challenges.

The third and final reason is this: purpose is what makes us human. Committing your life to making an impact will make you happier.

As Arthur Brooks, who teaches a course on happiness to MBA students at the Harvard Business School, put it in *The Atlantic*, "Enduring happiness comes from human relationships, productive work, and the transcendental elements of life." He adds that it's not the kind of work you do that matters, "but the sense it gives you that you are earning your success and serving others."

Engage in "Good Trouble"

Living a life full of impact really depends on you—on your hard work, of course, but also on your unique skills and experience. While none of this is easy, it is moral, just, and necessary. And it will become easier and easier when we can collectively agree to change the metric of success.

Our society still defines success in the shallowest of terms: the dollars in your bank account, the house and car you buy, the number of "likes" you get on social media, and perhaps little else. Now is the time to rethink how we define success individually and collectively.

Real and meaningful success is about doing unstinting good in the world, measured against only one metric: a balance sheet of real and positive impact.

It's tempting to adhere to systems of priority that dictate that we emulate the Elon Musks of the world or strive to launch the next Uber. And sure, that path might help build rockets for the 1 percent, so they can relocate to Mars after we've made earth uninhabitable. For too long, we've allowed the titans of Wall Street and Silicon Valley to co-opt the language of impact by falsely telling us that their success is about solving problems that matter, not about their money and privilege.

As you start or continue your impact journey during this unprecedented time when we are witnessing a renewed racial justice movement, keep in mind legendary US Congressman John Lewis's urging to engage in "good trouble." The systems on which we have built this world should enrage you, just as they enraged Greta when she chastised world leaders at the UN in 2019 with her "How Dare You?" speech. Don't let that rage take over and stop you from taking action; instead, use it as fuel to inspire you to take on the impact journey of a lifetime.

Seek to understand why the systems we've set up are unjust for the majority of the planet and how you can change them. Resist the urge to follow the crowd by defining success in terms of the size of your first paycheck.

We need you. We need all hands on deck to solve the enormous systemic challenges affecting the most marginalized communities, instead of the marginal headaches of the most fortunate.

My decade and a half of working in the social impact arena while trying to change it has helped me develop a nuanced approach to how you can become an effective problem-solver, focusing on those problems that actually matter. And while it is my hope that my advice will be of help, I also draw on the journeys of dozens of other problem-solvers from all walks of life so their experience can guide you as well.

How the Book Is Organized

Each chapter is organized around a key step to help you create a life full of impact. Within each chapter, I offer frameworks and provide advice to help guide you, as well as present stories of incredible problem-solvers that illuminate this advice.

"Part I: Problems and Purpose" is all about asking yourself the right questions—those that illuminate your skills, experience, and superpowers, and those about what problems really matter—to help you uncover your purpose.

"Part II: Power and Privilege" asks you to dig even deeper, with the aim of helping you to consider impact as your metric for success across all aspects of your life—job and career, family and relationships, and your giving, investing, and purchasing.

Chapter Six is perhaps the most challenging chapter because it asks you to wrestle with your own shortcomings and privilege, as well as the hypocrisy and shortcomings of the social impact world itself. In order to change the oppressive systems this world is built upon, often you still have to understand and play by the systems' unfair rules to get things done.

Finally, "Part III: Solutions and Grit" helps orient you to think lean and simple when looking for solutions, as well as to measure success, learn from failures, and invest in yourself by adopting what I call the "problem-solving mindset."

It would be convenient to be able to immediately jump right into Part III and solution-making, but this is how many well-meaning attempts at solving problems end up in the graveyard of good intentions. It's of critical importance to take the time to ask yourself the right questions and work to understand both yourself and the systems you are up against before you go off to apply your genius.

But rest assured that you are not alone—you can take comfort that the problem-solving generation is made up of millions like you who want to live a life of impact. You can build on the shoulders of your elders and the innovators whose experiences you will discover here. It's in their stories—and in your own—that the magic lies.

PART I

PROBLEMS AND PURPOSE

AMANDA'S FIGHT

Many people might have been intimidated by the prospect of taking on the government, but to Amanda Nguyen, it was "a no-brainer," given the challenges her Vietnamese refugee parents faced on their path to America. She observes, "I grew up with stories of how freedom isn't free—how you have to fight for it, every inch [tooth] and nail, to hold onto it."

Integral in her decision to work on rewriting laws affecting rape survivors was the notion that as a US citizen, she had the tools to create change. "I was lucky to be born in a country that wouldn't imprison me for speaking out against injustice. In fact, it was founded upon this fabric of pushing for a more perfect union."

For Amanda, the most important element was the mindset that as a US citizen, you have the constitutional right to petition the government for redress, no matter how you may have been gaslit into accepting the status quo. When most people think of walking into the United States Congress, they think of austere halls of cold marble—an unwelcoming prospect. But in fact, those halls are full of public servants that are meant to serve *you*.

But Amanda's perspective was, "This is what we're taught in elementary school, that 'Anyone can become President.' And somehow along the way, we are socialized to forget that." With the current lack of civic education and engagement, this disconnect, Amanda posits, "is on purpose. This ignorance really helps people in the status quo keep their power."

What helped Amanda in her efforts to change federal and state laws governing the rights of rape survivors was the belief that her quest was something much bigger than herself—that history was on her side. She believed, critically, that she had a right to walk the hallowed halls of those state legislatures and the US Congress. As she puts it, "You change the law by believing not only that it's your right to do so, but also that in fact, it's your responsibility."

Amanda clung to the ideals of one of her civil rights role models, Dr. Martin Luther King Jr., who like her, worked to change unjust laws. Though Amanda and her colleagues at Rise Justice Labs strive to raise civic awareness, her activism is not about protesting and shouting except when it's singularly focused on her mission to pass better laws.

Having this "North Star," as she describes it, helped define her strategy. For example, as Dr. Martin Luther King Jr. prepared to cross the Edmund Pettus Bridge the first time, he held off because the press had not yet arrived. He wanted people to see the brutality. It was a strategic decision, and for Amanda, this strategic approach (which I like to call solutions activism) is key.

For Amanda, the first step on her journey to seek justice was understanding how laws are written and who has the power to change them.

CHAPTER ONE

Reveal Your Superpowers

> "Yesterday I was so clever, I wanted to change the
> world. Today I am wise, so I am changing myself."
>
> —*Rumi, Persian poet of the thirteenth century*

Start by Looking into Yourself

What do you need to become a problem-solver? What specific actions can you take to make a positive impact?

Before jumping into the problems or even finding solutions, it's important to first look into yourself.

When we meet innovators and leaders, it is natural to want to bottle their essence, replicate it, and spread it so that we can emulate their success. What makes impact innovators like the ones I met during my time at the Clinton Global Initiative special? This is the wrong question to start off with in the first place.

Margaret Mead answers this well: "Always remember that you are absolutely unique—just like everyone else."

What works for Amanda and other problem-solvers won't necessarily work for you, and it is easy to forget that for many changemakers, success wasn't the result of an extraordinary thought or a moment of inspiration. Rather, it was through years of trials, tribulations, and varied experiences that they acquired a unique set of skills relevant to solving real problems.

There is a question I am asked all the time, by all kinds of people: "How can I get a job in social impact?" or the broader, "I want to do more good in my life and have an impact. What can I do, and where can I start?"

In most cases, when I prod for more detail about what type of role or organization the person may be interested in, I often get vague answers such as "policy," "an NGO," "a foundation," or "something involving human rights." It's like asking someone to be more specific about their desire to work in fashion, but not hearing anything back about what profession within fashion is of interest or what they have to offer to the space. They can't say whether they think they have the skills and temperament to be a model, a fashion designer, a marketer, or a seamstress; whether they want to work for Chanel or for H&M; or whether they want to start something from scratch themselves.

Many people seem to think that a desire to do something good is in itself enough. Clearly, it's not, because these people are not working in social impact (or at least, not yet). So my first piece of advice to anyone who either wants to get into the social impact world as a career or wishes their life in general to have more of a positive impact is to start with this one question: What are my superpowers?

Or to put it in more down-to-earth terms: What unique skills, lived experience, resources, power, and added value can I bring to the problem-solving table?

When I say the Answer is *You*, well, you do have to start with understanding the *You* part first. Don't worry, you don't need to be a superhero to have superpowers—far from it. Everyone has their own superpowers, even if they don't know it yet.

Julia Kumari Drapkin's Story: Making Sense of Our Changing Climate

Solver Julia Kumari Drapkin is the founder and CEO of ISeeChange, a tech company that crowdsources climate data and insights on its platforms and apps. She began her career as a science journalist with a keen interest in sustainability, due at least in part to her upbringing on a barrier island in Florida. In 2011, after a few years covering climate change while living in DC, Julia started to despair that no one seemed to be talking about climate change adaptation, even after yet another billion-dollar disaster year marked by flooding, tornadoes, and strange dust storms.

She observes, "As a reporter, you can only take a story so far if you can't get specifics. Reporting on a flood, I would ask scientists: 'Is this climate change?' They would hedge and get really muddled. It was frustrating. Things are a lot different since then. We've come a long way in our analysis of the severity of the problem."

Even with twenty-first century technology, including social media, satellites, and sensors, the journalistic and scientific analyses of climate change were still too "top-down." She asked herself this question: "What if we created a system where communities can reach halfway up and get to solutions in the middle?"

Julia decided to develop an idea for a bottom-up approach to climate change. As she searched for backing to build her concept into a reality, she applied to the Corporation for Public Broadcasting's program to reinvent

public media and was fortunate enough to be one of ten producers selected. But her application to conduct her research in her new hometown of
New Orleans didn't fly. Instead, she was encouraged to go to a rural town
in western Colorado. Her first impulse was to refuse: "With ten years'
experience, I thought I'd passed that moment in my career." But once
she got over what she calls her "ego moment," she told herself to do the
due diligence. "I called the station managers of the radio stations in this
tiny town. I talked to the people who lived there and then to the climate
scientists I would probably interview."

The spring of 2012 was the warmest ever recorded in the continental
United States. In the Colorado community where the fates had sent
her, Julia discovered (or rather rediscovered) ecological forecasting,
the method by which farmers and ranchers weathered the year-to-year
extremes by writing everything down, including stories that enabled them
to retain a record of their own experiences as a guide. Top-down climate
models created by scientists established baselines, useful reference points
pointing to what the average climate should look like in any given month.
When the actual climate is far off from the baseline—whether it's too
cold, too rainy, too dry, or too hot, a onetime event, or consistently way
off as we have seen in recent years—then the models need to be updated
to reflect the new reality of a changing climate. As Julia sees it, "When
we get further and further away from the baselines' holding, our stories
become the new data."

This was a key moment when Julia started to realize what her own unique
superpower to address this problem was: being able to connect the dots,
which stemmed from her unique collection of experiences throughout
her life and career.

Steve Jobs made a quintessential observation on perspective at the point
when he was looking back over a life marked by unusual twists and turns,
beginning with his having been adopted. As he said in his seminal 2005
Stanford commencement address: "You can't connect the dots looking
forward; you can only connect them looking backward. So you have to

trust that the dots will somehow connect in your future. You have to trust in something—your gut, destiny, life, karma, whatever. This approach has never let me down, and it has made all the difference in my life."

For Julia, the dots were coming together. Growing up, her father, who was fascinated by Mayan culture, had taken her all over Central America. At Tulane in New Orleans, where she received a full scholarship, Julia studied Mayan language, anthropology, and archeology for her undergraduate degree. The ecological forecasting technique used by the farmers in Colorado was similar to methods the Mayans had been using thousands of years ago, as documented in the famed Madrid Codex.

After graduation, and years before that trip to Colorado, Julia spent a summer running an archeological field campaign in the drought corridor in Guatemala, the source of many Central American migrants to the US. The men working with her knew the soil well and saw its exhaustion.

She felt that she was observing something more important than archeology: "As the environment changes, it changes people. Basic! When you think about climate change, that's what we're talking about. But when you saw the migrations north reported in the *New York Times*, there was no mention of drought. There was no mention of the extremes to which people in this community had been pushed. We're just missing the very basic notion that climate change also changes people."

Connecting the dots of both her experiences working with Mayan archeology and with the farmers in Colorado, Julia realized she was uniquely placed to work on a solution. Ecological forecasting and recording become the basis for her platform ISeeChange. Users can take a photo on their phone during a flood event, for example, and weigh in with first-person observations: "I don't remember seeing water on my street, but now I can't get to work."

Julia explains: "You start doing that during every rainstorm and comparing this rainstorm to the last one. Other members of the community are posting data alongside your story and photos. Then you're starting to understand how these events add up. You're getting nuanced information you need to know about what's wrong and how to adapt. The accumulated knowledge makes you a more informed and prepared citizen."

ISeeChange has many interesting applications, both for individuals working to better understand how climate change is affecting their community and for corporations and local governments, such as those of New Orleans, Miami, and Boston. These clients can use ISeeChange to access better and more precise local data to make more informed decisions on climate adaptation measures.

Julia is also interested in the link between climate and conflict. "Human beings are just products of the environment—we're animals. The human body really doesn't have too many ways to adapt to increasing temperatures. Climate change affects every one of our functions: our brains, our bodies and conflict. As we increase temperatures, we see a correlation with increased conflict, [including] personal violence, domestic violence, and murder rates. Understanding that relationship is part of what we hope to do at ISeeChange. 2016 was one of the hottest years on record in the United States. In New Orleans, it was also a record-breaking year. Our AC broke. My husband and I don't fight—but that summer, we fought!"

The challenge of understanding and adapting to climate change is more urgent every year. Julia's story stretches from Florida to Guatemala, then to Colorado and now Louisiana; but through all of this, she built up not only her understanding of the problem, but also her own unique superpowers: connecting the dots and looking for likeness rather than difference. Her upbringing on a Florida barrier island gave her real insight into the effects of climate change on coastal communities. Her education as an archeologist and anthropologist trained her to look for clues in the environment and to engage with people directly affected by the phenomena she wanted to study. And her career as a journalist gave her the ability to listen and bear witness, but also encouraged her belief that citizen journalism could be a solution.

Julia was never worried about fitting in because she never has. As a young woman of Jewish and Sri Lankan ancestry, she rarely met anyone like her growing up in her community in Florida. As she puts it, "In very disparate domains or [when dealing] with very different areas of expertise, I look for ways I belong. My brain is reprogrammed for that. I will go and sit in a group of NASA scientists, and it will take me [no more than] a hot second to figure out what they're talking about." Then as she grapples with the problem, she sees what they share: "It's looking for likeness rather than difference that has really allowed me to plant the seeds of innovation. It's often sitting in a room and not feeling I belong, until I figure out that I do."

So What Makes You Special?

Understanding and auditing your own skills, experience, resources, and power are critical, as idealism and enthusiasm alone are not enough.

Now the good news: not everyone is (or needs to be) a veteran climate journalist like Julia, a multilingual UN policy wonk, a monitoring and evaluation specialist, or a community activist. In fact, the problem-solving table is poorer if it only has these people sitting around it, so let's help you build your own seat.

Whatever your skills and lived experiences, you have a role to play. You can be a software developer and use your skills to work on educational technology (a.k.a. edtech), a lawyer or accountant who either volunteers or works for a nonprofit, or a filmmaker who makes a documentary on one of the impact innovators featured in this book. You could be a nurse like Sydney Gressel, a chef making meals with José Andrés and his World Food Kitchen, or a contractor building affordable community housing— the possibilities are endless.

I was initially a management consultant and then joined Save the Children as an internal consultant working with their "Country Offices" around the world helping to merge their programs; who even knew that such a job existed at a children's nonprofit?

And it is not only about working full-time for an organization or starting one, although those are key approaches to making an impact, given that either would occupy the majority of your waking hours. It's also about what you do in your spare time: where you volunteer and invest your money, what you buy, and how you live. We'll cover how you can create yourImpact Balance Sheet and leverage your powers for good in Chapters Four and Five.

When I talk to people about how they can help, I usually start by suggesting that there are many ways they can support a nonprofit or a social enterprise while still working at their current job or as a student.

Isis Bous's Story: A Lawyer Can Be a Force for Positive Change

As the daughter of two Egyptian engineers who emigrated to America, Isis Bous was given what she calls "three allowable job options: lawyer, doctor, and engineer. Doctor and engineer lost their luster somewhere around calculus for me, so that left me with lawyer." After graduating from law school, she wanted to find a job in international law "to somehow touch back to my roots. I wanted to work in the Middle East."

While still a student, Isis attended a conference in New York City where she heard a compelling speaker named Mark Zaid, an attorney working on national security issues. He was involved in cases like the bombing of Pan Am Flight 103 by Libyan operatives. A lot of his work involved suing governments and holding them to account, whether in the US or abroad.

Isis was particularly impressed by a case involving a diplomat from the Eastern European country of Georgia who killed a seventeen-year-old girl in Dupont Circle in Washington, DC, in a drunk driving incident. Mark ended up successfully stripping the diplomat of his immunity so that the girl's family then had the right to sue both the Georgian diplomat and his country to obtain relief.

After hearing him speak, Isis told a friend from law school, "I'm going to corner this man and I'm going to get an internship."

"I had no idea what I wanted to do, but I was sure he'd let me work for free. And that's what I did. I started working for Mark in my second year of law school."

When she graduated law school, she was able to start working with him full-time. What she learned in that job was crucial to her future career path: she hated appearing in court, where she was intimidated by the formality of a courtroom and feared she would forget something crucial. Instead, she gravitated to "transactional things" like contracts, which she found interesting "because they are like puzzles, where you figure out how to take them apart and put them back together so that they're unbreakable."

Her boss's focus on litigation allowed Isis to carve out her own niche in his firm doing the contract work. But in the wake of 9/11, after which suits involving the US government went nowhere, he lacked enough work to keep her on.

After working for a class-action firm and then for the Middle Eastern Broadcasting Network, Isis wound up quite improbably at the Mortgage Bankers Association right before the financial crisis of 2008, which was caused by poorly regulated sub-prime mortgages. There were a lot of questions as to what exactly the members of the Mortgage Bankers Association had done (or rather not done) to avoid the crisis and the resulting Great Recession.

At that point, Isis decided, "I didn't ever want to be in a position where I felt like I was working for the bad guys. Given everything that was going on, I just didn't want to be in that world anymore. So that was probably where I shifted. I started to freelance and to do a lot of volunteer work."

Isis recognized that the best way she could help was to apply her legal superpowers for good. And while some of you may think the world does not need any more lawyers, believe me, the social impact sector always welcomes them with open arms.

Isis put out feelers in her network. By chance, her kickboxing instructor's girlfriend responded to one of her emails and was able to introduce her to a DC-area social impact incubator. On a volunteer basis, Isis began to support social entrepreneurs (for example, by helping them to incorporate or writing their bylaws). She recalls, "These were the kinds of people I wanted to be working with. These were the organizations I wanted to help."

The work was mostly unpaid except for the odd freelancing contract, but this experience gave Isis the confidence that she could use her legal training in the field of social impact. She took a job at a large charitable organization, which she figured would be perfect: "I thought 'Great, now I'm working for an organization that's doing real good in the world.'"

But though she loved the work, she also discovered the downsides of working for a large bureaucracy: "It's like a government agency in and of itself. You come to realize that even in these huge organizations that are doing amazing work, from the inside out, they can be just as obstinate and difficult."

A couple of years later, she saw a posting for a job at the LexMundi Pro Bono Foundation, whose sole mission is to provide pro bono legal services to social enterprises through its network of over a hundred corporate law firms around the world. Isis realized that this could be her dream assignment at last—one that would pay her for what she'd been doing on the side for free. After several rounds of interviews, she was hired as the foundation's executive director, thanks in no small measure to her years volunteering with social entrepreneurs.

What Isis finds most rewarding are the moments when she can help an entrepreneur—now including MIT's own Solver teams—to better shoulder major stresses that might be keeping them up at night. She remembers conversations with people near tears, telling her, "I don't know what I'm going do, and I'm terrified."

Every day, Isis harnesses her legal superpowers to do good, as well as another superpower—one a friend dubbed her "divine nonchalance." It's not that she doesn't care, or that she doesn't work hard. What she does have is the ability to keep moving forward. As she says, "It never works out to plan, but it works out." She has the ability to tell anxious social impact clients: "You know what, it's going to be fine. Oops, that blew up over there. That's okay, we'll clean it up."

We All Have Something Unique to Bring to the Problem-Solving Table

Sometimes my advice to my lawyer friends who are looking for more meaningful work is well received, but often my friends protest that they want to do good, but not by working as a lawyer. Unlike Isis, they don't actually like reviewing page after page of contracts or renegotiating termination clauses or indemnities. I get that; if you write contracts all day long and you do not actually like it to begin with, you may not want to do more of the same in your spare time as a volunteer.

But consider this: Do you really want to be a lawyer (or an accountant or a salesperson, or whatever your current field of work is)? That's a different question altogether. Your best bet is to apply your current skills and experience rather than changing tracks or fields of work!

I always tell people it's hard to change five things all at once when you think about your job: what field you are working in, job function, geography, salary, and level. That does not mean it's impossible, but it's often easier to change just one or two of these things, and you might end up having to take a hit on your salary or level before going back up. By all means, though, if you actually would rather become a chef or a filmmaker, please go do that. You will still be able to do good in the world with your new skills.

Regardless of what lived experience you have when you begin this journey, you can always cultivate the problem-solving mindset, learn new skills, gather new experiences, and fill any gaps you may have by finding fellow travelers and partners in change who complement your unique superpowers. We will explore this further in Chapter Nine.

Why "Superpowers"?

When I say everyone has their own unique superpowers, I am dead serious. Why do I use the term "superpowers"? There are so many reasons, some of them will be cliches to the comic book aficionados, but here goes!

First, it's not about you being a superhero or going it alone. There are enough comic books and movies showing how the superhero fails when they go it alone. Rather, just as with the X-Men in their comics, the power is in the collective when everyone works together.

It's also clear that in the comic books, everyone has their own unique superpower: one can fly, one is invisible, one has red laser beam eyes that burn stuff (but in the service of good!), one reads minds, and so forth.

Superheroes also have a clear purpose—or rather, it usually takes them half the movie to discover their purpose, which is often the case in life, too.

Often, a superhero's purpose is connected to their own life story and lived experience, but the challenges they face cause each of them to extrapolate from their unique experience to understand problems affecting millions of the most marginalized. As these superhero characters go along, we discover that they all have their own weaknesses and shortcomings, their "kryptonite" of sorts. They don't get anywhere in terms of saving the world until they recognize their shortcomings, come off their idealistic high horse, and realize that they need to compromise and work with others, whether these are superhero friends, frenemies, or someone who was there all along. From that point, cue the hero's journey with a renewed sense of optimism until they ultimately prevail. You get the gist.

But for fans of these heroic tales, what I think makes this analogy really worthwhile is that we all know that "superheroes" are made, not born. It's their journey that shapes them: their wounds, their trauma, their trials and tribulations, and it often takes years for them to undergo this journey.

You have probably had enough of the superhero analogy for now, but let's double down on *power* a little more, this time through the more serious academic lens of colleagues at Harvard and the University of Toronto.

The book *Power for All* by Julie Battilana and Tiziana Casciaro explores this concept of power in depth. They define it as "the ability to influence someone else's behavior" and seek to offer a more timely, democratized vision of power, one where everyone has valued resources to offer and thus has access to power.

My vision aligns deeply with theirs in the sense that, as stated earlier, I believe that everyone (including you) can play a role in addressing the world's challenges. You have your own unique skills, experiences, and resources to offer. Together, these make up your superpowers, and starting from these is key.

I also like Julie's model of social change movements. In a 2017 *Stanford Social Innovation Review* article written with Marissa Kimsey, she maps out three distinct roles: agitator, innovator, and orchestrator. "An agitator brings the grievances of specific individuals or groups to the forefront of public awareness. An innovator creates an actionable solution to address these grievances. And an orchestrator coordinates action across groups... to scale the proposed solution." The key is to recognize that to get anything done in the social impact world, you need all three roles to work in concert.

Under their framework, I am an orchestrator doing my best to support innovators. I rarely work with agitators unless they cross into the territory of the innovator, like Amanda Nguyen of Rise Justice Labs. While she agitates, she also works on the solution and engages with those in power to effect change. I would certainly be a terrible agitator myself, but I think it's always worth thinking about this framework when working to reveal and develop your own superpowers.

YOUR SUPERPOWER AUDIT: PART 1

So how do you find your own superpowers? Overall, you need to do a radically honest audit of yourself. Let's start with the easier and more obvious questions:

1. What are the skills and experience you bring with you from your current and past jobs and/or education?

2. What do you do well?

3. What do you enjoy doing?

And now, some harder ones which may take time to investigate:

4. What is your story?

5. What have you learned from your lived experience?

6. What are the wounds and trauma you carry with you that have shaped your journey and thus your superpowers?

These questions are important to get you started. And before we dive deeper, I want to share a real-life story illustrating that sometimes what you think is holding you back can be exactly the place to look for your superpowers.

Yuriko Oda's Superpower

"Being a wheelchair user" is Yuriko Oda's superpower, but it took time and the help of her husband for her to embrace it.

At age twenty-two, Yuriko was diagnosed with a rare degenerative disease called distal myopathy. She has been in a wheelchair since 2006, becoming progressively more and more paralyzed. She started the app WheeLog! to help other wheelchair users navigate the world by providing crowdsourced maps with markers for accessible restaurants, bathrooms, and routes in her native Japan, where one in sixty people—two million—use wheelchairs.

But her path to becoming an innovator wasn't always straightforward. When she was first diagnosed, Yuriko didn't want people to think of her as someone with a disability or as someone weak. She did not want to go outside or be a burden on others. Her husband pointed out the error of that perspective. "It's the people who think of those with a disability as weak who are weak people themselves," he told her.

Initially, Yuriko felt confined at home in her wheelchair because she needed so much support to go out. Things changed in 2006 when Yuriko had a son and wanted to take him to the beach. She was frustrated until one day, as she recounts it, "I found an accessible beach on a website, so I could have a wonderful time with my family."

That's when she realized that information could change the lives of wheelchair users—and that she wasn't the only one affected. Where were the accessible routes, and which ones might have bathrooms? Information on barrier-free sites was scattered all over the internet, never in one easy-to-find location.

And with that, Yuriko changed her mind. She took what she had initially seen as a weakness and turned it into her greatest strength. By claiming her superpower, she is restoring a sense of purpose and independence to other wheelchair users as well.

Initially, Yuriko started a YouTube channel called *Wheelchair Walker*, where over two hundred videos showed people in wheelchairs how to get on planes, as well as where to find accessible hotels, beaches, and tourist attractions abroad. But Yuriko's YouTube channel had its limitations, and she aspired to create something more useful when out and about, which ultimately led her to start WheeLog!.

At the same time, she also served as executive director of a patient group for people with the disease that afflicts her, embracing the "agitator" in her, as well. Yuriko explains, "It's a small patient population because it's a rare disease, so it wasn't profitable for the pharmaceutical companies to develop a treatment. I was very active, exercising leadership to encourage one of these companies; now they're in stage three clinical trials. In this way, I learned about structures, with no limitations or constraints. If you keep trying, you can make change."

Now with WheeLog!, wheelchair users and their families and friends can help map and crowdsource the routes to their favorite accessible restaurants and sites, pointing out any issues along the way. For instance, for a route to be accessible, the gap between the pavement and the road needs to be a little less than two inches. A pavement with a higher gap, or even a small step between a pavement and a building, will render the space inaccessible to wheelchair users.

As someone who is not wheelchair-bound, I rarely notice these steps when I am out and about. Yet this is often the problem with design, whether in urban planning or any other field: if you do not involve a diverse array of people in the process, making certain to include those with disabilities, the result will probably be something which does not work for everyone.

Using WheeLog!, wheelchair users can discern which routes are step-free and thus can choose to go out without a caretaker. The app tracks the appropriate routes using GPS and Google Maps. The data from the app also enables Yuriko to advocate for better infrastructure and inclusivity in public spaces, pointing out where there are inaccessible areas and how these could be fixed.

She stresses that people without disabilities can also be "part of the solution." If WheeLog! is just for people in wheelchairs, it might not scale. Yuriko says, "I always want to engage everyone and create an opportunity for non-wheelchair users to contribute to the app. For example, they, too, can post a picture of a bathroom in a restaurant. In making the app accessible for everyone, we want to create a world in which everyone cooperates with each other to make a difference."

YOUR SUPERPOWER AUDIT: PART 2

As you continue to ask yourself what your superpowers are, here are more big questions to reflect on:

1. Who can you call upon to help? Who do you need alongside you to be your best self?

2. What resources and power can you access? We will come back to this more in Chapter Four.

3. What are the ecosystems and institutions you can influence and change? Think about your family, your community, your country, and the organizations for which you work, either paid or as a volunteer.

Sometimes, if you can put your ego aside, your Superpower Audit will highlight a hard truth. It can reveal that you are not qualified to solve the problem you care about—at least, not right now, with the skills and the resources you have, and with the predefined solution you may have in your mind.

But despair not! You have time and curiosity; with those, you can listen, learn, and adopt the problem-solving mindset. Over time, you will develop the skills and experience you need.

Your Superpower Audit will also help reveal areas for which you need to find collaborators and partners who have the skills, experience, and resources to complement your shortcomings. You may also realize along the journey that while you had your heart set on solving a problem in a particular way, there may be another adjacent problem or solution that makes more sense for you and your superpowers to focus on. Revealing your own superpowers to yourself is key to really understanding what makes you uniquely qualified to solve a genuine problem that affects the most underserved, one that could become your purpose.

As Spiderman's Uncle Ben says, "With great power comes great responsibility." So the next question is this: using your superpowers, what problem are you going to solve?

CHAPTER TWO

Solve Problems That Actually Matter

Miranda Wang's Story: Reinventing Plastics

Inventor, entrepreneur, and Solver Miranda Wang is the founder and CEO of Novoloop, a company that uses biochemistry and bacteria to recycle plastics. She started on her way early: at age twelve in the eighth grade, she met her future business partner and co-traveler Jeanny Yao. By high school, they'd joined the environment club, and one of their school visits was to the local waste management facility near their homes in Vancouver, Canada. This was not every teenager's idea of a fun field trip.

As an aside, in the summer of 2006 when I was an English teacher in China, I once found myself with over a hundred students at a crocodile farm. Cue open pits of crocodiles and children running all around the place during what was meant to be a "field trip." Yikes, what were they thinking?

Back to that Canadian field trip: Miranda had an epiphany while touring the facility, where plastic waste was piled in a huge pit and then sent to China once it had been (fairly badly) sorted. "Originally, I'd imagined there must be people or some advanced technology that would pick apart all these things you get in packaging. But when I went there to see for myself, I realized this was just not happening. It really struck a chord of something moral in me. Nobody cared about the way humans treat our things. It was all based on what we can get from them and how useful they are to us. When something's no longer deemed useful, we don't care what we do with it. There's something really wrong about that."

Her interest continued through high school, and in eleventh grade, she enrolled in an advanced biology class. One day at a bus stop, she had an idea: "I thought, can we use biotechnology to address this plastic recycling problem? If an apple or any kind of organic compost made of carbon is something that can be broken down in days, why can't plastics be broken down the same way?"

It was actually a really good question, and asking a good question is always the starting point to solving world challenges. Miranda and her friend Jeanny wrote to Dr. Lindsay Eltis, a biochemistry professor at the University of British Columbia. Undeterred by their youth, the professor agreed to help them, which meant Miranda and Jeanny were able to spend some time in his lab and conduct research based on soil samples they collected along a very industrialized river estuary in their area of Vancouver.

Their thinking led them to a couple of key questions: Can we find bacteria that feed on and thus break down plastics, just like the ones that break down other carbon-based materials such as apples? And where was the most likely place to find these bacteria? It turned out the answer was a very plastic-rich polluted area.

Miranda explains, "We were trying to grow bacteria on these plastics. At the end of four months, we were very surprised to find that quite a few kinds of bacteria can survive purely on plastic chemicals. That was the starting point—year one out of ten." This is how Novoloop began, now scaling up quickly with a team of eleven to work with waste disposal companies to collect their polyethylene materials, break down the plastic and use the resulting chemicals to create higher-value materials like nylon. Given that over 90 percent of plastics now wind up in landfills, incinerators, or the ocean, the valuable chemical process they have developed over the years has a huge upside.

For many, a moral imperative like the one Miranda faced as she looked at piles of waste provides the spark that inspires them, although developing a solution can take many years. But what I especially like about Miranda's story is that she really looked at how to address the problem upstream—at its source.

Many of you have probably stopped using plastic straws, perhaps thanks to a famous image of a turtle with a straw stuck up its nostril, and many restaurants now offer paper straw alternatives. It's a good start, but eight million tons of plastic flow into the ocean every year, and straws comprise just 0.025 percent of that. Your clothes are a far worse contributor. (Spoiler alert—a lot of clothing is made of plastic, and nylon and polyester fibers degrade into microplastics even as you wash them, let alone when you throw them away.) The fashion industry produces 20 percent of the world's water waste, and second to petroleum producers, it is the largest polluter in the world.

To add insult to ecological injury, a lot of plastic is produced and then discarded before it even ends up in the hands of a consumer, and thus contributes to what we call post-industrial waste (as opposed to post-consumer waste).

So yes, by all means, continue using paper straws because it's an important message to companies that people do care about sustainable alternatives to plastics. But it's also important to always think about the problems further upstream and their root causes, which is why Miranda's work in plastics recycling is so critical, so that we avoid plastics getting into the ocean in the first place or using virgin plastic to begin with.

But What Are the Problems that Actually Matter?

Before you can start off solving a problem, it's worth thinking about this question deeply since you don't want to waste your time solving something trivial. Neither you nor the world have time for this anymore. It's worth considering this question both from a macro or global perspective, as well as from a community and bottom-up standpoint. Let's start with the global level.

At a macro level, one can debate whether climate change, or education, or poverty, or pandemic prevention is the greatest challenge of our time. There are whole armies of people whose job it is to study these issues and try and set the world's social impact agenda. Many of them work for the United Nations.

In fact, almost all the world's governments (178, to be precise) came together at the UN in September of 2015 to approve seventeen Sustainable Development Goals (SDGs), representing the key challenges the world needs to tackle by 2030. The goals range from eradicating extreme poverty to providing clean water and sanitation, as well as taking action on climate. The social impact wonks (a term used here amicably, given that I consider myself a proud wonk) also defined 231 target indicators within these goals (for example, reducing the global maternal mortality rate to less than 70 per 100,000 live births).

I hope you will not fault me if I tell you I cannot remember all of them! I think it's a rather complicated framework with too many targets and goals. Further, despite the breadth of the SDGs, there are still important things that were left out. For example, Goal 3, "Ensuring Healthy Lives," omits mental health almost entirely, except for a mention of one indicator relating to suicide.

Another issue is that while the UN engaged many experts in designing the SDGs, it was still very much a top-down political process—a negotiation between countries and experts rather than something bottom-up and democratic. That's not to say that what is funded through global aid programs is not important. For example, in the area of health, a lot of government money has gone to HIV/AIDS research and treatment with impressive success. Another success in recent decades is the lowering of the infant mortality rate thanks to low-cost interventions: increasing the availability of skilled attendance at birth, infant vaccinations, and oral rehydration tablets, since according to the World Health Organization, one in ten babies worldwide still dies of diarrhea—nearly a million a year.

But there are still huge gaps that this top-down approach fails to address. For example, most global health aid budgets are still funneled into responses to infectious diseases, whereas the vast majority of people in developing nations die from chronic diseases like heart disease or cancer. Almost three times as many people die annually from heart disease and strokes as from AIDS, tuberculosis, and malaria combined. And three quarters of these deaths are in developing countries, according to the Population Reference Bureau. Yet chronic diseases receive only a tiny fraction of global health aid funding.

There is also still very little funding directed to mental health. And you may not be surprised to hear that preparedness for pandemics in particular was severely underfunded and underinvested, although I gather the world's governments may have learned their lesson, one well-articulated by Temie Giwa-Tubosun of Nigeria's LifeBank.

Temie points out the perils of short-term government and multilateral thinking, shortcomings that have been tragically highlighted in 2020. As she sees it, there is a critical need to build an affordable primary health system that is durable, not just a new system responding to an epidemic each time one shows up. "I would rather the world health community stop solving single problems and instead solve the basic system, [then] that can then be either dialed down or dialed up to respond not just to pandemics, but also to epidemics and diseases."

It's easier to say, "Let's eradicate polio," an issue Bill Gates has hung his hat on, but the real victories in global health are not disease by disease, but in building resilient, affordable, and quality health systems that everyone can access—ones that can treat infectious, chronic, and mental-health diseases, can help prevent people from getting sick in the first place, and instead promote overall health and well-being.

The SDGs also suffer from another big shortcoming. It's estimated that to achieve the SDGs by 2030, there is an estimated annual funding gap of 2.5 trillion US dollars! Who pays for this is unclear, and we are certainly very far from closing the gap. Governments, multilateral organizations, corporations, and investors all should give or invest more to close this gap. But it's my firm belief—and in a sense, a founding belief of MIT Solve as well—that that we will not achieve the SDGs with the solutions we have today no matter how much money we throw at them, even if that money suddenly materializes (which it won't).

We're missing innovative solutions—and we need to invest in innovation designed by, with, and for the most underserved communities. The innovation gap is just as important, if not more important, than the funding gap. If we could start to close the innovation gap, we could also reduce the unit cost of solving a particular problem and thus reduce the overall cost of achieving the SDGs.

Despite the exponential pace of technological innovation in recent decades, we are not funding or engaging in enough innovation to solve the problems of the poorest and most marginalized communities. While over 70 percent of the world's population lives on under ten dollars a day, most research, technological development, and innovation are designed to solve the problems of the top 30 percent. Just like trickle-down economics, we assume that "trickle-down technology" will work—and it just doesn't.

When you rely on trickle-down technology, there is the faulty assumption that innovations will soon become cheaper and easily adopted by the remaining 70 percent of the population, including the most underserved. If this were true, we would have already solved many of the world's biggest challenges. We need to fundamentally rethink what problems we focus on, and then design and fund research, technology, and innovation for the underserved, tapping into the talent and ingenuity of the people who experience these challenges every day.

Rather than going through all the layered complexity of the seventeen goals and 231 target indicators the UN has set out, I would summarize the macro level as one overarching goal: tackling inequality, injustice, and extraction in all their forms, most notably in connection with education, health, economic prosperity, and climate.

Then we can move on to what I find more interesting and where I believe real innovation for the underserved lies: the community, bottom-up level. These are the challenges faced by you, your family, your loved ones, and your community.

Unfortunately, I don't think you need to look very far. Even if you grew up with privilege in a high-income country such as the United States, you would have to be extremely sheltered and uninterested in the world around you to not see and recognize some of the issues facing the most underserved in the communities you live.

Take a hard look around you. Reflect on your family's and your own struggles. Meet people in your community. Volunteer with local grassroots organizations such as schools, clinics, religious institutions, after-school clubs, or small nonprofits. Listen. There will be no shortage of problems big and small, and among those, there will a problem that could become your purpose.

Some problems you will hear about time and time again; some will resonate immediately, while others may stay in the back of your mind for a few years before you make a connection to your own lived experience, conscious or not. The key is to find *your* problem and purpose among the numerous problems faced by communities all over the world, in the sea of injustices upon which we have built this world.

How Solver Teams Find *Their* Problem (and How You Can, Too)

Every year, MIT Solve runs "Global Challenges" on topics related to learning, health, economic prosperity, and sustainability. Some are very tied in to current events (for example, in 2020, we ran a Challenge on Health Security and Pandemics, while in 2021, we ran one on the theme of Anti-Racist Technology in the US). Other topics may be just as important but get less media airtime, such as the Circular Economy, which focuses on reusing, repairing, and recycling . (Miranda Wang from Novoloop was selected through this Challenge!)

Anyone anywhere can submit a solution: nonprofits, for-profit social enterprises, academic projects, and even individuals. The Challenges attract thousands of solutions from well over a hundred countries every year on Solve's open innovation platform.

The judges are a diverse set of leaders and experts across sectors and countries, such as Queen Rania of Jordan; Ngozi Okowea-Iwaele, who was at the time chair of the Global Alliance for Vaccine (GAVI) and is now head of the World Trade Organization; Indra Nooyi, former CEO of PepsiCo; and MIT faculty such as Sanjay Sarma and Linda Griffith. The judges whittle down the applications to select the top sixty finalists, who are each invited to present their solution to the judges and an audience of over five hundred social impact leaders from all fields. It takes place in New York during the UN General Assembly Week, which is the third week of September. (Throughout the pandemic, it has, of course, all been remote and virtual.)

The finalists have three minutes to pitch their solutions to the judges. The judges then have three minutes to ask questions, all in front of a live audience in the room, as well as thousands more online via livestream. Think of it as a social impact version of *Shark Tank*. The energy is exciting and infectious, and the stakes are high; in 2020, for example, over two million dollars in prize funding from the Gates Foundation, General Motors, Vodafone, and other funding partners was at play. It's also a grueling process. The finalists pace the room as they rehearse and prepare—some are quite visibly stressed, but their ambition is utterly inspiring!

Yet as my colleague Sara Monteabaro, who leads Solve's work with partner challenges, says, "People come together to learn from each other, share with each other, and grow together. It ends up being a starting point for a lot of relationships. It seems to be both a culmination of the hard work the teams have put into their solutions and a launching pad for the next stage."

One of the first exercises we do during orientation is called "A Story of Self, Us, and Now." It was developed by Marshall Ganz, who teaches a similarly named and highly popular class for Harvard graduate students. Interestingly, he came to academia after a career as an activist, beginning as an organizer in the Civil Rights Movement and working on staff for sixteen years for United Farm Workers. He also helped organize several political campaigns, including those of Nancy Pelosi for Congress, Jerry Brown for governor of California, and Barack Obama's grassroots campaign for both presidential runs.

Using Marshall's Public Narrative worksheet, Solver teams learn that mastering public presentation is not about self-expression per se, but is instead about how to inspire others to join you in shared action. With the steps Marshall outlines, you can move from your "Story of Self" to the "Story of Us," in which you identify some of the sources of your action and what makes your story applicable to many, ending with the "Story of Now," in which urgency drives others to join you in your enterprise for change. He asks: What urgent challenges do you face? And how do you define successful action (i.e., your mission)? A contrast should be drawn between the world as it will be if you don't act and the one you hope to create if you do (your vision). Participants are asked to describe the preferred outcome in a couple of sentences.

In a way, this process is also one employed by some of the most compelling politicians when they run for office, or perhaps by anyone crafting a public persona with roots in their own story. In fact, the framework was popularized during the first Obama campaign in 2008, to which Marshall contributed. As he articulates it, "A good public story is drawn from a series of choice points that that have structured the 'plot' of your life: the challenges you faced, the choices you made, and the outcomes you experienced."

The key to the power of this moment in orientation is when Solver team members move from the "Story of Self," centered on the problem they are individually tackling and why they chose it (including details about their families and other parts of their personal biographies), to the "Story of Us" and what they have in common. Solver teams hail from different regions, use different technologies, and address a range of problems for a wide variety of underserved people: refugees, people with disabilities, people living on under two dollars a day, and more.

When they're selected, they marvel at the diversity. Yet in the course of this exercise, participants come to realize they share many things, the most profound being that their story is a shared one with resonance in the commonalities of how and why each got started, and how they found their problem and their purpose.

Sometimes the problem is very personal and proximate: a family member, friend, or someone in their community faces a real challenge that affects them personally. Sometimes the problem comes to them without much notice or much choice, say, when fleeing war as a refugee or when a loved one receives a heartbreaking diagnosis. Sometimes the problem isn't quite so close and only emerges over the course of years after seeing instance upon instance of the same issue and connecting the dots.

In all cases, each Solver team found a problem that resonated profoundly with their "Story of Self" and then looked for solutions in their community; in the process, they spoke with countless individuals and institutions concerned with their chosen problem. When they realized their chosen problem was not being solved at all (or at least not quickly enough), they decided to get into the game and work towards a solution based on their superpowers.

In this sense, finding a solution became a necessity and an obligation, because whether it took years or just an instant, they had found a problem that became their purpose. And when a problem becomes a purpose, you have no choice, really, but to try and solve it.

Clara and Carlos Pereira's Story: Giving a Voice to Those Who Can't Speak

Clara Pereira was born with cerebral palsy in Recife, Brazil, in 2007. For her father, software engineer Carlos Pereira, that was the beginning of their joint mission.

When baby Clara finally emerged, Carlos could see right away that something was wrong; his daughter was rushed to the NICU, where she stayed for a month. Brain damage was confirmed. At the time, Carlos remembers, "I didn't know if she would walk or talk, or if she would understand anything."

But once he finally held Clara in his arms, it was of course love at first sight. "I didn't know what her future would be, but in that moment, I had this commitment: I will do whatever it takes to help my daughter." In that moment, Carlos not only fell in love with his daughter, but also with his purpose. He found information online about a stem cell treatment that might help Clara. But it cost $40,000, and he had only $30 in his bank account.

Carlos made a YouTube video that attracted 200,000 views. He said to his wife, "You know what? If every person who has watched this video donated one *real* (the Brazilian unit of currency), at twenty *reals* to a dollar, we could make our dream come true and get Clara the stem cell treatment."

Next Carlos, created a website called "One Real for One Dream," asking people to donate so he could raise the whole $40,000. And they did—Clara was the first Brazilian to receive this stem cell treatment. She was all over the TV stations and the papers. As Carlos remembers it, "You couldn't hide from my daughter!"

Some foreign investors who had opened a rehabilitation center in Europe took notice. They asked him, "Carlos, we saw what you're doing for your daughter in Brazil. Do you think it would be a good idea to open a rehab center there?" Carlos convinced them that his hometown of Recife was the best place for such a center. After meeting only twice with the investors, they agreed to make a large investment and to send over two tons of medical equipment. Carlos quit his job and renovated a huge space so the local community could have a top-notch facility for people with disabilities. He hired a speech therapist, an occupational therapist, and other professionals. Clara was among the center's first clients.

Although the rehabilitation center was helping her and other patients, Clara was still struggling; she could not communicate well, and it was hard to learn. There were alternative communication devices out there for people who were nonverbal, similar to the ones used by British scientist Stephen Hawking, who suffered from ALS. But these were extremely expensive, and they were for the most part not available in Portuguese.

Carlos approached companies in the US, pointing out that there are fifteen million Brazilians who are nonverbal. There was a market, and he was ready to help bring some of these devices to his country. The response? "We are not interested in Brazil."

So Carlos taught himself to code so he could generate software to help Clara. After working all day at the clinic that he ran with his wife, he'd come home and sit down at the computer. When they started to test the software that would become Livox in the clinic, he recalls, "It was like the pieces of the puzzle were coming together."

There were challenges. People with motor disabilities like Clara's touch devices with their whole hand, dragging their fingers, and sometimes twitch involuntarily. Carlos came up with an algorithm he called Livox Intellitouch that analyzes how many fingers are touching the screen and for how long, and adapts based on the user. Carlos and his colleagues also came up with technology that works with only a front-facing camera; that way people who could not operate their limbs could use Livox, including patients with ALS. A device that might cost $10,000 to $18,000 in the US can now be replaced with Livox's software, which works on a $100 tablet from Amazon.

A few years ago, Carlos and his family moved to Florida to perfect the software with the help of a major grant from Google. Through AI and machine learning, the software can now learn a user's preferences. If Carlos asks Clara, "What do you want for dinner?" her favorite dishes will come up as options first, and the specific dishes can be adapted to a particular country or culture. Carlos explains: "If it's lunchtime, Livox knows that she is Brazilian, so it would show foods for a Brazilian to eat."

Carlos's drive to help Clara communicate became his purpose, and he used his skills as an engineer to solve the problem when he found that no one else would do it. What started out as Clara and Carlos's Story of Self quickly became Stories of Us and Now, as Livox is currently used by thousands of individuals with nonverbal disabilities, along with their teachers and their families. It's available in ten countries and is compatible with twenty-five languages. Clara's medical condition, a disability which means that she cannot speak or move much, affects an estimated seventeen million individuals globally; there is still lots to do for Livox, Carlos, and Clara.

Don't Confuse Your Passions with Your Purpose

I very much like Nathalie Molina Nina's distinction in her book *Leapfrog Hacks*: passion is for "bliss businesses" and first-world problems, for ladies who brunch and trust fund kids with a lot of money who can afford to fail. Most people cannot just quit their jobs and start a business based on a passion, and I would not advocate doing so in the context of thinking about the real problems that face most underserved communities.

Instead, Nathalie recommends taking on "a problem you want to punch." Obviously, this is not about literally punching anyone you think is guilty of causing this problem, even if you are tempted to do so. Instead, she recommends writing down lists of things you notice and really want to punch over a number of days, including injustices that enrage you, inefficiencies that beguile you, or system breakdowns that confound you. Some of these are problems other people want to punch, too. If enough people see it as a problem that needs solving, and if it's not just an inconvenience faced by the 1 percent but in fact a problem faced by the most underserved members of your community, solving it may be something worth pursuing. Overall, your goal is to distinguish a real problem from a mere passion in order to discern a cause that over time could become your purpose.

For instance, you might really hate walking your dog every night in San Francisco, so maybe you write this down as a problem you want to punch. That does not mean I think you should start a new dog-walking app, although that is in fact how TaskRabbit, originally called RunMyErrand, was started. Boston-based IBM engineer Leah Busque didn't have time to buy dog food as she and her husband headed out to dinner. Wouldn't it be great, she thought, if they could find a dog sitter for the evening?

In my mind, this is where the tech world goes wrong when it co-opts the impact lexicon of "solving a problem that matters." This kind of language conflates the mild inconveniences of the 1 percent with real problems, while leaving behind any meaningful definition of what *matters*. (I'll admit, I have used TaskRabbit myself for hanging up shelves and curtains, but I still don't think this is a problem that is worth your genius when we compare it to the big challenges facing us.)

Whether you live in the most expensive city or one of the poorest in the world, every day you choose either to see challenges or to literally walk on by. You can choose to notice people experiencing homelessness in San Francisco alongside the Facebook and Google buses as you walk your dog; you can choose to see the plastic bags and bottles in the street that will take thousands of years to degrade.

Kevin F. Adler's Story: Helping Unhoused Neighbors

Speaking of San Francisco and deciding not to look away from real problems, Kevin F. Adler likes to say: "I never learned the word 'stranger.' "

This is the core philosophy of his nonprofit, Miracle Messages: people may be unhoused and experiencing poverty, but the real problem lies elsewhere—in relational poverty, the profound lack of human connection that people who become unhoused frequently experience. As Kevin puts it, "The problem we want to solve on some basic level is complacency. Those who are homeless are not problems to be solved, but people to be loved."

Kevin had an uncle who suffered from schizophrenia and experienced homelessness on and off for thirty years. But as Kevin was growing up, he never saw his uncle as a person experiencing homelessness, but rather as a beloved family member. After he passed away, Kevin had a realization: "Everyone I'm walking by, this is someone's son or daughter, this is someone's brother or sister."

While working in edtech in San Francisco, Kevin started to dive deeper into the problem. He began talking with people he met on the street, which ultimately led to his deciding to begin the Homeless GoPro project. Over the course of a year, he gave GoPro cameras to twenty-four unhoused people to document their experience of life on the street. The concept he began with was, "I just walked by you. You're still here. What's on your mind? What's in your heart? What's your life like? I want to know your story."

When Kevin got the footage back, he was shocked by what he heard: over and over, it was some version of the same story, the same Story of Self becoming a Story of Us: "I never realized I was homeless when I lost my housing, only when I lost my family and friends." This insight—that relational poverty matters—was a crucial ingredient missing in how most public and nonprofit services that work with unhoused people operate.

In order to learn more while further testing his insight, Kevin went back and asked each person a very simple question: "Do you have any family or friends with whom you'd like to reconnect, even if you presently don't know how to reach them?" When Kevin sat down with a man named Jeffrey, he discovered that this man hadn't seen his family for twenty-two years. He recorded a short video message for the man's nieces, nephews, sister, and father. Then Kevin sat on the video for a week. "I didn't do anything because I didn't believe him. And I didn't think I had any business getting involved further than I already had. I was complacent," he explained, even after he'd spent a year listening to the stories of people like Jeffrey, added to what he knew about his own uncle. As Kevin relates, "I still did not have the level of trust and confidence in our conversation to put myself out there on his behalf."

But a week later, on Christmas Eve, Kevin posted the video on a Facebook page connected to Jeffrey's hometown. He regards what happened next as a miracle, which is where the name of his organization established later originates.

Within an hour, it was shared hundreds of times and made the local news. Former classmates started commenting: "I went to high school with Jeffrey. I work in construction. Does he need a job?"

"I work at the congressman's office if he needs healthcare."

In the first twenty minutes after Kevin's post, Jeffrey's sister was tagged on the Facebook page. Kevin called her the next day and found out that Jeffrey had been registered as a missing person for twelve years; his family had been looking for him. As Kevin observes, "There he was, in broad daylight, downtown San Francisco, a few days before Christmas, with thousands of people walking by doing their Christmas shopping."

That first "miracle" compelled Kevin to leave his job at a Silicon Valley education start-up and start working with his unhoused neighbors full-time, "because I knew Jeffrey wasn't the only one—and this shouldn't have been happening. We shouldn't be so hyper-connected, desiring to solve all these world problems, while someone like Jeffrey is living and dying on the streets, and thousands of people are walking by him without even knowing his name or his story."

As Kevin sees it, homelessness is in fact "not the driving force in what I do. It's my belief in the intrinsic value of each person and the interconnectedness of us all."

Get Proximate to Problems

Really seeing and bearing witness is hard enough. The plain and simple utter unfairness of this world is difficult to swallow, so it is easier to push the unfairness and contradictions out of your mind. But being present to what is before you is the first step. It can be even harder to understand why these challenges are not being solved and how systems are breaking down—or even, in many cases, working exactly as they were set up to do in creating injustices.

Take the time to really study the problem and to gain perspective and proximity by listening to many afflicted by it. Doing so allows you to distinguish the real problems affecting the most marginalized from the marginal headaches affecting the most fortunate.

Dr. Angela Jackson of New Profit provides an excellent definition of a proximate leader in a 2020 *Stanford Social Innovation Review* article written with John Kania and Tulaine Montgomery: "someone who has a meaningful relationship with groups whose identity, experience, or community are systemically stereotyped, feared, dismissed, or marginalized."

Angela, herself a proximate leader who you will hear about later, points out that being proximate means more than observing or studying such groups; it's about being part of them and/or "being meaningfully guided by that group's input, ideas, agendas, and assets." For her, proximate leaders recognize the genius and talents within communities and avoid the trap of misunderstanding as viewed from a dominant cultural lens. They are then best able to use their and the communities' experiences, assets, and knowledge to develop solutions that will stick.

So as you think about the problems you hope to address, think about your proximity to them and invest time in creating meaningful relationships, listening, understanding, and codesigning with those whom you seek to serve.

Rajesh Anandan's Long-Winding Story: Fighting for Jobs for the Neurodivergent

For Solver Rajesh Anandan of Ultranauts, it took years to home in on the problem. He offers advice on what *not* to do if you want to make change: "Don't start with an idea, as in let's come up with a new app or a device to solve this problem that doesn't actually affect me, and I don't really actually know anything about it, but I read an article. If you don't have firsthand experience with a problem, take the time to understand how this challenge manifests and spend time with the people who are actually impacted by it so you have real firsthand experience before you even think of solving it."

It's important to fall in love with the problem, not with the solution, whether that's glitzy technology or an inspiring movement you think might help. And by love, I mean the kind of love that keeps you awake at night, the kind that stays with you no matter what and makes you do things you once thought were impossible. Ideally, it's not an obsessive, unhealthy love, but that is a possible side effect you risk when working to do good in the world. We'll come back to how to take care of yourself in Chapter Nine as you face the harsh realities of trying to change the game.

Taking the time to really understand the problem might very well take years of witnessing and listening before you even come up with a solution you can act on. This was the case for Rajesh, in fact. When he and his roommate Art Shectman went to MIT for their undergraduate degrees, some of their class-mates were wired differently; they excelled academically but then struggled to navigate through society and typical workplaces after graduation. Years later, after several stints in the corporate world, Rajesh started working for UNICEF and came upon data that indicated a real need for work for people with disabilities, including those on the autism spectrum.

The World Health Organization estimates that globally, one in 160 children is on the autism spectrum—a staggering number that includes four million Americans—and many of these children will grow up largely unemployed or underemployed. Climate activist Greta Thunberg has shared that she herself is on the spectrum.

Before taking on climate change as a personal and then global cause, Greta really struggled at school and in life; as recounted by her mother, Malena Ernman, in the book *Our House is on Fire*, she had few friends and often sat at home in a gloomy fog, and even developed an eating disorder. But as Greta learned more about climate change and it became her purpose, she woke up. Now she sees her "disability" as a positive; she uses the hashtag #AspiePower. She has frequently responded to the negative comments directed her way as her international profile has risen: "When haters go after your looks and differences, it means they have nowhere left to go. And then you know you're winning!"

What if we could harness the unique skills of neurodivergent talent such as visual pattern recognition, creative problem-solving, and heightened focus—all skills that make for good software engineers—and adapt the workplace to become more welcoming to the wide range of people on the autism spectrum? With this insight, Rajesh and his partner saw both a business opportunity and a chance to have a real impact on the lives of an underserved and massively underemployed population. He and his partner founded Ultranauts, which now employs over a hundred people, 75 percent of whom are on the autism spectrum.

It's important to recognize that the problem does not always need to be one that affects you or a loved one directly, even if we need a lot more proximate problem-solvers to get in the game. The key overall is to make sure it's a problem that will keep you going; and for that, it's important that it still resonates with your "Story of Self." Rajesh's "Story of Self" was not initially linked to autism, but is in fact rooted in his childhood in Sri Lanka, where he grew up in the midst of a civil war. His mother is Sinhalese and grew up in the south, while his father, who is Tamil, is from the north of the country.

Rajesh explains: "In the south of the country, I had the wrong name, and in the north, I spoke the wrong language. The civil war triggered massive civil riots. Civilian mobs went door to door in the south, armed with voter registration lists to hunt down Tamil households. Then they'd set them on fire. This happened when I was eleven. No surprise, I have a very deep-seated intolerance for intolerance. It's really dangerous and unproductive when people start to get hung up on their differences and allow those differences to keep us apart. At a very basic level, that experience has shaped a lot of what I do now. It's about finding common ground and appreciating real value in the uniqueness we can all bring to the table—and being able to harness that value by working together."

As he recalled the Solver orientation and the Marshall Ganz exercise, Rajesh was struck by the fact that even given the diversity of the Solver teams working in various geographic areas using different technologies and business models, his cohort all came together around fairness. In the team's collective vision, as Rajesh puts it, "Each company and organization was striving to ensure that the work of the future was going to be more equitable and accessible to everyone, not just limited to people who were born in the right place at the right time or in the right way."

Rajesh notes that what makes Ultranaut's design and business principles really exciting is that, by envisioning a more equitable workforce for neurodivergent talent, they're creating a blueprint anyone can access. Many engineers—including Rajesh and his team—now design products and services using a framework called "user-centered design," which means that at each stage of the design from conception to pre-production to post-production, the product/service is tested to ensure it works well for users (e.g., it's easy to understand, simple to use, and people want to actually use it, etc.) But Rajesh goes further: he sees neurodiverse talent as an edge case, meaning that if he can design a workplace that works for people on the autism spectrum, it will be a work environment that works for the rest of us as well. Innovations developed for neurodivergent talent can benefit workers everywhere, making diversity, inclusion, and basic fairness guideposts to a more dynamic future workplace. "If you imagine the workplace as a system, we're trying to design a system that works for what you might call in a product lens [or focused

The Answer Is You

design study], 'an extreme user'—a user with a different set of needs. If we do that, it's just better for everyone."

For example, from the beginning, Ultranauts was designed as a fully remote workplace, because many people on the autism spectrum struggle with the stress and environmental stimulation of a commute and an open plan office. When the pandemic unfolded, this decision seemed more prescient and practical than ever.

Keep Learning about Real Problems— and Yourself

As you go along your journey, start with your lived experience, and then reflect on what you care about and why. Keep coming back to the problem(s) you want to punch and choose the hard ones first, because everything else is at the margins. As you continue to stay curious, listen, and learn, you will see problems come up again, again, and again.

Take the time to really understand if these problems are paramount, not only to validate whether they are real problems that affect the most underserved, but also to discover if they affect the many—if your chosen challenge is something that resonates not just with you (and your Story of Self), but with your community and the world (the Stories of Us and Now).

You may grow frustrated that a problem keeps happening and that there does not seem to be a solution; but out of your frustration and your desire to do something about it, your purpose will appear. Take the time to home in on the nature of the problem and to develop your superpowers, because it's at the intersection of your superpowers and a problem that really matters that you will find your purpose.

CHAPTER THREE

Find Your Purpose at the Intersection

Temie Giwa-Tuboson's Story: Delivering Blood to New Mothers

In describing her motivation for starting LifeBank, Temie Giwa-Tuboson uses the word "passion," but she defines it not in terms of the fleeting fancy of the fortunate, but as "something you can't stop thinking about. Whatever keeps you up at night, that's the problem you need to solve—or at least try to."

Temie never set out to be a maternal health entrepreneur, but rather hoped to be a diplomat, a career choice to which she aspired after attending a Model UN session at college in Minnesota. Following her graduation, she also considered a career in immigration or civil rights law, inspired by Gani Fawehinmi, a prominent civil rights attorney in her native Nigeria.

She decided to go on to graduate school and chose the Middlebury Institute of International Studies in Monterey, California, an excellent program for would-be UN workers. Over the summer of 2009 after her first year of grad school, she returned to Africa to intern on a healthcare project funded by the UK's Department for International Development. She was sent to Kano in northern Nigeria for three months. "I was just dropped in and had to develop my skills in the middle of nowhere. At the time, I had no interest in healthcare."

Her job was to do household surveys to figure out how local people accessed healthcare. When she and her team entered a village during the day, they often encountered very few people because so many were on their farms. But as she recalls, "You would find the women, and you would be able to speak with them frankly."

One day, they saw a group standing in front of a house; a young woman in the house had been in labor for days, but her labor was not progressing. Though she desperately needed to be taken to a hospital, there were no resources. As Temie remembers it, "I was really heartbroken. I thought about all the things I'd learned that summer about health structures, finance, and systems. I was so shaken because I saw the human costs of not having those things—which was the life of the baby, who had died already, and the life of a mother who was waiting to die. I felt so horrible that I just went and locked myself in my hotel for a few days."

Temie went on to reflect, "This was my first understanding of the way what I'd learned in college and grad school, and even in the Model UN, all just came together. That's where my passion for healthcare began."

After changing her focus to healthcare for her second year of graduate school back in Monterey, Temie went to work in the nonprofit sector and returned once again to Nigeria, but her true purpose was still percolating in her mind. That all changed after she herself became pregnant and experienced extensive complications, including gestational diabetes, eclampsia, and a baby born early in the breach position. She even had childbirth fever. "Everything that could go wrong, did. I remember specifically bargaining with God or the Universe or whatever that if I survived, I was going to do something about maternal healthcare."

Two years after the birth of her son, she founded LifeBank to try and solve the biggest killer of women in childbirth in Africa and globally: postpartum hemorrhage. "With access to blood, nine out of ten women with postpartum hemorrhage could be saved," she told me. "Those are staggering numbers. Women in developed countries in the 'Global North' don't generally die from postpartum hemorrhage because there is a great structure to get blood to the women who need it, quickly and in good condition."

Recalling the woman she'd met in Kano all those years ago, as well as her own personal experience much later, Temie saw a life-threatening and fixable problem, one that stole her sleep and almost stole her life. After years of seeing the problem time and time again and developing her own unique skills and superpowers, she was finally ready to attack it head-on.

What Is Your Purpose?: yourImpact Matrix

Finding your purpose is not easy, and for many, it could take years or even a lifetime to uncover. In a sense, perhaps a life well-lived is one where you are constantly asking yourself, "What is my purpose, and am I living it?"

Enter what I call yourImpact Matrix. Ta-da!

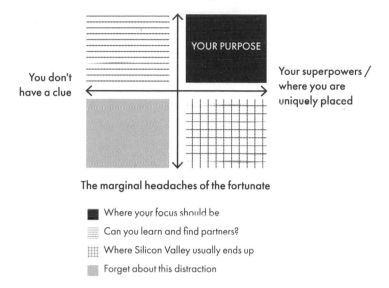

Real problem affecting millions or
billions of the most marginalized

YOUR PURPOSE

You don't
have a clue

Your superpowers /
where you are
uniquely placed

The marginal headaches of the fortunate

■ Where your focus should be
≡ Can you learn and find partners?
▦ Where Silicon Valley usually ends up
▨ Forget about this distraction

You'll see the horizontal axis points to something we discussed back in Chapter One: your own unique superpowers.

The vertical axis is the subject of Chapter Two, a real problem that matters. The key over time is to find the intersection between real problems that affect the most underserved and your superpowers. When both of these align in the upper right quadrant of the matrix, that is your purpose.

Now it might take a long time for your purpose to emerge, but have a go now: Where do you think you stand? Are you in the upper right, upper left, lower left or lower right?

Upper right? Incredible! This is where you need to stay, so keep doing what you are doing. There is still a lot for you to do and learn, as problems don't get fixed overnight. But stay the course, find co-travelers to help, and take care of yourself as you go.

Lower right? Well, hopefully you are making lots of money, but I gather you are reading this book because you want to measure your life by moving in the direction of making an impact; so start thinking more about those real "problems you want to punch" and how you can use all your powers for good.

Upper left? Okay, you've identified a problem that's affecting millions of underserved people, but you are lacking the skills and/or experience needed to address it. So is this the right problem for you?

Sometimes the answer is no; it's not something well adapted to your skills, resources, and lived experience, and never will be, at least in terms of truly becoming your purpose. But it might also be that you need to spend a lot of time learning and acquiring the right experience, which you can do.

That is the journey, and the following chapters should help you, too. And if you are in the lower left quadrant: while it's good to know you are there, it's time to stop wasting your time and energy and start moving—ideally diagonally!

Like the superhero's journey, the quest to find your purpose—that intersection between a real problem and what you're really good at—often takes many years, as it did for Dedo Baranshamaje.

Dedo Baranshamaje's Story: Finding Purpose Via a Flash Mob

Dedo Baranshamaje was born in Burundi and raised across Europe and the US. "Oftentimes, as every third culture kid knows, I could see how my value changed based on people's perception of who I was. When people saw me as a kid from Burundi, no one cared. When people saw me as a gay man, that was even harder in certain situations. But when people saw me as a gay educated Burundian from the diaspora, then the conversation changed. I was still the same person, but the perception was very different depending on what I put forward. And my access was very, very dependent on that."

His family background dissuaded him from following the route of multilateral institutions globally. Multilateral development money rarely went to those who really needed it on the ground. So Dedo tried the social entrepreneurship route while he was in college. "When I reflect back, I was obsessed by this idea of unlocking potential because I could see that every time I came back to Burundi during vacation, the only difference between me and my peers who stayed there was just access to opportunities. We all have the same potential. My first social enterprise was about investing in young people and connecting them to jobs, banks, and microfinance institutions so that they could start their own businesses."

It failed quickly. "I could have meetings with anyone that we could want, from the head of the World Bank to the biggest CEO of a private company, to anyone in government. But even with that level of access, it was really difficult to broker trust with investors to fund us to do what we wanted to do."

This dynamic came up again when, upon graduating college, Dedo received a prestigious fellowship with Global Health Corps. He was attached to work with small local organizations in Burundi. As Dedo relates, "The mission was unbelievable, and the work was really good, but they were struggling to raise funding to run their programs because they didn't have access to the opportunities and networks to which other larger international organizations have access."

Dedo ended up transferring to another organization because they couldn't pay his salary. He moved on to work for an international organization where he had more resources, but he was disappointed. "The difference was that the small local organization was responding to the needs of the community with little money, while the larger international organization was responding to the needs of the donor. I realized that there was a problem around grant-making and change-making. Oftentimes, funders and donors think about grant-making, but change-making is a whole different ballgame."

The larger international organization was getting the funding and then subcontracting local organizations to do the work, but it was not asking the local organizations who knew best what was happening on the ground the key question: "What is the problem you're trying to solve?"

As Dedo puts it: "There's a little bit more mistrust because the process is designed around mitigating risk and making sure that the money is accounted for. That ends up being a burden for the small local organization. The space for locally led organizations is very small, if you consider that out of the whole of international aid funding, only 2 percent goes to local visionaries and entrepreneurs on the ground. The rest stays between expatriates and large organizations. That is a problem that should not exist. It's just based on trust."

So Dedo sees the problem he is trying to solve as "brokering trust between local social entrepreneurs, funders, and government in such a way that they can collaborate to create change. There's so many visionaries and innovators out there, but we don't have very clear systems or a process to find them."

If Dedo's mission seems similar to Solve's, it's because it is. He works for the Segal Family Foundation, whose mission is singularly focused on funding African social entrepreneurs, who they call African Visionaries. Dedo's mission and mine overlap wholeheartedly.

His definition of these visionaries very much echoes Dr. Angela Jackson's definition of proximate leadership: "What do they have in common? One, they have the cultural competency that is required to engage in conversation and understand what is going on. Two, they use the relationship economy that allows them to connect with whoever they need to connect with, be it the government and/or the private sector, in order to move the needle. And three, they have unique experience around what actually is a problem."

Through the Segal Family Foundation, Dedo and his team support many of these visionaries across the African continent. One is Grace Francoise Nibizi, who is coincidentally also from Burundi. Having worked for the UN and bilateral institutions for many years, but with no certainty of where the money was going, she decided to start her own social enterprise, SaCoDe, to provide community services, jobs, education, and especially quality healthcare and certified hygienic products to girls and women. Lack of these crucial items for girls has been linked with lower school attendance.

Dedo explains: "Most organizations are throwing money into making reusable sanitary pads. Francoise is saying, let's reduce the pain first, as cramps are in fact a big issue, and let's start with proving that with the pads, we can have more girls be confident and stay in school. Let's also move away from reusable sanitary pads because they're not sustainable in places where water is scarce." One of Francoise's key innovations was to make underwear with pads included, since many girls in rural areas lacked both.

Her organization also makes sure there is an online platform where girls can connect and share stories, talk about their sexual health and reproductive rights, and get referrals. Francoise started SaCoDe in her own garage with less than $2,500 and has since scaled up to include the entire country of Burundi. Dedo applauds her efforts. "She has built an incredible social enterprise that produces products and services for women, and that is also thinking about scale."

Through early "failures," both as a social entrepreneur himself and then working to support small local organizations, Dedo identified a problem: the disconnect between proximate activists, entrepreneurs, and innovators doing great work on the ground and the global funding community looking for trusted partners. This often resulted in their funding typically going to larger US-based or European-based nonprofits.

Dedo then gradually uncovered his purpose as he zoned in on his superpowers, many of which stem from his upbringing across three continents and cultures. He always thought his superpowers were being a good listener and thinking everything was possible, but his true superpower, which was there all along, became clearer to him during the COVID-19 crisis. "Being originally from a conflict and war setting, living across the world, experiencing adversity and resettlement following elections in Burundi, and being in West Africa during the Ebola crisis gives you resilience. It gives you that sort of resilience that you can reinvent yourself anywhere you go, in any situation. I'm an extrovert, and so during COVID, everyone thought I was going to suffer living in Malawi by myself, but I was like, 'This is our new life now? Sure! Let's run with it!'"

His real superpower is that in moments of adversities or trouble, Dedo becomes creative. "I see opportunities. It's something that has continued to be the theme throughout." His creativity was on full display when he was working for Population Service International (PSI) in Burundi in 2011–2012, before ultimately having to leave the country again in 2015 during a contested election. At PSI, he and his co-fellow Leah Hazard were tasked with bringing healthcare services and products to people who need it—communities of color, minorities, women, and young people.

Dedo explains, "Condoms are such a taboo thing in different cultures. I've even seen it in my own relationships around the world. It's not something that is only exclusive to poor countries. But what happens in those places is that sex is so taboo that people can't even buy health services and products."

His boss asked him and Leah to think about a campaign to help educate young people about HIV and how to protect themselves. She was probably expecting them to come up with a ten-page proposal for a campaign, but Dedo and Leah had another idea; they said to her, "Let's do a flash mob." They went ahead with this inspiration, and as he relates, "It was highly, highly interactive, and fun, and we showed condoms to everyone. Young people were singing 'This time, baby, I'll be bulletproof...' "

The resulting flash mob video de-stigmatizing condoms was the most popular YouTube video in Burundi for a very long time. Dedo explains, "I like the idea of just coming up with simple solutions that work and seeing how they actually change the conversation."

After having been defined for so long through others' perceptions, Dedo's other superpower is that he is comfortable in any room, with anyone. "It's just the ability to treat everyone fairly; be it the CEO in the boardroom, a field officer, or smallholder farmers, they are all equally smart and driven. They just need a mirror."

Due to his superpowers—being resilient and adaptable to any situation and any person—he is the ideal person to broker trust at all levels of the system, from the local visionary to the billionaire. "How do you broker trust at scale? How do you drive more capital to entrepreneurs who need it? And how do you create narratives that actually build trust?

"I am inspired really, really deeply by these entrepreneurs who are starting in the last mile off the beaten path, but who really are committed to it, and who are going to figure it out anyway, with or without support."

And his initial obsession—his mission to unlock potential—has not changed. When his social enterprise failed, he explains, "I joined all these other organizations, but it was still the same thing. How do I unlock potential for the entrepreneurs at the bottom while working for larger international organizations?"

yourImpact VISION, MISSION, AND VALUES

Once you have some sense of a real problem and your superpowers, you might try a simpler version of the Marshall Ganz Stories of Self, Us, Now exercise. I do it annually around the new year, and it helps me refine my purpose. I call it *yourImpact Vision, Mission, and Values.*

If you've ever either done paid work or volunteered at a nonprofit, you probably know that a vision, mission, and values statement are how nonprofits articulate their goals. Sometimes they are meaningful, and sometimes they're a bunch of buzzwords the organization puts on their website as marketing-speak. When done well, I think the exercise can help you express your purpose once you have identified a real problem.

yourImpact Vision should answer the question, "What do I want the world to look like?" This can be broad or specific, but I would say that you should always start with something ambitious and audacious, and even perhaps seemingly unattainable. After all, you want it to be part of your life's purpose, so begin with something you will not see come to fruition in one, two, or even five years.

In a sense, your vision is a positive mirror of your problem: If you solved the problem, this is what the world would look like. For Temie Giwa-Tubosun of LifeBank, her personal vision is that no woman in the world would die of postpartum hemorrhage, or expressed more positively, that every woman has access to the healthcare she needs to survive and thrive.

My vision is about equality of opportunity, a world where everyone, no matter their zip code, skin color, gender, or financial limitations (among many possible variables) can achieve their full potential.

yourImpact Mission should answer the question, "What role should I play in achieving this vision?" It's important to recognize that your mission will not fully encompass your vision. Or, put differently, your vision is not going to be realized solely by you or even your organization. To really identify your mission, take the time to understand your unique superpowers and the problem you really care about solving long term.

For example, Miranda Wang of Novoloop is not attacking the whole plastics crisis. She's not even attacking the most visible part of the problem, which is the tons and tons of plastics that end up in the ocean. Her mission to recycle previously unrecyclable plastics takes her further upstream. If and when she is successful, her solution will ultimately have a huge impact in reducing plastics both in landfills and in the oceans, as well as in curtailing the use of fossil fuels from which plastics are derived.

But she leaves fishing the plastics out of the ocean to others, and even as she is working on her part of solving this problem, she needs a ton of other people—corporations, governments, and more—to join her in her mission.

In early 2016, before I had ever even heard of Solve, I wrote up my own mission this way:

1. Identifying and supporting the solutions and innovators that can unleash big, bold change.

2. Moving capital, leaders, and systems across all sectors to invest in those solutions and innovators.

In a sense, it was incredible that a mere few months later, a headhunter contacted me about an opportunity to become the founding executive director of a new initiative MIT had just launched called Solve, which corresponded exactly with my mission! It may look like an utter coincidence, but it was not serendipity per se. I had been talking to a number of organizations about potential opportunities, but none of them had felt quite right up to that point, and I was clear enough about my mission to avoid getting sidetracked. So when the Solve opportunity came about, I was ready to say yes and to shape Solve's mission into my own, even if that meant packing up to move to Cambridge, Massachusetts, and accepting a new job there when I was utterly in love with New York City (as I still am).

Finally, your Impact Values should reflect who you are as a person and what you stand for. When looking to solve world challenges, the adage that the end justifies the means obviously does not hold true (if ever it did). How you achieve your mission matters. Conversely, violating or not holding true to your values should make you feel uncomfortable and help you make decisions about which red lines not to cross, which is important given that the social impact world does come with real paradox. (More on that in Chapter Six.)

For me, being optimistic, bold, ambitious, solution-oriented, collaborative, and human-centered are my core values. This is how I always seek to go about my mission.

In truth, your Impact Vision, Mission, and Values take time to develop, and they may evolve in small or big ways both as you explore how you can make an impact and move forward. But don't be afraid to try this exercise right now to see what you come up with as a starting point. Give it a try!

The point is that there are many real problems you can focus on to find your purpose. The only mistake is to stand by and assume that other people will do something about them. It's your responsibility, too—and you need to do something; in fact, the world needs you to do the best you can, as soon as you can.

Dr. Angela Jackson's Story: Making the Future of Work More Equitable

The car accident was serious; it could have ended Angela Jackson's life. But it also caused her to rethink her most basic priorities. "I was in a neck brace lying on the couch for almost four months. I had a lot of time to think about what I wanted to be in the world. I'm so busy, I haven't seen my family. So I made a decision that I would start doing things that weren't about money; that I wasn't going to wait to have the impact that I wanted to have."

After that decision, Angela first founded and ran an educational social venture; she then completed a PhD program. She is now a managing partner and impact investor with NewProfit, where she invests grant and equity funding in US-based proximate entrepreneurs reimagining the future of work.

The inequitable world of work is what she calls "a big, juicy problem. Seventy-three million US residents don't have a bachelor's degree; how are they able to connect to the jobs of the future?" Most adults acquire new skills through their employer; the problem is that 80 percent of professional development dollars are spent on the highest wage earners. Angela points out that this disparity leaves "very little for people who are living in the bottom 25 percent as far as income. A large percentage of these people are earning less than a living wage and are either working a less than fifteen dollars an hour job or piecing together multiple gig jobs to make ends meet."

Angela sees a more equitable future of work as "the issue of our time. It's not important just for these communities, it's important for our democracy. That makes me wake up and go to sleep thinking about it, but it also makes me excited. This is the problem I want to solve, because I think it's going to do good for the world."

When Angela thinks about the future of work and workers in the US, she remembers her grandfather and her community. "I was raised by my grandparents about forty-five minutes outside of Chicago. My grandfather worked at the local Chrysler plant—a blue-collar job. He worked on the line, but at that time, he made enough because he was part of the union. We could have a house that we owned, and I had all the necessities."

She also saw what happened to the same community when the work disappeared. When the factories closed down, jobs with wages that sustained family life no longer existed. This made it personal for Angela. "I see how that's changed the prospects not only for people like my grandfather, but also for their children. What does it mean for kids when their parents are more stressed out, when they don't have incomes?"

Reflecting on her own career, she humbly recognizes how exceptional her opportunities have been compared to those of the people she grew up with. "I finished my doctoral work at Harvard University, and I'm working as an impact investor. But if you go back to my community now, and I visit frequently, a lot of people don't even think those options exist. When I was living there, I didn't know they existed either."

She adds, "I always think about people living outside of the coasts, in rural and underinvested communities—how if they could tap into some of these life-changing experiences, that could really put them on the road to a different trajectory." She advises that it's critical to find "what you're passionate about, what problem you want to solve in the world, and how you can make that your career. Find people who share that passion, because they've done it, so they know the roadmap—and that excitement will be the driver."

Growing up, Angela never knew she could make a living solving problems she cared about and understood from her own experience, such as the future of work. In her last year as an undergraduate, she worked as a substitute teacher in a couple of different local high schools for extra money. As she describes it, "One was the 'good' high school, and the other one was the high school that 'the bad kids' went to—predominantly Black and Brown kids." Some of the students were only a few years younger than she was, yet they had already decided what was possible for them, which pained her. But Angela found energy in "sharing with them, hearing their stories, telling mine, and really thinking about some widened pathways for them."

After college, she taught for a year in Chicago but lacked a safety net. She figured that she needed to "go somewhere and make a lot of money, so that I could then give back. In my mind, that was how it worked; you do well for yourself, and then you can give back."

She went into corporate America, working for the multinational telecommunications and consumer electronics company Nokia and volunteering on the side. Working in the private sector, she had all the trappings she thought she would want in life: an apartment in New York, material things, and international travels. But after the car accident, Angela committed her life to impact and took a sabbatical year off. While living in Paris, she came up with her first social venture, the Global Language Project.

"It was really based on my experience growing up in a very disinvested area of rural America. I didn't hear anything about the future of work or being a global citizen. How could I create a program to help children think differently about their opportunities?" Her goal was to help kids expand their horizons by learning to speak a second or third language. It was the first time in her life that she had done something where money was not the primary objective and it was really all about impact. Today, Angela says, "I tell people it was the hardest job I ever had, as well as the most fulfilling thing I've ever done. Now I understand you can have that intersection of profit and purpose in life. When you work at that intersection, at least for me, it gives you more than you could ever give—it gives meaning to your work."

But there was still a rude awakening ahead for Angela. She was spending a majority of her time—about 80 percent—with funders. "I thought I would be able to sit in the back with the kids and learn Mandarin and add that to my repertoire; but as the organization grew, I found that I was spending most of my time outside of those classrooms."

She spent a great deal of her time educating philanthropists. Her challenge was to try to build a case for something she knew all about as part of her own lived experience and explain why the venture mattered to people who didn't share that experience. She encountered a philanthropist in New York City who seemed to understand Angela's project. "We bonded over our love of living in Paris. But then the conversation took a turn to politics, which I had learned you try never to talk about in professional settings. We were at a restaurant on the Upper East Side in New York, and she told me, 'You know, I just never go above 96th Street. I did once, I went to 125th Street, and it took me an hour to get there. I just don't think I can make those trips anymore.'"

Angela—who lived above 96th Street in Harlem at the time, as did many of the kids with whom she worked—observes, "This woman had the ability to write a check that could solve all of our fundraising issues. But where is the line between having some type of alignment on values, and what's important? That was a pivotal moment for me. Even if she can write that check, I don't think she can be a partner with us in the work if she is unwilling to visit the communities where the students lived."

Thus began Angela Jackson's questioning of philanthropy, which led her to undertake a PhD reflecting on this crucial question: "How do we intentionally use capital and service as levers for change?" As Angela says, "There's a lot of power in dollars and how we invest them. They say you vote with your dollar." She set out to help philanthropists think about how we can create a more equitable future based on new ways of deploying capital.

Angela sees her ability to connect with people as one of her superpowers. When she speaks with potential investors, she says, "For me, it's not like I'm asking them for money. That might be the end result; but the way I approach them is based on relationships—learning about a person and sharing my story and my 'why.' " It gives people who control significant financial resources an opportunity to have a greater impact. And when you do this, as she puts it, "You bring together what some people might see as odd bedfellows. That's when magic happens; because when you think about systems change, it's not one entity. It's really going to be an ecosystem working together to move mountains."

The people she encounters who are "on fire, those are the ones working at that intersection of what they're passionate about and what they believe in and making an income doing it.... Some people say we shouldn't tell kids to dream like that. But that's exactly what we should do, because that's the work that you're going to do when it's really hard. And when you're being pulled at the margins, when it's most challenging, that's when it's going to be the most gratifying work."

PART II
POWER AND PRIVILEGE

AMANDA'S TRIALS

Amanda Nguyen found her purpose—or rather, it most unfortunately found her—through the double injustice of her experiencing both a sexual assault and then the Kafkaesque justice system that revictimizes and retraumatizes survivors.

So how do you exercise your rights, change the law in the United States for rape survivors, and seek your own justice?

First, Amanda sought to understand power. She researched the hierarchical structure of the US government, both in Massachusetts and at the federal level. She built out her own key stakeholder map, taking into account not just each member of Congress or state legislator, but also each legislator's chief of staff, legislative director, legislative assistant, and legislative correspondent. Amanda kept reminding herself that she was fighting for a community. "This was bigger than me. These members of Congress needed to be part of the cause I was fighting for."

She and her team kept detailed Excel spreadsheets on all legislative staff members, all the way down to the interns. As she put it, "It's a grind. But we had to learn the rules of the game." Amanda and her team met with anyone and everyone and sent out flurries of emails in what she dubs her key technique: "pestering for progress." She kept going, no matter the setbacks, having learned that, "Everyone says no until you find your first yes."

It's important to note that the pestering was strategic. "One of the most annoying things, at least [it's] a pet peeve for me, is when people say to call your member of Congress if you care about an issue. It doesn't actually help if you call a member of Congress." Amanda and her colleagues at Rise Justice Labs have been able to pass thirty-three laws across the country in record-breaking time because they put in the work to understand the rules of the game—the only way to win. Amanda explains, "There is a very specific procedural rule that inhibits 99 percent of bills. It's called 'agenda-setting authority.' It is really critical to understand if you want to move a bill through. What the agenda-setting authority means is literally that—the power to set the agenda in order for bills to be voted on."

In the US Senate, for example, if the Senate Majority Leader (at the time, Republican Senator Mitch McConnell) blocks a bill from being put on the agenda, it will not come to the larger body for a vote. At the federal level, the Senate Majority Leader is one of only four people who can advance a bill, one of the others being the Speaker of the House (at the time, Democratic Representative Nancy Pelosi). Committee chairmen/women are also key. Sexual violence issues come under the jurisdiction of the Judiciary Committee, at the time led by Senator Charles Grassley, a Republican.

The other critical piece of knowledge is that only a majority member of the chamber can sponsor a bill, an accepted rule on both sides of the aisle. In a Republican-dominated Senate like the one Amanda had to work with, for example, if a Democrat cares about a bill and wants it to move forward, they have to cede the lead sponsor position to a Republican. This unspoken rule within the US Congress is also applicable to every state legislature.

Amanda points out that at the time, when she would see a Democratic Senator standing with a group of survivors, for instance, and claiming to introduce a bill, it was probably just a way to get a sound bite for a campaign because they knew full well that Mitch McConnell wasn't going to put it on the agenda if a Democrat sponsored it. This is the dirty truth about politics, in her view: "It is a game, and both sides play it. There are no angels on either side, and the ones who get hurt are the American people."

Amanda had to learn not to take political betrayals personally, no matter how hurtful they might be; she made a choice to work within the system, as imperfect as it is. She defines herself as a "pathological optimist," a necessary stance for everyone engaged in the search for social justice. And as in all social justice activities, persistence is crucial.

Even while living in DC, Amanda kept traveling back and forth while fighting for a bill in Massachusetts that would allow rape kits, including her own, not to be destroyed at the six-month mark. But she was running out of time, as her kit was now at risk after being wrongly removed from the forensic lab despite having been granted yet another extension. The day set for the bill to be heard was the last date on the legislative calendar in June 2016. "My own justice was on the line. If the bill passed, my rape kit would be saved."

However, if the bill was not voted on that day, Amanda and other survivors and allies would have to wait for the next legislative session. It would mean starting the whole advocacy process again, potentially with a whole different legislative staff. More importantly, it would be too late to save Amanda's rape kit. While sitting at the airport on the way to Boston to advocate one last time for the bill, she got a call from one of the state policy advisors informing her that the Speaker of the Massachusetts House of Representatives wasn't going to bring up the bill for a vote. Amanda broke down and cried in an airport bathroom cubicle. He had the agenda-setting authority, so it would never even be voted on. But then she got messages from other rape survivors saying, "Just go. Just be present. Just stand there outside the door of the floor and have each and every one of them have to confront your face, your being, as they walk off the floor."

She was the last person to get on the flight.

CHAPTER FOUR

Choose Impact as Your Metric for Success

Luis Garza's Unlikely Story: Venturing into Early Childhood Education

"Dude, Instagram is being acquired by Facebook for a billion dollars, and I'm changing diapers. I definitely did something wrong in my life. No?"

No, Luis, you did not. It's all about what metric you choose to measure your life by.

Luis Garza grew up in Monterrey, Mexico, never thinking he would end up working in early childhood development or even social impact, but his early learning app Kinedu has now been used by over seven million parents to help their children in the most formative years of life. He was lucky enough to be educated at some of the foremost US schools: Stanford for his bachelor's, and then Harvard Business School for his MBA. While at Stanford, he took some classes with Kevin Systrom, who went on to found Instagram, spawning an entire generation of "likes" and changing the world in one way—literally one filter at a time.

The pull toward measuring success through money and likes on social media is difficult to shake for many, especially when you are always encouraged to compare yourself to others. Luis observes, "I never had the goal of being in social impact; I'm as capitalist as you can get. In many ways, the biggest value a human should have is liberty. It's freedom, essentially."

Personally, I think the desire to do good was there all along, even if Luis didn't know it at the time and wasn't familiar with social impact lingo. Indeed, he believes strongly, "If you cannot exercise your freedom, you're not free. If you don't have health, you're not free. If you don't have the ability to leverage your brain because your education has been half-a**ed, then you're not free. We have to help people be free, and we have to provide an equal first stepping-stone so that everybody can exercise their freedom. That's the type of mindset I grew up with."

Luis grew up in a Catholic family that was financially comfortable and that always stressed service to others. As he describes it, "It's this mantra that if we have been fortunate, we have to help others be fortunate. We have to give back to the society that has given us so much."

While at Harvard Business School, he was unsure of his future path, but was secure in the realization that he wanted to help others have the kind of opportunities he'd had. As a proud capitalist, he figured "the best way to do that was to help people have great careers by creating jobs and companies. There are two ways to take a stab at that: venture capital or being an entrepreneur." Though he was drawn to venture capital, he chose entrepreneurship. He explains, "My thought process was that the only way I was going to learn was to actually do it."

While on Christmas break during his last year at Harvard, Luis reached out to a man who'd run nonprofit schools for low-income families, recognizing that parents in those communities didn't have many options when their children were aged three to four. "He wanted to start lower-income day care solutions for these families, and he was so passionate about it. He's such a good storyteller that I fell in love with the project." Luis pledged to spend his last semester helping to craft a business plan and raise capital. "That way, I thought I was learning how to start a company."

Eventually the project refocused from creating low-income day care chains to corporate-sponsored day care chains, on the basis that corporations would be able to afford to pay for them to provide for their employees. At the end of the semester, Luis was convinced to join the company as a cofounder. As he put it, "I had other options, but I was so intrigued by what he was doing that I felt that it was the right path for me. I got into early childhood through the entrepreneurial mindset. But once I was there starting to research the importance of early childhood and talking to families, recognizing the impact I was having, I just went deeper and deeper down the rabbit hole. I don't see myself coming back out, because it's one of those businesses that lets me sleep well at night. And if we can make it work, then we'll be making a sustainable machine for good in the world that can scale and reach more people."

Interestingly, when I worked at Save the Children from 2009–2012, about a third of our work was in response to emergencies (i.e., the latest cyclone or conflict) and two thirds was in development (i.e., longer-term work in education, health, child protection, and more). One evening in London, I was having drinks in a pub with Save the Children's Director of Emergencies. (That is what one does in London, you go to pubs with your colleagues starting at around five-thirty.) He told me, and I am paraphrasing based on memory: To be honest, Alex, everything we do at Save the Children that isn't early childhood development is an emergency. In everything we do after the first five years of a child's life, we're trying to catch up with the fact that due to the unfair lottery of birth, children weren't given the same opportunities to begin with.

It's been shown time and time again—for example, in the work of Nobel Prize-winner James Heckman—that early childhood development is the best investment philanthropic organizations and governments can make, since it yields tremendous returns both in reducing social and economic inequality and spurring economic growth overall. Despite this, early childhood education is the most underinvested area of education. At a stage of life where parents are as much the educational providers as teachers, both have less support and fewer tools. Luis asked himself, "Knowing this, how can I not be working in early childhood?"

Luis Garza faced challenges nearly every step of the way. One of these was confronting ingrained cultural attitudes. "My country is traditionally very misogynistic in the way it looks at women in the workplace." When he pitched ways to support women workers and families, he got responses from executives at big companies that made him wonder if he was up against too high a wall. "It seemed impossible. This was never going to work."

On one visit, Luis was told: "You know, for women here in the company, we do a Mother's Day party, and we do cake and give them sandwiches, and we're happy with that." And this company was not the only one that thought they needed to do very little to support working mothers and parents, even though helping women and families benefits both employees and employers in terms of retention, productivity, and reducing burnout. Luis was speechless. He explains, "But ten years ago, that was the reality in Mexico. That was one of the reasons I went from building physical day care centers to Kinedu."

Indeed, after a few years, and despite some good progress opening physical day care centers, Luis grew frustrated by the speed at which they could grow if they had to depend on corporations "who got it" becoming willing to extend day care benefits to their employees. As he worked every day on the day care centers, a related opportunity emerged—one Luis thought could scale better and that aligned well with his skills as a software engineer.

As Luis saw the realities of day care operations firsthand and heard from parents and educators, he gained two insights. First, the majority of early childhood development happens—or *doesn't* happen—at home, rather than in day care centers, and is facilitated mostly by parents. Second, an ideal system for early childhood development would be to connect parents with the activities of day care centers so that parents and day care staff could work in tandem on supporting a child's milestones.

Those insights became the for-profit app and software system Kinedu, a project Luis spun off on his own from the initial day care business to provide a program parents could carry out at home. He and his team considered the fact that day care centers gave out handouts, sheets of paper, or PDFs of daily activity ideas. So why not an app? Every step of the way, they added functions to help parents understand how to stimulate their young children. Once they had an app, why not do a video? Next, why not videos with voice-over, and while they were at it, voice-overs in both English and Spanish? As Luis says, "With a click of a button, you're in any market you want."

Kinedu launched in English and Spanish, offering a program for the first twelve months of a child's life that provided parents with customized plans to help their children learn and grow. It took off, and they went on to extend the app to the first four years of a child's life, as well as creating a version in Portuguese for the Brazilian market. Luis explains that key changes in attitudes on early childhood are needed. "We need to help families understand that what you do in those first few years of life can be a big boost to your child."

Even after he developed Kinedu, Luis encountered resistance—sometimes in unexpected quarters. In a meeting with the team at the Harvard Center on the Developing Child, he showed a video about Kinedu in its early stages. He thought the meeting had gone swimmingly, but their response surprised him: "This is great! This is going to be a fantastic project, but we're not really interested in projects that do not support lower-income families, because high-income families have all the support they need."

While lower-income families do indeed need more support, Luis observes, "How many parents do we know who are high-income but have no idea how to take care of children or how to stimulate them—who don't know the importance of early childhood? They think that early childhood is just feeding your baby and changing diapers. My perspective is that this is a global problem of parents who are either not engaged or not informed. It's everywhere, in every country, in every level of society."

And in fact, Kinedu users span a whole range of incomes, from high to low, especially since Kinedu offers both a free version of its app and a paid one. From user research data, Luis and his team calculate that about 35 percent of their customers are using cell phones that cost less than one hundred dollars, as opposed to an iPhone that costs a thousand. Many are in Brazil, one of Kinedu's newest markets.

The second major overall issue he confronted was the way people perceived his work. As he relates, "I had so many comments in the beginning that it was just a toy—a little app. It's this small project." Even though he was convinced he could "conquer the world" with Kinedu, others weren't yet on board. "Convincing people that this could be something really big and impactful was a big challenge. It wasn't until we got the first big investor to come in that it started to feel real for my friends and family." Even Luis's father, who was supportive throughout his journey, challenged him consistently with questions like, "You got an MBA from Harvard. Why are you wasting it on doing a small app? You could be doing big things. It takes the same energy to think big as to think small." The negative feedback undermined his confidence at the outset, but he was energized by proving people wrong. "One of the things investors always said is that Kinedu wouldn't be successful in the US—and it's now our biggest market."

For Kinedu, the pandemic presented a number of challenges, but also real opportunities. Suddenly learning online and via an app became a widespread necessity, at least for families with internet connectivity and smartphones. Luis sensed an opportunity to achieve an even bigger goal, which he describes as "trying to change the dogma that quality learning has to happen in a quality childcare center." He observes, "You can be at home, or you can be at a center as well. You can be in a micro school, you can be in a pod—wherever you are, we at Kinedu can support the adults, the caregivers, in providing high-quality experiences. I do think that our mission is redefining the way it's done. The capacity for children to have quality care shouldn't be limited to whatever box they're sitting in."

Kinedu saw a lot more traffic during the pandemic lockdowns and extended its premium content for free during March and April of 2020, growing its user base to a figure that is now over seven million (thanks in part to an investment from Solve through our philanthropic venture arm, Solve Innovation Future). There was also an economic crunch for parents unsure of the future who were uncomfortable paying even thirty dollars a year. Kinedu was responsive and lowered prices by about 50 percent, with an immediately noticeable impact.

Before COVID-19 hit, Luis was already planning a new version of Kinedu for educators and day care centers. In light of the crisis, it was significantly revamped. "We were very fortunate we were building it in the middle of the pandemic, because we wouldn't have had the flexibility [to pivot to building in relevant new features] if this platform had already launched."

When a large school chain in Mexico asked to see a "roadmap" related to home and school, Kinedu was hired for a fifty-five-school system, catering to eight thousand children from infants to five-year-olds. Luis and his team were able to pivot from building what was originally envisioned as a curriculum management tool for teachers to creating a platform where you can engage parents, centralize the curriculum, and deploy an online early childhood program in schools. He points out: "In early childhood, tools like Google Classroom don't work because they think of the student as a user. A one-year-old is not a user of our platform; it's the parents or the educators." Now Kinedu is deploying what they call "the online preschool experience, educator-led, but implemented by parents."

When Luis looks back on the times people told him he was wasting his degrees on a small app, he recalls asking himself, "What if I don't try, and I end up forever regretting not trying?" Despite the challenges of entrepreneurship, he offers this encouragement: "You have to start. If you have an idea and you think it's worth it, you should pursue it. Most people don't start at all."

yourImpact Balance Sheet

To help you choose and see impact as your key metric for success, let's help you create what I call *yourImpact Balance Sheet*.

For those of you who are personal finance aficionados like me, you will likely have heard of *Your Money or Your Life* by Vicki Robin and Joe Dominguez. Published originally in 1992 and still popular today, the book's premise is simple—it asks readers to think about money in much broader terms.

The central idea is to redefine your relationship with money, and not just in terms of dollars in your bank account. It's not just what you earn, what you spend, your assets, and your debts, but also your time—what the authors call your "life energy"—and your satisfaction and fulfillment. From there, you can see whether the trade-offs you are making with regard to money are worth it. Let's say you're working over ninety hours a week: you earn good money, but you hate your job, and you never get to see your loved ones. Is your money worth your life?

I think this idea functions even more effectively when you choose impact as the core metric to think about your life, and when, like Luis, you might have a hard time shaking off the traditional definitions of success and the comparisons to other people's lives, houses, cars, and vacations.

The first critical thing to do is recognize that your life and your potential for impact are more than just your job.

That can be a hard one for some people. When I meet new people at a conference or party, I sometimes ask what turns out to be a very difficult question. Instead of saying "What do you do?" or "Where do you work?" (the usual introductory questions that often pop up in casual conversation, at least in the US), I ask, "Who are you?" This stumps most people. I am sure some people might even find it rude or intrusive, but that in and of itself is interesting to me: why is it okay to ask people what they do, but not okay to ask them who they are?

When we define people by what they do, we are measuring their success by their productivity, and often that productivity is narrowly defined as their job. I imagine this can sometimes make mothers who are not working a paying job feel bad, or shame people who are currently unemployed, even if by any reasonable measure it should not.

Two scenarios often ensue in response to my unsettling "Who are you?" question:

1. The person often recognizes that this is not the standard question. They ponder it, then comment that it's hard to answer. After a few minutes, they answer it as if it were the usual "What do you do?" question, perhaps with the addition of something short in front, such as "I am a father of two" to try and curtail the implication that who they are is in fact "just" their job.

2. They break down in a semi-philosophical meltdown about their inability to define themselves in any way that isn't about their job or their productivity. Then, they reflect on how terrible it is that they have been captured by the capitalist system, American consumerism, and so on.

A few people do offer different answers. My former colleague at the Clinton Foundation, Elsa Palanza, came up to me one day and described a wonderful brunch she'd had sitting next to my dear friend Qusai Hammouri, whom she found to be incredible and inspiring (which they are!). I made a comment about how busy Qusai was at the hospital.

Elsa was surprised: "Why is he at the hospital? Is he okay?"

Me: "Because he works there."

Elsa: ?!?!?!

Me: "He's a pediatric spinal surgeon. He fixes kids' spines and resets the odd broken bone."

Elsa: "What?! This never came up. We talked about art the whole time, and he told me about his paintings and how he curates art shows at his loft in Bushwick. I thought he was an artist!"

Me: "He is an artist! He's also a pediatric spinal surgeon, and that occupies quite a bit of his time, too."

Elsa: "He's even more incredible than I realized."

Indeed! But the broader point is that Qusai (who now goes by he/him as a doctor and they/them as an artist) does not define themselves solely (or sometimes at all) by their day job. They are not ashamed of their day job, and obviously they do *a lot* of good there, especially given that they work in a Staten Island hospital where the majority of their patients are low-income. But Qusai primarily identifies as a gay Muslim immigrant, a Jordanian and an American, a Bushwick resident, a chef and a generous host, a friend and family man, an uncle, an artist, a curator, an entrepreneur—and maybe last, a pediatric spinal surgeon.

Of course, your job occupies a large majority of your waking hours, so your work will always be (and should be) a primary lever of power for your impact, positive or negative. But you may not always have enough influence at your job to be able to have a positive impact, and you may not be in a position to quit your day job at the moment. You may also work long hours or have to work two (or even three) jobs. That might not leave a lot of time for other side activities, especially if you are taking care of children or other family members.

I do not want to minimize these circumstances and say everyone can start a social enterprise on the side of their main gig or change jobs immediately for better impact. But even if you have little time to spare and you can't quit your day job, there are many areas in your life where you can have impact and where you hold power: your family, your community, and your purchasing decisions.

CONSTRUCTING your Impact BALANCE SHEET

Step 1: Reflect on who you are. By that, I mean: What identities are most important to you? What power do you hold in any or all of the identities and dimensions of your life? You should think of every core area where you spend time (and/or money)—every identity that matters—as a lever you can and should pull. You have *power* in all these places whether you are currently using it or not. And whether you realize it or not, you are having a positive or negative impact across all these core areas.

You can seek to move the needle toward more positive impact once you have mapped out your life on yourImpact Balance Sheet. One commonly used tool I employ to think about core areas of power is what is called a Wheel of Life. My friend Shabrina Jiva, a certified executive coach, first introduced me to this exercise a few years ago. Although there are several versions (many available online), these are the core areas I thought would work well for our purposes:

- Career/job
- Money—giving, investing, and purchasing
- Love relationships
- Family
- Friends
- Spirituality and community
- Learning and personal growth
- Side activities—entrepreneurial ventures, volunteering, social, cultural, art, sport, fun

You may decide to add or subtract core areas, but if you remove any, then think about why you may want to take out a particular item. Is it an area of your life you're neglecting in terms of the positive impact you could be having?

Based on the above, let's use these areas and write them down as rows to construct yourImpact Balance Sheet, using this example as a framework:

yourImpact BALANCE SHEET

Core Area	Impact	Fulfillment	Earnings/ Year	Cost [time + money] \ Year	% of Time Spent
	score + or - 10	score + or - 10	$/year	$/year + hours/year	%
1. Career/Job					
2. Giving					
3. Investing					
4. Purchasing					
5. Relationships					
6. Learning					
7. Side Activities					
8. Spirituality/ Community					
9. And More					

Step 2: Once you have your levers of power, score these in the first two columns in terms of impact and fulfillment on a range of 10 to -10, with 10 being the best you can ever achieve in terms of positive impact and fulfillment, and -10 being the worst in terms of negative impact; zero represents neutral.

For example, let's start with that first row—your Job/Career. Does your job have on balance a positive or negative impact in the world? Are you working for a human rights nonprofit but traveling all the time while doing so, which does not help the environment? Perhaps that's an 8.

Are you working for an oil company, but in their innovation department that investigates renewables? Maybe that's -2, or perhaps it's 4. It depends on how you feel about it, and also on the commitment of the company you work for. Is your department a tiny part of their budget, hence more about greenwashing than real positive impact? Or is 90 percent of their R & D focused on renewables?

How fulfilling is your job, again on a scale of 10 to -10? For instance, you may love your job and your colleagues, but you're working over ninety hours a week and in a different city every week. Perhaps that's 4. Or it may even be -2, because you have two delightful kids at home. Or it might be an 8, because you're twenty-four and love the traveling and racking up the hotel points—it's up to you. Or perhaps you like the content of your job, but the workplace culture is toxic, and you did not get that promotion you wanted. Maybe that's a -5.

Then go across all the core areas in the rows—your money, relationships, friends, and so on—and score these on the 10 to -10 range in terms of impact and fulfillment. Don't worry if you are not always sure. This is meant to be a quick exercise to see where you stand now, and to help you focus.

Step 3: In the next column, calculate how much each core area brings to you in terms of earnings per year. Of course, a large part of this is likely your job, but if you have side gigs, entrepreneurial ventures, or investments, the earnings they generate should be included, too.

Step 4: In the last column, note how much each core area actually costs you in terms of life energy (i.e., time and money). In *Your Money or Your Life*, Vicki Robin points out that it's important to take a good look at all the tertiary time each of us spends on a job besides the official hours we work. For example, the actual life energy cost of a job is not just forty, sixty, or ninety hours a week in the office or at your computer. It's also how much time you spend commuting and traveling, how many hours of sleep you lose doing it, how much stress you endure, and how much physical or psychological therapy you have to do because of your demanding job. You will, of course, also have to spend money on commuting, as well as on buying the right suits or clothes that fit the part, a chunk of change on said therapy, and so on. You might find that your job is costing you a lot more than you realize when you stop to figure it out.

Step 5: Lastly, note what percentage of your time you spend on each of your core areas.

Now, take a step back and ask yourself if yourImpact Balance Sheet works for you.

Are you having a positive impact in your life, and are you spending the majority of your life energy and time on this? Are you enjoying the journey as you go? Is the trade-off of money earned vs. money and time spent vs. impact and fulfillment actually worth it? Where could you have more impact? Where could you redirect more of your life energy to spend on things that better align to your purpose?

You have a finite amount of time each week, each year, and each decade. And unlike the majority of people in the world today, you have a choice about what you do with your waking hours—at least some of them, even if you might have some unavoidable obligations. How can you move the needle in yourImpact Balance Sheet in small or big ways to maximize both your impact and your level of fulfillment?

In her book, Vicki Robinson goes even deeper; for example, when thinking about purchases big and small, a nice dress you like might cost two hundred dollars. And say you calculate your actual net revenue per hour as fifty dollars (after all the commuting time and other costs are subtracted from your pay). Is that dress worth four hours of your life, or would those four hours of your life be better spent on volunteering, spending time with your kids, and/or giving to support two hundred children getting lifesaving early childhood vaccines? And is that house in a nicer area, which costs an extra $500,000 (when you count the price plus interest payments) compared to where you live now, worth four years of your life, or would you rather be able to retire sooner and help others get their own house to support the creation of intergenerational wealth?

Most importantly perhaps: what would the ideal balance sheet look like, and how might you be able to get there? How can you choose impact as your metric for success and prioritize that while still feeling fulfilled and having enough to provide for yourself and your family?

Do not worry if you are not where you want to be yet. yourImpact Balance Sheet is just a snapshot in time. It's a a diagnostic that allows you to track your progress as you go. Try it for yourself, and let me know how you get on!

The good news is that finding and living your purpose can make you live a longer and happier life. As a June 2020 article in *The Washington Post* points out, "Although diet and exercise are certainly vital for health, science shows there is another longevity ingredient we often overlook: finding purpose." Ten studies involving more than 136,000 people found that "having purpose in life can lower your mortality risk by about 17 percent—about as much as following the famed Mediterranean diet." This is good news for Akshay Saxena, who spent quite a lot of time trying to define his core metric for success.

Akshay Saxena's Story: Struggling with What Success and Impact Mean

"I spent most of my twenties oscillating between [two priorities,] figuring out what is the point of living: whether it's to accumulate lots of wealth, or whether it's to do good. And if it was to do good, then *how* to do good?"

I met Akshay Saxena in 2006 in London. We were both employed at the Boston Consulting Group (BCG)—I worked out of the London Office, while he worked out of the Mumbai Office. We had both been seconded to Save the Children, meaning BCG was paying our salary while we worked there for a few months. I was on the team that supported Save the Children's field and regional offices, helping them merge their operations (a process somewhere between a joint venture and a post-merger integration, which is why they needed consultants). Akshay was working to launch and support new "Member Countries," which involved fundraising operations in India, South Africa, and more. In theory, this would help make Save the Children less Western while also helping raise more revenue.

We spent many hours debating our respective life purposes, and to a large extent, we still do. For Akshay, the journey was first "making peace with how much money I wanted. Breaking out of needing to earn money was a very important reckoning." Although he grew up in a cramped apartment in the suburbs of Delhi, his family was middle class for India in the '90s: "We were well-to-do, but every month, balancing the books was an important part of our existence."

When he started work at BCG after graduating from one of the best engineering schools of the country, IIT (Indian Institute of Technology, similar in that sense to MIT), Akshay's paycheck allowed him to stop counting every rupee for the first time in his life. He had certainly never before stayed at a five-star hotel. "Living in fancy hotels, flying all over the country, wearing a suit—a lot of these trappings of wealth were things which we were told we aspired to, that we wanted to live a good life. A good life was not having to worry about what you were spending, not having to economize on which brand of cheese you ate—a lot of the things that became part and parcel of growing up in the India of the '80s and the '90s."

But for Akshay, these trappings got old quickly. After six or eight months, he was bored. "I'd come to the realization that I'd actually shockingly achieved that goal with my first job. There was no aspiration after [reaching that milestone]." He started to examine what he was really doing and concluded, "This is not to pass judgment, because all work is valuable in some ways, but the day-to-day of advising corporations on how to be very efficient just wasn't very interesting."

Seeking meaning, Akshay took up the opportunity to be assigned for a few months to Save the Children, which is how we met; but he quickly became bored there, too. For him, there were still many similarities with his previous work at BCG, in that there wasn't much innovation in play at either organization. "A lot of it was taking innovation that had happened perhaps a decade or two ago and just making sure it scaled—which is really important, but not something I could get excited about. My desire to be an engineer was about solving difficult problems."

After Save the Children, still unsure of his path, Akshay started an MBA at Harvard Business School. During the summer after his first year, yearning for an environment of innovation, Akshay joined a biotech company founded by two Stanford professors called Heartflow. He was their first employee. Pretty quickly, they raised hundreds of millions of dollars, so he never went back to finish his second year of business school and instead started working there full-time. After three years at Heartflow, and with most of his shares vested, Akshay had made enough money to pay down all of his debt; and the opportunity to solve a really big problem in India beckoned.

While in business school, Akshay and a few of his friends had founded an education start-up called Avanti as a side gig, one focused on low-income students. In 2013, things were starting to take off both in terms of growth and impact: "What we were finding was really exciting." He decided to take the plunge and return to India to give Avanti a go full-time. "The primary driver was the realization that I care much more about leaving the world more equitable than about leaving my children richer. Once that choice was made, the easiest place to start was academics, because we understood the problem of getting kids through hard tests."

Akshay and his cofounders had all graduated from IITs, which are extremely prestigious; admissions to these technical schools are competitive, requiring excellent scores on a public exam taken at the end of high school. Unfortunately, as Akshay and his colleagues understood well, those test scores were overly determinative for each student's opportunities going forward. "The broader problem that we're really interested in solving is one of equity, especially in the context of India. We're obviously a pretty poor country. We're also an extremely inequitable country. So even though the country's actually growing from a GDP perspective and people have made money, we've done a pretty good job of leaving the poor really far behind. As a consequence, we tend to mirror a little bit of what the British Raj said, which is that the only real way you can escape extreme poverty is if you're academically good. Then, through a series of exams, you can gain access to the best institutions for undergraduate education."

These institutions are still largely publicly funded and affordable. But if you don't get in, your options become much more limited if you cannot afford private college or are seeking vocational qualifications. As Akshay observes: "It's very murky if you don't go to college. There's no certification, there's no accreditation. And while all these good things exist in the public college ecosystem, it's very, very small, which means that access is gated by how well you do in public schooling—and public schooling is really bad. So there's a systematic bias against people who aren't wealthy or aren't from the middle class actually bettering their lives."

This is the daunting challenge Akshay and his team at Avanti are trying to solve. For the first five years of the organization, they focused on the easiest kids, the ones who had already tested very well to gain entry into public magnet schools in India. They tried to support these low-income students with after-school programs so they could make it through the highly competitive national exams—the ones to qualify students to get into the IITs as well as universities for other high-demand fields including medicine. Using a collaborative approach and self-directed learning, Akshay and his team had some success in their endeavor. Then they decided to tackle a much more complex problem: helping low-income kids who were not already attending good schools.

In Akshay's view, for decades, or even a century, the education system in India has developed "a muscle memory of being really ineffective. And the problems are well documented. There are massive problems with teacher incentives and teacher absenteeism, and the home environment is not conducive to study. These kids in public schools are basically learning the same way as Indians were in the 1960s and '70s and not doing very well. So how do you create equity in what I believe is among the most inequitable schooling systems on the planet? It just so happened that this was the problem I started with. But I think I now have my reasons to continue solving it. There are many, many problems to solve. This is the one I think I am best equipped to solve now."

Seen through the lens of Marshall Ganz's "Story of Self," Akshay's childhood was undoubtedly a key influence in his mission to disrupt India's broken education system, since as he describes it, "Even though I did really well in school, I spent most of my life hating school." Even in college, he enjoyed things like basketball, theater, and debating, none of which had anything to do with academics. "My overwhelming sense throughout my schooling, and I think most of college, was that I was wasting my time in the classroom."

But in his teens, Akshay had the opportunity to step away from formal schooling. His father was a merchant ship captain, and Akshay, his brother, and his mother accompanied his father on the ship for months at a time. During that time, he taught himself primarily by reading books, "learning whatever the hell I wanted to learn." He realized why he felt he'd been wasting time in traditional classrooms: "I was constantly trying to fit what I was learning to tests. I was being forced to learn within bounds. You're spending more time preparing to score well on your final exam than really learning. The way we learn in classrooms makes no sense. The curriculum was really outdated. This was reinforced when I went to college."

Setting out to build Avanti differently, Akshay and his cofounders got really excited when they put kids in a self-directed learning environment and saw the results. "We actually saw that work a lot better than instructional teaching." Their research over time has borne out the validity of this approach. "If there's one driving mission for me personally, it's that since kids spend so much time in classrooms and in structured learning environments, we need to find ways for those not to be a waste of time and not to be actually detrimental to them."

Once Akshay knew he could always make enough money to live comfortably, he chose impact as his core metric of success. His mission to redress educational inequity in India was built upon "the personal experience of wasting away years of my life in a dreary classroom, where it was borderline depressing. For that not to happen to anyone else is a big motivator."

Why Wait? Start Now on Making a Positive Impact

Think about Akshay's dilemma for yourself: should you wait until you make a good amount of money to take care of your family before giving back?

Bob Harrison, the former CEO of the Clinton Global Initiative (and a great boss), used to do brown bag lunches every semester for interns. A few dozen idealistic twenty- to twenty-five-year-olds would roll into our offices to start careers in social impact through a coveted internship—or so they thought.

Counterintuitively, Bob advised these interns against starting their careers in social impact. He would tell them: Go make money. Go learn some skills. Then give back through government, philanthropy, nonprofits, or all of these avenues, a path he himself had followed to towering success.

Bob always wanted to make an impact and have a career in public service. But when he graduated, he felt nonprofits and governments did not offer good training options, unlike corporations that invested in the professional development of their junior staff. He also valued the financial security a for-profit career afforded: it gave you options later in life. Thus, he worked his way up on Wall Street over twenty years, ultimately becoming a senior partner at Goldman Sachs in the firm's investment banking division, as well as global cohead of its Communications, Media, and Entertainment group. He then retired from banking at perhaps the exact right time: after Goldman's lucrative IPO in 1999, but before the 2008 financial crisis. He could retire several times over compared to most people, but instead of doing so, he decided to give back through a second career in public service.

The 2008 Democratic political campaigns welcomed him with open arms. Bob would regale the interns with tales of his time during the campaign season, first with John Edwards, then Hillary Clinton, which is how he met the people in Clinton world, started working at the foundation, and then ultimately became the CEO of Clinton Global Initiative. In addition to his role there, Bob also came to chair the board of trustees of Cornell University, his alma mater; this was a major role, especially as Cornell was at the time opening their tech campus on Roosevelt Island in New York City.

Bob's decision to make good money first and then give back is completely valid; many people decide to do this, or certainly aspire to. And when it's not always clear how you can get a job (at least one which pays much at all) in social impact, or that you will learn any valuable skills whatsoever in the more junior positions, the decision to first "establish yourself" seems completely fair. That is in fact why and how I got started as a management consultant: no one would pay me to do anything remotely interesting in social impact after I got my master's degree. I had to think about where I could go to learn something that might be useful for later, while getting paid decently.

But I would like you to get out of the mindset that this has to be an either/or—that you have to put doing something good on hold for years or decades until you have first made a ton of money. *It's a false dichotomy.* You can still do both at the same time, even if the time and resources you can initially devote to having an impact may be limited. Some examples:

1. Many of you may have family, relationship, and community obligations. You can still do a lot of good while providing for them.

2. There are also jobs that pay well (even *very* well) in social impact, where you can earn enough to live and provide for a family.

3. As per yourImpact Balance Sheet, even if your job does not allow you to make much of a difference, there are many other core areas of your life in where you can have a positive impact through the time, money, and life energy you expend outside of your job and those areas can be a great start, as we will discuss in Chapter Five.

Bob also recognizes that today, there are many more options out there to acquire professional skills and also make a good salary in the nonprofit and public service arena—something that was far more limited when he was starting out.

If you choose to go make money first and then give back later, always keep in mind the following as you go. First, how much money is enough? How much do you need for you and your family to be comfortable? How many years is it okay to have a neutral or negative impact in your day job (if that is the type of day job you have)? Will your giving back later compensate for those neutral or negative years? How many years is it okay to put off living your values and your purpose? Can you be fulfilled putting this off? Is delaying directly working for impact a way to learn how the system works so that you can change it from the inside?

That last question is particularly interesting, because you could recast it differently depending on how cynical you might be. Is it okay to make money upholding and profiting from a rigged system, and then declare yourself the savior who will go and fix it? We will come back to this when discussing the Impact Paradox in Chapter Six.

For me, no matter what path you choose, creating a life full of impact starts now, even if you can't quit your day job or choose not to at this time. You can and should start making a positive difference as much as possible now, even if the changes you make are small and gradual. The journey always matters as much as the destination; the real metric of success should be about impact, even if it takes time.

Just like Akshay Saxena and Luis Garza, Julia Kumari Drapkin of ISeeChange thinks that recasting the metric for success makes for more powerful outcomes: "One of the things that I really started to do naturally at a certain point was to get out from under the labels that define success. I was going to be an archeologist who was featured in *National Geographic*. I was going to be a journalist for the *New York Times*. I was going to work for the UN. Those things don't matter once you get in there and see how they work, or how they don't work. And you realize that it's better to have the opportunity that you want to have. A label isn't my work—I don't need a big name or a logo attached to myself to know that I can have an impact or inspire meaningful change. We actually don't have time for that."

CHAPTER FIVE

Start with 10 Percent of Your Time and Money

As discussed in the previous chapter, many of you may not be in a position to quit your day job. And in fact, until you have a better sense of your purpose (i.e., both a feel for a real problem that matters and a measure of your superpowers), I would advise not jumping in headfirst to start something new. (Well, not unless you have a trust fund, then by all means go ahead, and please start giving a good bunch of it away.)

In his book *The 10% Entrepreneur*, Patrick J. McGinnis advocates that we should all become 10 percent entrepreneurs, and by that he means we should all diversify our opportunities and spend 10 percent of our time, capital, and resources on entrepreneurial ventures. It's really a pretty simple concept, and I think this framework works even better if you replace "entrepreneur" with social impact or social entrepreneur.

Rome was not built in a day, and you can't get to 100 percent impact either on yourImpact Balance Sheet or in your life in ninety days. But can you make a number of changes quickly to get to 10 percent? And then work your way up from there to 20, 30, 40 percent or more? 10 percent is a Saturday or Sunday morning, and perhaps a mid-week evening, too.

Starting with 10 percent is ideal because there is less pressure and risk, you will learn a lot, and you can test things out.

And it does not have to be your own entrepreneurial venture. In fact, many times it might be better if you do your research and join something that's already up and running that corresponds to what you think might be your purpose. You can help out by volunteering, mentoring, giving or investing money.

If you do want to start something yourself, I hope it's because you have taken the time to understand your target problem and the solutions currently being tried, and you think there is something new you can add as a social entrepreneur. Then 10 percent of your time, capital, and resources is still a good way to get started. It will scratch your itch to do good and have an impact, and if it doesn't work out, it will not be such a risk or a time commitment that you jeopardize other obligations you might have. If it shows promise, then you can make the decision to jump in with both feet and/or find others who can help.

This is what both Akshay Saxena and Kevin F. Adler did when they started out; both Avanti and Miracle Messages were initially side ventures to their day jobs, and it's only when the ventures showed promise in terms of impact that they decided to take the plunge to 100 percent full-time work on their respective endeavors.

Akshay reflects, "I think there's a false narrative about tossing your life away and jumping headfirst into stuff. It's a very romantic narrative. Most people don't do that. Most people have real constraints. Many of them have to do with money, personal life, and family relationships." On the other hand, he cautions against the other extreme. "I think conventionally smart people fall into this trap of trying to analytically arrive at or optimize to the right decision. You can't, because there are too many unknowns. If you try to analyze your way to a decision, you are almost never going to make it."

Conversely, he says, "Entrepreneurship is a little bit about madness. It's about taking risks and emotional leaps of faith. But you can't take such big leaps of faith that if they don't work out, you're unable to take another one, because you're likely going to have to take three or four or five or six before you actually arrive at something."

"Having a side hustle, or at least exploring something on the side" is a little like the Goldilocks-style middle way. Akshay admits that he still does this, even with the success of Avanti.

If you reprioritize some things in your life, you'll be surprised to find that 10 percent is possible, and perhaps you can do even more. Of course, some of us have obligations between work and family that make it hard to even give 10 percent. But try to do as much as you can, and see if you can double-book yourself. For example, if you have children and they take up 100 percent of your outside-of-work time, could they participate in your 10 percent somehow, such as through a volunteer gig that also welcomes children?

Volunteer Based on Your Superpowers

Volunteering 10 percent of your time is a great way to get started in social impact, and the beauty of that is that it's usually free (although it's even better if you can give money to the organization as well).

How do you find a good volunteer opportunity?

First things first: Go back to your purpose and yourImpact Vision, Mission, and Values, as well as your unique superpowers. What problem do you want to solve, and what can you bring to the table? Then do your research and talk to people in order to identify organizations that fit your purpose and your skills. Ideally, you are bringing relevant skills and experience to the problem-solving table right from the start, and these are exactly what the organization needs. You could offer hard skills and experience in specific useful fields like accounting, law, or marketing, or softer skills such as coaching and mentoring the organization's staff or its program participants.

If you have years of experience as an executive running big organizations or starting entrepreneurial ventures, your skills as a coach or mentor to early-stage start-ups, not to mention your funding connections and other useful resources, will be hugely valuable. But even if you are a student or a recent college graduate, you have more to offer than you might think. You could share relevant experience on how to write essays, where to apply for scholarships, and what college is like. This is particularly valuable for young people who might be the first in their family to think about going on to higher education.

With Miracle Messages, Kevin F. Adler's organization, you can also sign up to be a "Miracle Friend," where you are paired through a buddy system with an unhoused neighbor whom you speak to once a week over the phone. This is based on Kevin's core theory that "relational poverty is a form of poverty, and that relationships and social support are essential to get by—for people on the streets, or for anyone."

The Miracle Friend project, now up to two hundred volunteers, was developed during the pandemic to help combat isolation in places like shelters and hotels. Kevin compares it to a Big Brothers Big Sisters program for the unhoused, but on an equal footing: "Miracle Friends is not like mentoring. It's really pure neighbor. That led to the kind of trust, communication, and information sharing that allows us to do really interesting new projects like the Miracle Money project," a direct cash transfer program where unhoused neighbors receive five hundred dollars a month for six months.

Overall, you are most useful when you stick to your skills and experience, and when you have or can establish good relationships and proximity to the population served.

In terms of proximity, that could mean that you grew up in this community, or you now live there and have spent a lot of time getting to know your community members, or perhaps you or your family have faced similar issues.

Say you are a graphic design wizard who lives near a nature reserve where you often hike that has lost a lot of trees during a storm. Yes, spending an afternoon planting trees for a tree-planting organization is a good thing to do if you care about trees. You should care because trees remove carbon from the atmosphere. Planting trees is one of the best things we can do for climate change, and good forest management is important for avoiding floods and fires. But overall, you're probably relatively bad at planting trees unless you grew up tree-planting. The organization will still need to have someone overseeing the work and teaching you how to do it right, and that person could probably do it five to ten times faster than you. Given your skills and experience, you're better off helping them with their logo, branding, and marketing materials, so that they can raise more money to plant more trees.

Now say you, the graphic design wizard, are frustrated, and you really want to move into tree-planting full-time. Then yes, volunteering to do tree-planting would make sense in terms of being able to learn skills you need for your new career. But keep in mind that the organization will still need to invest time in you. So for this example, I would advise that 1) you still help them with some graphic design along the way if they need it; 2) you consider donating some money to compensate for your training; 3) you commit to a significant number of hours so that your learning curve quickly goes down and you require less supervision.

By and large, be wary of costing an organization significant time (or even more time than you give them) in terms of planning, organization, training, and supervision. And keep your commitments in terms of time and activities so that people can rely on you and are not chasing you down. You should apply the same level of professionalism to your volunteer activities as to your work and studies. Show up, be on time, come prepared having done any needed research in advance, be courteous, understand you are there to help, and don't expect things to be done for you or that there will be nice snacks. This should all be obvious, but many people think that showing up on time, or at all, is voluntary (i.e., optional). It's not—you're wasting precious resources that could have been directed to the people the organization is trying to serve.

Don't impose things on the organization that you think could be valuable to them, for example: "I think you need a new digital tool. I can do this for you, it won't cost you a thing." Good, if they agree and have always wanted to do this but never had the resources. But maybe it's not a priority for them; and even if you do it for free, your proposal will still cost them staff time for set up, training, oversight, and more.

Like all good relationships, volunteering with an organization is about good communication and expectation management at the beginning and throughout. Do we share the same values and destination? What can I bring to this relationship? What can you expect from me? What commitments do I make to you? How is this going? What do you need more of from me, or from others?

Recognize that as a volunteer, you will be receiving just as much (if not more) than you give, but the equation should not be costing the organization significant time or money—two of the resources that are usually in short supply in social impact. As a volunteer, you will be richly rewarded through the joy and happiness you get from doing something good, from meeting new people who might have experiences quite different than yours, and from seeing the humanity, potential, and opportunity that exist in this world. You will also be able to learn about the problems you care about and current solutions. Over time, this will serve you well as you refine your purpose and own solutions. You will be able to make connections, and in time, these volunteer activities may serve you well if you decide to apply to jobs in the social impact space (as they did for Isis Bous of the LexMundi Pro Bono Foundation), or if you decide to launch your own solution.

Your time is obviously not the only thing the social impact sector needs. Now let's now take a look at how you can use your money for good.

Hala Hanna's Side Gig Raising Money for Her Home Country

On August 4, 2020, a massive explosion caused by the detonation of a cache of ammonium nitrate rocked Lebanon's capital, Beirut. This caused devastation in a city already suffering from the global pandemic, an economic crisis with massive street protests, and the neighboring Syrian civil war, which had increased Lebanon's population to almost seven million by adding over a million Syrian refugees (in addition to 300,000 Iraqis and Palestinians already in exile in the country). Lebanon has the highest number of refugees per capita, with one refugee for every four nationals. In the bomb blast, almost two hundred people died, thousands more were injured, and huge amounts of property were destroyed.

Hala Hanna is the Managing Director at Solve and my number two (we'll come back to her career before Solve later). She grew up in Lebanon, and her family still lives there. In response to the tragic explosion, Hala and her husband Habib Haddad, also Lebanese, posted a note on Facebook offering to match any donations made by friends to support disaster recovery and recommending four potential charities. It took me all of five minutes to click the links she had shared and to decide to make a donation to the American University of Beirut, Hala's alma mater. I had visited its lovely campus back in 2011 when I myself had spent several months living in Beirut while working for Save the Children right at the start of the Syrian civil war. I might have given my donation to Save the Children, but with a recommendation from Hala, I felt very comfortable contributing to a local organization as she had done all the research for me. Making it as easy as possible is a good way to bring in your family, friends, and network to give to a cause you care about.

But Hala and Habib did not stop there in terms of leveraging their power and networks. In their nearly nonexistent spare time, given that they are raising a toddler, they banded together with two Lebanese friends to form Beirut Box, a local restaurant initiative to raise money to support disaster recovery in the aftermath of this tragedy that had hit right in their hometown. They reached out to a few Boston restaurants with Lebanese connections, asking each to create dishes designated as a "Beirut Box." Proceeds from the dishes, ordered directly from the restaurants, went to the Beirut Emergency Fund, providing relief assistance on the ground in Beirut through local non-governmental organizations.

Like Sydney Gressel's Frontline Foods initiative that I mentioned in the introduction, Beirut Box is also a way to support locally owned small restaurants and help these restaurants stay in business during the pandemic. "We hope that this is not just about food and not just about money, but also about starting a conversation," said Hala's husband, Habib. "[It's about] people trying to create that empathy connection that all humans are longing for at the end of the day."

Giving: Good for You and for All

Like Hala and Habib, you can do a lot more than you think with your charitable giving, especially if you do it strategically and intentionally. Many nonprofits rely heavily on small donations to continue and expand their work. Collectively, individual donors make up 70 percent of all contributions in the US, according to Charity Navigator, while corporations contribute 5 percent. Foundations (16 percent) and bequests (9 percent) fill in the rest. And this is probably a gross underestimate in the sense that, in many cultures, you give to support your family, as well as your community and your religious institutions; but these donations might not be tracked in the statistics, especially if those gifts aren't tax deductible.

Because many individual donations are small amounts, we often discount their collective power. When we talk about philanthropists, we almost always exclusively think of millionaires and billionaires—those well-heeled people who don nice dresses and penguin suits for galas where they congratulate themselves for being so generous. But in fact, almost all of us are and should think of ourselves as philanthropists, and many of us have something that is very valuable when giving—proximity. Just as Dr. Angela Jackson supports proximate entrepreneurship, let me urge you to all become proximate philanthropists, too, and to claim your power as a philanthropist, both individually and collectively.

Why should you give more?

Besides the fact that your money can help more people, there is a pretty straightforward selfish argument to contributing more: giving feels good. When you give, you feel happier and more at peace. It connects you to the problems in your community and helps you learn and listen. This means you can come to better understand both the problems that could become your purpose and the solutions that could help.

Especially if your job is not particularly impactful and you are very busy, giving is a great way to start finding your purpose in social impact. It can also be very much a social, fun, and communal activity. You can participate with other donors on a board (for larger charities there may be several types, such as the real governing board, but also a youth board and several advisory boards) and give input on strategic projects. Or, as already discussed, you can participate as an active mentor or volunteer.

You can also give through a giving circle, which according to Sara Lomelin, executive director of Philanthropy Together, is "a group of people with shared values that come together to create change. They pool their money together and decide as a circle where it should go. Their efforts, discussion, and collective gift transform into community power, proactive change, and civic action." Now the good news with giving circles is that even if you don't have a ton of money to give, by multiplying your money and your action by ten or twenty or a hundred people, it can become a decent sum. For example, Impact100 is a network of giving circles where 100 women each give $1,000 a year (or $3 per day, less than a Starbucks latte). That's $100,000 a year for each chapter. Now, they have over sixty chapters in the US alone. I myself am part of a giving circle which focuses on impact investing. (What is impact investing? More on this shortly.) It's partly a way to give back and partly an avenue for me to learn more about and support early-stage social impact ventures, ones at even earlier stages than the social entrepreneurs I work with at Solve.

So how much should you give?

Of course, it depends on your income, your dependents, your debts, and your circumstances. Many religions talk about this, and their teachings often mention 10 percent of your income as a number for which to strive. In Christianity and Judaism, for example, this is known as tithing (*tithe* literally means "tenth" in Hebrew). Islam designates *Zakat*, a required minimum contribution by Muslims of money and property or goods that can help other needy Muslims. *Sadaqah*, a term used in the Qur'an for both *Zakat* and charity, can be in the form of money, deeds, property, or salutations. You may not hear as much about giving in the Buddhist tradition, because it's not done publicly for acclaim or self-satisfaction. Giving, or generosity, is one of the Perfections (*paramitas*) of Buddhism, but to be "perfect" it must be selfless, without expectation of reward or praise.

I like 10 percent, because it matches the 10 percent of your time, capital, and resources advocated by Patrick J. McGinnis in *The 10% Entrepreneur*. Do not worry if you are not close to that. The average American gives 2.1 percent of their disposable income to charity. This figure hasn't budged in years. In fact, as you get richer, the percentage tends to go down, not up, which is pretty depressing. In tough economic times, lower- and middle-income people tend to increase their giving, presumably because they are closer to understanding the need, which again speaks to the value of proximity. Higher-income people gave less between 2006 and 2012, even though the need was higher during the Great Recession. Further, in the United States, Black people give a lot more of their median family wealth, around 8 percent in recent studies, as opposed to 2 percent or so for white families, and 5 percent for Latinx families.

So how much do you give? How close is it to 10 percent?

It's completely okay if you have not given 10 percent or can't give at that level at the moment; but can you increase your giving by 1 percent of your income this year? And every year after that, can you increase it by another percent? (By the way, this is a good technique to increase your retirement savings, too.)

Finally, how should you give?

In a short sentence, align your giving to yourImpact Vision, Mission, and Values! If a friend asks you to give to a charity they like, or to buy a gala ticket and you want to go, sure, do that, but also think about how your giving can be more strategic and help advance your purpose. Do your research, listen, and learn. Find organizations that match your purpose and in which you can get involved if you want to do so. Think about your proximity to the organization and how it resonates with your Story of Self.

Whatever commitment you make, monetary and/or voluntary, be sure to stick with it—don't waste an organization's time by making promises you can't keep. For these reasons, I would go deep rather than broad (I.e., make bigger donations to fewer organizations you really care about rather than going broad and making lots of small donations to whoever asks).

Unrestricted multiyear recurring donations are particularly valuable to nonprofits, which sometimes have donation matching requirements or get grants from foundations and government agencies that may have big restrictions and may not cover the full overhead the nonprofit needs to do their work. There is always this false narrative that a low overhead is good, and a number of foundations will cap their overhead rate (i.e., the money devoted to non-programmatic staff and activities). But who funds the accountant to do the budget and the finances? Who pays for the HR staff, or even rent? And would you rather have a good finance manager and executive director who are paid decently or the cheapest people money can buy? After all, the best CEOs of the Fortune 500 are paid millions of dollars, so great nonprofit staff should also be compensated for the value they create, not paid based on penny-pinching. Yes, a nonprofit has to use their money as responsibly and as effectively as possible, but having good staff will likely help, not hinder, that; and you should look at metrics other than the overhead rate to judge a nonprofit's impact, which we will come back to in Chapter Eight.

There is a growing movement in philanthropy that ought to take over if I have my way. It's called "trust-based philanthropy," which according to the Trust-Based Philanthropy Project led by Shaady Salehi is about addressing the inherent power imbalances between foundations and nonprofits and proactively working to cede power and control to create a more equitable nonprofit/funder ecosystem.

It's pretty simple in my view: do the research, find a nonprofit whose vision, mission, and values align with yours and whose team you like and respect, and give them money, over several years if you can. Then trust them to use it well (that is to say, as they see fit). Don't put in overly burdensome restrictions (such as implementing match requirements, requesting intermittent reports, or dictating how the money is used). These create more overhead and headaches for the staff who have to spend time managing you. Instead, ask for feedback and treat the organizations to which you donate as real partners, not subservient recipients.

Also, seek to multiply your giving through your network. Does your company offer matching funds for donations? Can you get your family and friends to contribute even a little extra? If you want to get this all organized, consider starting a giving circle yourself! Sara's organization Philanthropy Together is there to help, but an online or in-person fund-raiser is a good enough place to start.

Iman Usman's Story: Doing Good while Making a Profit

Philanthropy and giving are not the only ways you can use your money for impact, and this is where impact investing comes in.

At Solve, 60 percent of our social entrepreneurs are for-profit or hybrid organizations, and many are supported by investors who are looking to both make money and do good at the same time. For example, in 2020, Iman Usman's Indonesian-based edtech company Ruangguru ("teacher's room" in English) raised a $150 million series C funding round from General Atlantic and CGV Capital, among other investors. It was in fact the largest series C of any company in Southeast Asia at the time. The best news was that this was for a company whose mission is to promote learning through an online platform with animated videos, quizzes, and infographic summaries in order to level the playing field for millions of underserved students. In Iman's own words, "What we're doing essentially is trying to leverage the use of technology to provide better access to quality education."

Like other Solver teams you have been introduced to, Ruangguru is not a charity or a nonprofit. It makes money by charging a small monthly subscription fee for each student who uses the platform. Through the app or website, students can access personalized and adapted content that follows the Indonesian curriculum. If a student did not understand their calculus lesson that day at school, if they need to prepare for a forthcoming exam, if they want to learn more about a particular topic of interest, they can get on Ruangguru to find tailored videos, quizzes, and more. Think of it as a more personalized version of the popular Khan Academy, or perhaps as a Netflix for education that follows the Indonesian curriculum!

Getting funding was no easy feat when Iman started. For the first year, they chose to "bootstrap," as he put it, to validate their concept before bringing it to investors. Iman notes, "What made it so fascinating is that it was the same year when Uber came into Indonesia. Then there were one or two e-commerce platforms who got very big funding, on the hundred-million-dollar scale, which was actually huge for Indonesia at the time. People started seeing the potential of technology. But edtech was not seen as an interesting sector because people always think, 'It's just for altruism, there's no business in that.' It wasn't like today, where we see a couple of edtech unicorn companies."

Ruangguru has evolved a great deal since then—it serves over twenty million with a viable subscription-based business model, encompassing not only Indonesia but also Thailand and Vietnam, now with over four thousand employees! The company originally started purely as a for-profit business, but one seeking to balance profit with social and/ or environmental impact (what Michael Porter calls "shared value"). In the United States, there is a relatively new classification for such companies with dual financial and impact purposes; they can register as B corporations in Delaware and a number of other states. This model has been embraced by Ben and Jerry's, Patagonia, and Danone, to name a few of the largest who have done so. But in Indonesia, B corporations as such do not exist.

As Iman explains, "Value is created inherently in our business process. When we think about our customers, when we think about the pricing, when we think about the products, when we think of how to make it more accessible or affordable, it's not just because of the business strategy, but also because we want to reach out to the audience that really needs it." That includes ways to reach students and teachers who may have limited internet access. He and his team sought to make their app "bandwidth friendly, so it doesn't consume a lot of data that will cost students a lot." He points out that this is not the way most companies in more developed markets think about their services.

Despite huge growth and success, Iman wanted to do more, and he worried about reaching out to those who might not be able to access his learning tool in the first place. So in addition to his for-profit company, he and his team set up a nonprofit arm to focus on noncommercial activities that foster accessibility for students who are underprivileged, out of school, and/or otherwise marginalized. This is the project for which Iman was selected by MIT Solve in 2017.

When Iman saw the announcement for the Solve Challenge on "Youth, Skills, and the Workforce of the Future," he was intrigued. "We were also just reflecting in the company about the demography of our users. We wanted to make Ruangguru a lot more open and accessible. And when we looked at the demography of our users, we realized that majority of them came from affluent groups. So we wanted to use this opportunity to rethink and also revisit our strategies and what we were doing as a company so that we could reach out to those who really need it without sacrificing the business and its sustainability."

Iman was selected that year, along with ten other Solver teams out of hundreds of applications. With the nonprofit project and significant multiyear funding from Solve's partners, the Australian government and Atlassian Foundation, Iman was able to focus on providing a curriculum on employable skills for out-of-school youth, something that would not otherwise have been commercially viable.

"From the impact standpoint, we have been able to reach out to a lot more people. And if you look at the demography of our user base right now, even from the business angle, it's actually the other way around. 70 percent of our subscribers are now coming from middle- to low-income families." Whether for-profit or nonprofit, as Iman puts it, "At the end of the day, it goes back to whether you are basically creating value or not."

Good News: You Can Also Have an Impact Through Your Investments!

Impact investing, such as investing in a company like Iman's which seeks to have impact and turn a profit at the same time, is all the rage right now in the social impact field. It's about how you can invest money for positive financial, social, and environmental returns. Making money and doing good at the same time—wow!

Now let's assume you are not working full-time either as a venture capitalist or for General Atlantic. Instead, you are an individual who has some investments that are held as a diversified allocation in your pension/401k, along with maybe a little in a brokerage account. In the US, you would usually have a bunch of mutual funds and/or ETFs in those accounts.

If you are not sure what I am talking about, go check your pension/401k statements and do some reading. There are plenty of books and blogs to get you started (you will find a few recommendations in the *Helpful Resources* section at the end of this book). You need to take control of your personal finances, as money is a key lever for you to exercise power and have positive impact not only through giving, but also through investing.

Say one of the funds you own is an energy mutual fund. Instead of investing your money there, which will include a bunch of oil fields and coal companies, you can invest in a green energy fund that focuses on solar and wind. Or, depending on your risk tolerance and capital allocation, you could even invest directly in a solar off-grid, for-profit company that helps people access clean and affordable energy. (Keep in mind that most personal finance books and blogs would advise directing no more than 5 to 10 percent of your funds to venture investments, and that you should only wade into these waters once you have already accumulated a lot of capital across a diversified portfolio of equity, fixed income, real estate, and emergency cash.)

If this whole impact investing thing sounds too good to be true, I would say that to some extent, it is (although overall I am bullish on impact investing).

First, let's start with why it's too good to be quite true:

1. It's still a tiny part of the overall investing world.

2. It's still a tiny part of the overall philanthropic/social impact world.

3. Lots of stuff that is only doing a little bit better than the baseline of doing evil by default gets lumped into "impact investing."

4. It's really hard to do impact investing well if you are not part of the 1 percent (i.e., if you don't have private capital to deploy), because there are not that many true impact investments for the average retail investor in your pension fund/401k.

5. Because it's not that developed, it's (slightly) more expensive to do in terms of transaction costs.

6. The impact investing field has a chip on its shoulder because of point 1. So many actors in the field spend a lot of time trying to show that you can make "market rate" returns while doing good, instead of actually trying to change the system to focus more on impact.

7. Many problems facing the most underserved do need grant or government funding regardless, and not everything is a market, so this is not the silver bullet that will solve everything.

Okay, not a great start. So why do I care about impact investing? And why should you?

Every investment you make—in your pension and/or 401k, in your brokerage account, or as a private investor—has a positive impact, a negative impact, or a mix of both.

If your 401k or brokerage accounts are invested in a broad set of mutual funds, you're invested in a wide range of public companies that reflect your country market or the global market, say through the S&P 500 or the FTSE 1000, the respective large cap indices of the US and the UK. By default, that will include armaments makers, tobacco and oil companies, private prisons, and more. There will be companies whose human rights and environmental records are less than stellar.

Even the balance of your current savings account can be invested either in things that have a positive impact or with banks that still discriminate against Black, Brown, and Indigenous people. So if you're not intentionally invested for impact, by default, some of your portfolio is having a negative impact. What would you prefer to fund with your investment dollars?

Now, unless you're buying individual stocks or investing directly in companies (which I don't recommend unless you are very well-off and you really know what you are doing, even if the WallStreetBets-Reddit crowd might tell you differently), it is true that it's hard to know in detail what you are invested in. Transparency is a key issue the investment sector needs to resolve.

If you care about impact, you probably wouldn't buy a T-shirt from a company that's in the news a lot for employing child labor in its factories and which has been fined multiple times for polluting nearby rivers. You would likely find a T-shirt elsewhere, at least until there seems to be a *mea culpa* acknowledging what they've done wrong and a series of measures put in place (and whether or not these will be effective, who knows?). But if you're invested in a broad market index, you could very likely have shares in such a company without even realizing it. Why should your investments not match your values?

Now, if you want to be more intentional about being invested for impact, what can you do? As a retail investor, your options are somewhat limited, but growing. Let me be clear: nothing I tell you below should be construed as investment advice by any means. I am just using examples to illustrate the point. Please do your own due diligence or talk to investment advisors!

For your cash, there are banks that offer checking and savings accounts that focus on positive impact, such as Amalgamated Bank or the newer Aspiration, both certified B Corporations in the US.

In the fixed income space, there are green bond funds (for example, the global BGRN by iShares). In the United States, you can also invest in Community Development Finance Institutions (CDFIs), which according to Opportunity Finance Network (the largest association of CDFIs), "are private financial institutions that are 100 percent dedicated to delivering responsible, affordable lending to help low-income, low wealth, and other disadvantaged people and communities join the economic mainstream."

The good news is that the CDFIs typically hold a lot in reserves and have good repayment history, so they are considered quite safe investments—although as with any investment, there is always a risk. Calvert Impact Capital's Community Investment Note and the newcomer C-Note offer easy ways for retail investors to invest in a broad swath of CDFIs, as examples.

In stocks, provided you adopt a diversified passive portfolio strategy, there are ESG-screened funds available such as JUST or ESGE. These focus on three areas: environmental, social, and governance. Sometimes you have to pay a slightly higher expense ratio, but you can find some funds with expense ratios under 0.2 percent. The issue is that these are so far still pretty low in terms of the bar for making more of a positive impact. They screen out the really bad actors, but stay with a lot of companies whose records might not be stellar. And by and large, their strategy is more negative than positive—"take out the bad stuff" rather than "find and invest in the good stuff."

For many people, real estate (that is to say, owning a home) will be a main way to build wealth. In that realm, too, there are things you can do to improve your impact. These include: making sure your house is energy-efficient, perhaps by installing solar panels to heat your home; being sensitive to gentrification in the area where you choose to live and ensuring there are still affordable options for longtime and low-income residents; or supporting your local council in efforts to preserve land in your area.

For those rich enough to have a wealth manager, there are quite a few more options for dedicated portfolio construction. The big banks are not necessarily leading the way, but many are catching up; often they buy up smaller dedicated impact wealth managers to do so.

Casey Verbeck, a partner at Veris Wealth Partners (another B Corporation) who advises many clients on creating impact-aligned portfolios, says, "After working in the impact investing field for fifteen years, I continue to remind myself we have a choice to make—a choice to invest from the principle of building a better society, preserving our natural resources, and moving away from our extractive economy. Each of us can choose to look at our wealth as an opportunity to make significant positive change while also understanding that impact investment is a smart and proven way to invest. Making a choice to align your wealth with your values is one of the most empowering steps forward any one person, family, or endowment can make."

Through impact-aligned asset managers, you can also adopt active shareholder approaches. Rather than divesting from bad stocks, asset managers can use their client's ownership of stocks to demand change through participating in shareholder meetings and putting forward resolutions. Matt Patsky, the CEO of Trillium, uses research to support their "shareholder advocacy team to engage with companies on issues where their ESG performance scores indicate they are lacking. Our shareholder advocacy team also uses our clients' power as asset owners to propel changes in public policy."

With more capital and with sound financial advice, you can also make investments into private equity or venture capital funds like Bain Capital's Double Impact Fund, or even into direct deals to early-stage social entrepreneurs, all of whom are laser-focused on positive impact while still established as for-profit businesses. Early-stage is, of course, riskier; so I would say invest no more than 5 to 10 percent in this way once you have built a good nest egg already (but if you have a wealth manager, you probably have already done so).

What's interesting is that for all the talk about impact investing, few people are actually *doing it*, at least in an intentional way, across their whole portfolio. I have to admit I am not 100 percent invested for impact myself, although In recent years I have moved a lot of my portfolio in the right direction. The good news is that a number of impact-aligned strategies have shown over recent years that they can match or even outperform the "market" based on adjusted risk/returns. In fact, during the 2008 financial crisis, and when the markets tumbled briefly in March 2020 at the beginning of the pandemic, a number of impact aligned portfolios fared better (i.e., they lost less money).

The New York Times reported in August of 2020 that "Impact investments, which aim to promote a social good or prevent a social ill, have significantly outperformed traditional bets during the coronavirus pandemic. And their returns are enticing hesitant investors to rework their portfolios. Overall, 64 percent of actively managed ESG funds beat their benchmarks versus 49 percent of traditional funds through the first week in August, according to research from RBC Capital Markets."

This makes intuitive sense, especially if your time horizon is decades, which it should be. Climate change is real, and more and more governments will take action and regulate to mitigate and adapt to it. More and more people will care, especially young people. Renewable energies will get subsidies and will be chosen more and more by both individuals and companies, while polluting industries will get taxed more. Thus, over time, your portfolio will do better with a pro-climate strategy, even if today in the US, oil companies are subsidized and fracking has proven to be a short-term boon. Exxon, once the valuable company in the S&P500, was kicked out of the top index, dropping below 500th place in 2020. For me, it's short-term thinking not to invest in pro-climate strategies—even if you only cared about making money, which I hope you don't!

Don't discount other investment pools where you might have influence: the investments your parents and family make, for example, or the endowment of your university or other institutions with which you might be affiliated. You will have likely heard of student divestment campaigns. Some successful examples include: Columbia University divested from private prisons; the New School divested its $340 million endowment from fossil fuels and reinvested it in climate solutions; and Oberlin invested $5 million in responsible investments. Overall, on-campus strategies have become increasingly sophisticated, moving on from protests about university divestment to having students file shareholder resolutions on behalf of their institutions' investments. This is the same sort of shareholder activism Matt Patsky from Trillium describes.

Again, this makes sense to me, because many universities are nonprofits have missions stating their intent to better the world through education and research. Their core constituents are students, researchers, and professors, so why would they make money through investments that in part harm the world? More optimistically, how could their investments reflect their values and even align better to the core mission, (e.g., making investments in education technology or spin-offs from the university's own medical research labs)? Side note disclaimer: MIT's endowment is not impact-aligned, so there is work still to be done.

Find out more about the institutions to which you are connected—discover what their investment strategies are and whether their strategies align with their own values. And if they do not, help them see how they could do better. The important thing to remember is that through either your own money or funds over which you have an influence, you have power to have a positive or negative impact. Be intentional and use that power for good!

Even Your Purchasing Decisions Matter

Many of you will have heard of Marie Kondo, the Japanese folding wizard, especially after her Netflix show debuted in 2019. Her premise is simple: we have too much stuff cluttering our closets, our homes, and therefore our minds—and we are not enjoying these things enough...or perhaps at all. By cleansing our stuff as radically as we can and only keeping things that "spark joy" in us, we will live better, simpler, happier lives, we will save money, and in the process, we will have more space and time for creativity.

I love this idea, especially as my parents are what I would call "intellectual hoarders." Our apartment in Paris is filled to the brim with books. That's good, in a way, but the books are rarely taken out of the bookshelves and read. They are more of a display of the collective accumulated knowledge of the family, or rather likely the aspirational knowledge, as I wonder what percentage of the books have ever *actually* been read. I imagine I could spend three years reading full-time to get through the collection, and even then, I wouldn't be sure I'd read everything. I think my parents are still hoarding more books in the cellar! There are also lots of magazines and newspapers, some of them aged five years or older; a record player, even though I do not think anyone has put a vinyl record on it for over thirty years; tea sets my parents haven't used since I was born; and the worst in my view, boxes that still sit unpacked from when we moved apartments in 1998.

I have big arguments with my mother about all this. (There is no point talking to my father, although that lets him off the hook.) I wound up buying her the Marie Kondo book, which promptly just created more clutter (i.e., one more book in the apartment). I can't say I apply Marie Kondo's advice perfectly to my life, either, as I still have too much clothes, even though during the pandemic I managed to live for months in the same five outfits (but my gold dresses will someday bring me joy when I get to go to a party again).

I think it's worth adapting and expanding Marie Kondo's core concept to social impact by asking these key questions:

Does this new purchase or possession I already own spark positive social impact in the world? And to expand on this idea even further: Do my new or existing relationships, activities, and investments spark positive impact, too?

Ideally, every new thing (as well as activity and person) you bring into your life should seek to spark positive social impact. But first, you should look at what you have and radically declutter. That can feel very overwhelming, and it's a real process to change your habits over time. So, let's Marie Kondo your impact, starting by evaluating what you have!

In terms of your things and your purchases, again, everything you own or purchase can have a positive or a negative impact. First, the most obvious: the Western-style level of conspicuous consumption is by nature very detrimental to climate change. Even if you are not in the top 1 percent economically, you might very well be in the top 1 percent or 10 percent in terms of your carbon contributions to the world if you travel a lot for work, own a larger house that needs a lot of air conditioning or heating fueled by coal plants, eat red meat every day, and regularly purchase a lot of clothes. The book and website for *Project Drawdown* are very helpful here, because they divide climate action into specific areas consumers can address, including transportation, food, and buildings.

To give you a more jolting example, one of my favorite speakers at the Clinton Global Initiative was Cindy McCain, wife of late Senator John McCain. She and the Senator joined us at CGI University in 2014 when the program was held at Arizona State University in Tucson, Arizona, in the McCain family's home state. Cindy is an impressive, towering blonde woman, and an active philanthropist who supports the fight against human trafficking.

While participating on a panel, addressing hundreds of eager university students from around the world, she asked them the following question: "How many people have iPhones?"

Probably almost half the students raised their hands. That does tell you something about privilege—even though many of the students were from far-flung countries, they (or at any rate, their parents) could afford iPhones.

"Okay, keep your hands up. And now if you have a Samsung, raise your hands." At this point, most of the students had their hands raised.

"Keep your hands up! How many have another smartphone?"

I seem to remember that by that point, everyone had their hand raised.

Cindy, in an acerbic tone, said: "You are all raping the Congo!"

Cue shocked student faces. She then went on to explain how the race to extract cobalt and other precious minerals for smartphones has served to fuel the continued violent, two decades-long civil war in the Democratic Republic of the Congo (DRC), which has claimed the lives of six million people and exiled an estimated five million refugees to neighboring countries, as well as internally displacing half a million more. Women and girls have been particularly affected by widespread systematic sexual violence, which is used as a weapon of war, hence Cindy's word choice of "rape."

So next time you are due for an upgrade and want the latest iPhone, ask yourself, "Do I need it right this minute, or can I make my current phone last longer?" Apple is particularly annoying about planned obsolescence, where by intentional design, your devices slow down after a year or two to encourage you to get the newest model. In a number of countries, they have been sued because of this. It's unfair to the consumer but also very negative for the environment and human rights overall.

When you Marie Kondo your life and possessions for impact, take it in small, digestible steps. Start with an overall audit and be systematic.

Choose a category you want to work on first, perhaps the one where your negative impact could be cut down the most or your positive impact could be the greatest.

Let's say it's fashion, a category widely covered on Marie Kondo's TV series (you will also learn how to fold things really neatly, yay!). According to the World Bank, the fashion industry is responsible for 10 percent of annual global carbon emissions, more than all international flights and maritime shipping combined. CNN reported that the purchase of a white cotton shirt results in the same amount of greenhouse gas emissions as driving your car for thirty-five miles.

Alarmingly, three quarters of clothes wind up in landfills or incinerators. It takes forty years for many textiles to decompose once in a landfill, and in that time dyes and chemicals in clothes actively contaminate the soil and water in the ground. Shoes in particular can take up to a thousand years to break down (thankfully, one of Miranda Wang's first potential products for Novoloop is in fact shoe soles!). The average American (pre-COVID at least) purchases sixty-eight garments a year, spending on average $1,700 on clothes annually. There are also widespread labor issues in the industry. Unfortunately, many major apparel brands still have abysmal records on human rights and continue to require constant oversight. As consumers, we often find this out only when things go very wrong, as with the 2013 fire in a Bangladesh apparel factory in which 1,132 workers were killed, as well as with regular child labor scandals. The most famous was Nike's in the 1990s; since then, the company has done a lot more than most to clean up their supply chain.

So how do you reduce your consumption of clothes? Well, let's first look at how many clothing items you purchased recently. How many of them do you actually wear? What's been in your closet for six months, nine months, twelve months, or more without being touched? In that sense, the pandemic might have shown you how little you needed to live with, and what clothes you actually gravitate to for comfort during unusual times. This does not mean you should throw out your suits if you are an accountant—at some point you probably will need them, although I am all for pajama-casual becoming the new fashion normal.

AUDIT: DOES THIS POSSESSION OR PURCHASE SPARK POSITIVE SOCIAL IMPACT IN THE WORLD?

To help you rethink your possessions and purchases in terms of impact, here are a few helpful questions:

- What can I repair that will then spark joy?
- What can I reuse for different purposes? (For instance, you could use your old ratty T-shirt as a rag for cleaning your car.)
- What can I give away to local organizations in need? (They will hopefully be very clear on the types of clothing that are helpful versus less so. For example, winter coats and socks are always popular.)
- What can I recycle? (Do some research on local organizations that recycle clothing in a meaningful way.)

Then, for any purchases going forward:

- Do I really need it, or do I already own something that works fine?

- Does it spark joy, as Marie Kondo would say?
- Does it have a negative impact, or is it more sustainably made?

Let me be clear: a T-shirt will never have a positive environmental impact in and of itself, even if it's made of recycled cotton with all-natural dyes. It still requires water and energy to produce and transport, so it still has a carbon footprint. Owning one more T-shirt in addition to the thirty you already have is still increasing your carbon footprint, even if by less than the virgin cotton T-shirt "Made in Myanmar."

Worse, if you buy a T-shirt and never wear it (or wear it only once or twice), your environmental cost per wear goes through the roof versus if you buy something you love and wear all the time. If you do need a T-shirt, it's better to buy a T-shirt you're going to wear every week for three years even if it's not recycled, compared to the recycled one you'll wear twice (although I do not quite have the numbers to show you this is a better deal).

The numbers are in fact what Alexander Frantzen is trying to do with his company Carbon Calories, which produces carbon labels (just like calorie count labels) for clothing that are based on the average number of wears. That denominator (i.e., the number of times you wear something) is key to the equation.

Your T-shirt could have a positive social impact if it provides fair wages and jobs to an underserved population, if all or part of the profits go toward a good cause, and so on. But the best way to minimize your carbon footprint is to buy less and to use more of what you already have, time and time again.

Buying vintage is great. On top of the shops that give 100 percent of their proceeds to charity, there are more and more websites at many price points, including for used designer clothes and furniture. You are reusing something that is already in existence in the world, and bar its transport, you could say that its environmental and social costs

The Answer Is You

are already accounted for, so you might as well maximize its use by giving it a new life.

Here is another myth to dispel: by and large most "buy one, give one" schemes are pretty bad. TOMS shoes became very popular promoting this model—for every pair of TOMS shoes purchased, another pair would be given to poor children by the company. The founding myth of TOMS was in fact that when Blake Mycoskie was traveling in Argentina in 2006, he "witnessed the hardships faced by children growing up without shoes."

The first issue with the buy one, get one model is this: why would you go through all the trouble to make expensive canvas shoes and sell them in the United States and Europe to solve a problem thousands of miles away? If you really wanted to solve the problem of shoeless children, why would you not establish a shoe company in Argentina with local ownership, creating jobs in the community?

Or better, why not support already existing local shoemakers in the country where there are the most shoeless children (though I would be surprised if that is in fact Argentina), rather than giving shoes away in a traditional neo-colonial model, creating an aid dependency and potentially destroying any local shoe industry, thereby actually causing harm? More importantly, who said that what low-income children in Argentina and elsewhere need the most is shoes?

As Vox journalist Amanda Taub noted, "When TOMS worked with an outside research team to evaluate the impact of its shoe donations, the researchers were unable to find a way in which the shoes had much of a substantive impact on poor kids' lives." The shoes were well liked, and the kids played outside a little more in them; but neither their school attendance nor their self-esteem improved. More worryingly perhaps, kids felt slightly more dependent on outside aid, something we should always avoid.

Bruce Wydick, who was commissioned by TOMS to lead the study, was a little more diplomatic, acknowledging the company's commitment to transparency and change. But overall, he admitted, "I have always been a greater fan of interventions that attack the root of poverty rather than give things away to the poor."

Unfortunately, the "buy one, give one" model seems so popular that it is here to stay. Right before the pandemic hit, in late February of 2020, I was at a social impact conference in Washington, DC. One of the speakers gave a talk about his "buy one, give one" enterprise. In this case, he sold blankets, and for each blanket bought, one would be given to a person experiencing homelessness.

Again, if you asked the administrators at a local shelter, "Would you prefer money or blankets?" what do you think they would say? Presumably, they would be able to use the money to decide what was most needed—food, medicine, blankets, socks, or coats—but they could also use the money for overhead to pay for the heating and electricity, the accountant, and more. Furthermore, if you are going to stand onstage boasting at a social impact conference about the impact of your business, it's best to do your homework about your core product—in this case, blankets, which were very visibly and undeniably Native American-inspired in their pattern.

After the talk, a friend who has done a lot of work with Indigenous communities inquired diplomatically about whether this speaker worked with Indigenous artists and communities. He was enthusiastic in his response, stating that they were now starting to work with an Indigenous artist on a new blanket. It seemed a little late for a company touting its social impact credentials not to have been working with Indigenous communities up until then, given the designs—and as my friend pointed out, given "the triggering nature of blankets in Indigenous history."

"What do you mean, in terms of Indigenous history?" the blanket entrepreneur asked.

My friend went onto explain how colonizers brought smallpox to the American continent, killing many Native Americans who had never been exposed to the disease until then. In some instances, in what could be considered early instances of biological warfare, British and American colonists gave items such as blankets from a smallpox infirmary as gifts to Native American emissaries with the hope of spreading the deadly disease to nearby tribes, the most well established being at the siege of Fort Pitt in 1763. There is quite a bit of debate as to the extent of this practice and whether the blankets themselves actually worked in transmitting smallpox versus its inadvertent spread. Regardless, to Indigenous people, the image of white people giving away blankets is far from positive and is seared into their collective consciousness.

While I do not expect everyone to know about smallpox blankets and what they mean to Indigenous people, I would expect the CEO of a blanket company to do his homework. The good news is that they now have a collection designed by an Indigenous artist, and 100 percent of the profits go to a local Indigenous organization, showing that there is always a way to make good progress (and perhaps my friend asking a few pointed questions helped him on the way—who knows?).

So rather than these "buy one, give one" models, look for companies who live their values throughout their supply chain in terms of social and environmental impact. If they give a percentage of their profits to a cause, good; but better that they give that in cash. Newman's Own, started in 1982 by actor Paul Newman, gives 100 percent of their profits in the food and beverage industry to local, proximate organizations, such as a summer camps for kids with incurable diseases and various organizations supporting animal welfare. (I like their pasta sauce, too.)

When you start applying Marie Kondo to your impact, you can also start to make an honest assessment of your resources, both financial and nonfinancial. What do you really need to live on? You might be surprised that you do not need as much as you think if you are able to make real changes in the world, and that purpose can feed your soul more than the newest car.

What can you devote to making the world a better place? What can you give without expecting anything back in terms of time and money?

This might feel initially painful. This is not about becoming Gandhi, Mother Teresa, or living like a monk. However, it does require deep, long-lasting changes if you are serious—cutting out the things that have a negative impact, and devoting your energy, time, skills, and money to those that do good.

CHAPTER SIX

Wrestle with Your Personal Kryptonite and the Impact Paradox

Digging Deeper into Hala's Story: Finding Her Place Amid the Contradictions of the Social Impact World

"It's 1989. I am four years old. That year was the best ever. There was no school. We would travel around a lot with my mum to all corners of our country, to my grandparents in the village, to our aunts in the city. That year was all games. One of my favorite games was to run in the middle of the night to the basement. There was music. We would share simple food; my favorite was pita bread and canned hot dog."

Solve would not exist as it is today without the hard work and leadership of my number two, Hala Hanna. I started telling you about her in Chapter Five. But I did not tell you much of her story, nor did I tell you how she tried many different approaches to impact, working both outside and inside the system, and the paradox that comes with that. Let's rectify that now.

Hala continues: "What I did not fully understand back then is that we were running to the basement because that was the only safe space in the building. That I did not have to go to school because my school had been bombed. And that we were not exactly traveling around, we were actually internally displaced, looking for a corner in the country that was safe enough for us while my father stayed behind to provide. That was growing up during the Lebanese civil war. My reality is a shared reality of all Lebanese kids who grew up between 1975 and 1991. In fact, I had it easy. It's the shared reality today of Syrian children since 2011. It is the reality today of twenty-two million children under the age of five. How did I make it out, from the basement of that building in a war zone to standing here today? I believe it's two things: The first is the superpower of children—resilience. The second is luck. I got lucky."

Hala has since used the resilience and luck she grew up with to devote her life to impact. She has sought to create opportunity for others, notably for refugee children, so that they, too, can fulfill their full potential without having to rely on luck. But the road has been winding, pivoting back and forth from activism to large bureaucratic institutions, starting her own data journalism social enterprise, Hulul (which coincidentally or not means "Solutions" in Arabic), and now working at Solve.

Along the way, Hala has learned a lot about herself, how to make change happen, and the difficult compromises you have to wrestle with along the way.

This is what I call the Impact Paradox, which, in its essence, comes down to this: To dismantle injustice, you have to understand, and almost always work within, the system that has created or maintains this injustice. You are trying to change the game, while still having to play by its unfair rules.

There are purists who will take exception to having to play the game, and perhaps that is how revolutions start; but almost always, agitating and activism, while paramount, also require an understanding of (and often compromise with) those in power.

Hala credits her parents, both doctors, with instilling a sense of service in her. "We wouldn't see my dad for days on end. And it's not just because he had to work for us to eat, but also because he considered it his duty to serve and to be there for his fellow citizens." At the same time, the Lebanese civil war and subsequent Syrian occupation thrust upon her the need to be an engaged citizen early on: "If you don't understand the world around you and why things are happening, then there's a total sense of loss of control. So my first protests were in high school."

When she got to college, Hala became even more engaged, but not politically per se. Instead, she chose to volunteer with nonprofit organizations doing poverty relief with families. For a long time, she also wanted to become an actress. She chose this art form to defy another deeply ingrained authority in the Arab world—patriarchy. Hala and her cohorts created a play that was so controversial that it was shut down. It was about the secret sexual lives of women in Lebanon: "We were a group of six young women between the ages of eighteen and twenty-five. It was our own stories, our own experiences of everything from what it means to masturbate, to what it means to get an abortion, in a context where this was just so incredibly taboo. We were sold out every single night. At the time, it was pretty shocking. My first activism was very loud and in your face. I became more toned down with time."

While she considered acting and journalism as potential careers, and continued her activism through street protests, Hala started taking more economics classes in order to understand the system through a better grasp of macro trends and data. She ended up majoring in economics, then continued her studies for a master's degree in international development, which brought her to Washington, DC. It was her first trip on a plane.

There she took classes on gender and economics, notably with Caren Grown, the Global Director for Gender at the World Bank, where Hala got a job upon graduation. Set up after World War II through the Bretton Woods Monetary Conference to help devastated economies recover, the World Bank's mission today is to reduce poverty and improve living standards globally—a dream job, it would seem, for someone wanting to have an impact!

However, after a few years traveling to Yemen, Syria, Senegal, and more, Hala became disillusioned; did any of the reports she was writing actually matter? What was changing on the ground? One of her bosses also told her not to specialize in gender, telling her it was "such a small niche." This, even though women make up half the population! Hala also found the World Bank to be hierarchical. She felt she would need a PhD to gain respect and advance there, so she applied and got accepted into one of the most prestigious programs, one at Harvard's Kennedy School. But just as she began her studies, Hala's activist streak came roaring back when the Arab Spring started. She recalls, "I had such high hopes." What was the point of looking at data for seven years when "the world is changing as you breathe, and I am sitting in Cambridge tweeting?"

Hala had witnessed how activism could get results—she had seen it move beyond protests leading nowhere. She and her classmates had felt victorious when the Syrian government left Lebanon in 2005 after a fifteen-year occupation. One day that year, she woke up early at five o'clock in the morning and took her parents' car to the site of one of the largest protests under cover of darkness; she knew they would be scared to let her go. She was one of the first people there.

Hala remembers, "I wasn't one of the organizers, I was really just one of the supporters. We were holding hands. Lebanon is very divided, and so just being in the same public square as folks from all of these very different denominations and beliefs was incredibly powerful."

The group confronted armed soldiers who held them back from going into the square to protest together. "It was literally pushing body to body with these soldiers—who were armed—until they gave in. They didn't shoot because they were on our side. It was this beautiful moment of national unity as well."

That day, a million of Hala's fellow citizens came into the square together. Shortly thereafter, US President George W. Bush gave a speech pushing the Assad regime to announce that they were leaving Lebanon. As Hala puts it, "That was a moment that fueled my belief that people in the streets could do something. And then the Arab Spring completely shattered that."

By the time Hala graduated from Harvard, the success of the Arab Spring was in jeopardy. Those in power—be it the generals in Egypt or Syria's dictator—were fighting back. She got what she considered to be another dream job: working as head of programs for the Middle East and North Africa at the World Economic Forum, which included writing the narrative of what was happening in the region, making sense of it, and selecting and curating the stories that would make it to the international stage. Although Hala was rejoining a big institution with plush offices—this time comfortably based in Geneva, Switzerland, rather than Washington, DC—she saw her role at the Forum as an activist on the inside, and in that sense, she thought she would have a greater capability to effect change than if she was protesting in the street.

Every year, the World Economic Forum hosts a legion of world leaders from government and business in the sleepy ski town of Davos, Switzerland, and there she could engage in parallel diplomacy. She recalled: "What matters is what you're doing in the background of what happens on the main stage. That was my way of contributing." But as the hopes and dreams of the Arab Spring largely faded, she felt that the job "was no longer something that I could recognize or relate to—that was a big blow. When people go into the streets, they have to build on something—and there was nothing. There were no institutions left to build on. There was no Marshall Plan. No one cared enough about Tunisia to put enough money for the second stage of economic development, even though Tunisia fared probably the best as they had strong enough institutions."

Like Amanda Nguyen of Rise Justice Lab, Hala sees solutions activism as a better path forward. "In a place like Lebanon, people have been protesting since October 2019, and nothing happened. But I feel that the Black Lives Matter movement has actually created a huge cultural shift. What recurring protests do is build the generational muscle of activism. When well-managed, and when there are people doing the legislative work, this can actually turn into change."

In 2015, Hala was frustrated. She had spent a decade going back and forth between activism and seeking to move big bureaucratic institutions from the inside, but the paradoxes there were manifold. The big institutions were initially set up to change the system, but they had somehow become part of the status quo and were thus perpetuating it.

She felt most useful through her work at one of the volunteer side gigs she had started while at Harvard: supporting and working with women parliamentarians and ministers, helping them increase the number and influence of women in political leadership positions as part of the Women Political Leaders Global Forum.

In wrestling with the Impact Paradox, Hala also had to wrestle with her own unconscious shortcomings. "I used to define myself as an international development professional. What really cured me of that was spending a summer in Liberia working for the Minister of Planning. I thought, 'I'm the product of post-war reconstruction in Lebanon, of course I will understand what Liberian post-war reconstruction is.' And it was so hard. This is why I believe so much in the concept of proximate entrepreneurship."

In that sense, "Solve is the best alignment so far in terms of where I can add value versus the impact I can have." Through her work, Hala is bringing what she sees as her superpower—her huge network of funders and powerbrokers, acquired through her years at big institutions—to support proximate social entrepreneurs bringing their own solutions to the problem-solving table.

She advises, "For young people who want to change the world, don't change the world. Change your community, and then you change the world through your community."

The Impact Paradox: Playing an Unfair Game While Trying to Change or Dismantle the System

Welcome to a big fat dose of reality, pragmatism, and confronting your shortcomings! Are you ready to put your ego aside and roll up your sleeves?

It's time to take a hard look in the mirror at your weaknesses and biases, and also to wrestle with many of the shortcomings of the social impact space itself, and confront what I call the Impact Paradox.

Don't worry, the next chapter is all about optimism, solutions, and why what you do individually and collectively does matter. But before you mount your shiny techno-utopian savior horse, it's key to understand and acknowledge the things that may bring you and the whole social impact space up short—and there are many.

Let's start with the social impact world. In all the work I do, I am constantly wrestling with the Impact Paradox, which is best summarized through this question: *How do you make an impact when to do so, you need to work within the system you are trying to dismantle?*

And a corollary: *What happens if your impact initiative, while doing good at the margins, might in fact be helping a malfunctioning system to sustain itself?*

These are critical questions, ones that Anand Giridharadas asks to some extent through his book *Winners Take All: The Elite Charade of Changing the World.* The basic premise is that elites—the 1 percent who have greatly profited from an unjust system they created—have recast themselves through philanthropy as saviors of the world, but will in fact only take actions and give to solutions that provide marginal change and do not threaten the overall system.

Ultimately, the system prevails, and they continue to profit from it to stay on top. This is not a new argument per se. See Leo Tolstoy: "I sit on a man's back choking him and making him carry me, and yet assure myself and others that I am sorry for him and wish to lighten his load by all means possible...except by getting off his back."

Anand's book comes alive through recounting his experience attending lots of social impact get-togethers with the who's who across the world. He even has a full chapter devoted to the Clinton Global Initiative in which he criticizes my team's choice of speakers for being too conforming to corporate interests whose good deeds were, in his view, mostly window-dressing. His book hits a nerve for most of us who work in social impact. There have been lots of discussions of Anand's book at social impact events while nibbling *canapés*, which I have to say is very meta, given that a large part of his critique is about social impact events where people nibble *canapés* rather than actually do anything to change the system.

I do think Anand hits on the Impact Paradox. There is real cognitive dissonance in the social impact sector, where to fix a problem, you might end up taking money from (or working with) the very people who created the problem in the first place. Is it okay to take money from an oil company to promote women's empowerment? Is that better or worse than taking money from them for environmental conservation, a cause that is diametrically opposed to their core business? Are you helping them buy a conscience? And even if that is the case, is it still better to take their money and engage them, hoping to create systems-level change? Is the alternative of boycotting such businesses, refusing to work with them or take their money, better? Is it even possible? And will your organization go bankrupt before you ever know the answer?

This paradox can also present itself in other ways. Is it okay to fly around the world to climate conferences and more broadly continue to lead a "Western" lifestyle of consumption, and are you a complete hypocrite if you do so? Or should you be like Greta, who will only eat vegan and refuses to get on an airplane? What about working as one of two people on the Corporate Social Responsibility team of a multinational organization, where your team's budget is less than the sum total of the money your company spends on ink cartridges annually? Can you actually change anything from within, or are you just there as a token nod to greenwashing, which allows the company to tout your work in ads and, in the process, helps them sell more stuff that harms the planet?

The US tax system is extremely generous in terms of charitable deductions, and many laud that as a good thing. But is the billionaire getting a massive tax break better at deciding where charitable money goes than a government, which is meant to use tax revenue to redistribute resources based on real need and democracy? And what if the billionaire is giving away millions to a nonprofit think tank that promotes thought leadership on issues that promote his own agenda (e.g., little to no regulation for the chemical industry where he made his fortune)? Would you go work for him if he also decides that he cares deeply about refugees' economic empowerment, a cause that is central to your purpose?

Should you work with governments that are not democracies? What if they are launching a promising education initiative and are ready to put in millions to help scale your program? And what if they now want to review the content and take out something in the history lesson to which they object? Is that something small—and who are you to decide?

For me, the Impact Paradox comes down to this unfortunate reality: to be able to change the game, you almost always need to play the game, too. And this is where I will disagree with Anand, whose book offers very little in terms of actual solutions, whereas I am (as you will have seen by now) all about problem-solving.

Theodore Roosevelt put it much better in his famous "Man in the Arena" speech in 1910: "It is not the critic who counts; not the man who points out how the strong man stumbles, or where the doer of deeds could have done them better. The credit belongs to the man who is actually in the arena, whose face is marred by dust and sweat and blood; who strives valiantly; who errs, who comes short again and again, because there is no effort without error and shortcoming; but who does actually strive to do the deeds; who knows great enthusiasms, the great devotions; who spends himself in a worthy cause."

Yes, you can be an activist, an agitator, and protest and shout and point out problems. And if this is you, you will likely rate fairly high on the idealism scale. Hats off to you if you will not compromise your ideals and sit down with those in power whom you are trying to tear down—if you choose to stay outside of the system shouting at it rather than get into its muddy and murky waters. We need you to point out the problems and to highlight the ideals for which we need to strive. This is a critical part of all social change movements, as Julie Battalina (whom I highlighted in Chapter One) says. Maybe you yourself can stay pure and not have to wrestle with the Impact Paradox.

However, to effect real change, you also need people to offer new solutions, to innovate, but then also to understand and work within the system and to compromise with those who do have the money, power, and influence, in order to get them to change things and scale the new solutions. Real movements involve strategy, long-term planning, and coalition-building, not just public outcry. This is why Amanda's work on sexual assault has been so effective—she was willing to compromise and sit down with those in power, even if she disagreed with them on many things.

Even if you are the activist/agitator type, it's important to understand the system to begin with, which is sometimes hard to truly do without being ready to work with the system (i.e., play the game first, at least to some extent). How do you build a new, fair system if you don't know why the current system is failing in the first place? How do you transition from one to the next? Can you reform the parts that are broken rather than trying to tear everything down?

In this sense, Hala Hanna's journey back and forth between activism and big institutions has been about gaining that understanding of the system and the different tools she has at her disposal, and then trying to find the best place where she can effect change.

It would be reductive to say there are easy answers. We all need to wrestle with the Impact Paradox, to think about when working within or outside the system makes the most sense, while taking our own values, skills, and experience into account. I would make a poor activist, and I am not a purist. I am a pragmatist who likes to get things done, who can bring lots of people together to move things along. This is why, per Julia Battalina's framework, I work well in my role as an "orchestrator." I also have a good sense of my red lines: who I would work with, take money from, and engage with, and who I would not. These are also things I research and discuss with my team so that we can make the best possible decision with the information we have.

My red lines and yours may be different. That's okay, providing that you understand where your lines are and that you can justify them honestly to yourself and to others—your team, your stakeholders, even the general public if one day the media picks up a story about who you worked with or took money from. It's possible you will still make mistakes, and through these you will grow and learn, so your lines might evolve. But as one of my old bosses used to say, "Don't ever do or write anything you would not be okay with ending up in *The New York Times*."

You have to remember you are playing a long game, and you need to be ready for some of your decisions to come back years later, in a day and age where everything is online and trackable. Anyone who is even vaguely a public figure and ever took a photo with Jeffrey Epstein or members of the Sackler family knows this all too well, let alone organizations who made the unfortunate decision to take money from either in order to advance their mission (including MIT, the Metropolitan Museum of Art, Harvard, and countless others).

If you do understand the Impact Paradox (i.e., you are clear on where you are ready to work with the system while trying to change it and where your red lines are), you are ready to walk into the arena, but always keep your mission in mind. It's crucial not to get lost. The risk is becoming too comfortable and then becoming part of "the system" itself, or getting dispirited and accepting marginal change as you start to believe it's impossible to steer the behemoth. Always remember that, as you play the game to get things done, you are still ultimately there to change its unfair rules.

And we need everyone to get in the game—to use their skills and superpowers to work together. That's how we can change the game for good.

How Dedo Operates in a Dysfunctional System to Support African Social Entrepreneurs

Dedo Baranshamaje, whom you heard about in Chapter Three, has seen his fair share of the Impact Paradox in action in a number of spheres: listening to stories about the ineffectiveness of multilateral bureaucracies, as well as his experiences throughout his own career with social enterprises, large international organizations, and now in his current role at a foundation.

"Philanthropy is dysfunctional. There is a utopian idea around building wealth and then spending it. Oftentimes, actually building wealth in that way creates a problem and then also puts you in a position where you have to go solve it. We have seen Mark Zuckerberg trying to figure out ways to work around democracy and you're like ?!?!" Indeed, the Chan Zuckerberg Initiative is now giving away millions to solve a big problem: voting rights and democracy. But some would argue Mark made billions creating some of that problem in the first place. (Certainly, Facebook the company could do a lot more to help than giving away a miniscule percentage of Zuck's fortune.)

Dedo also cautions against the idea that funders and philanthropists know best. "There is this idea that because you have the money, then you have the ideas, or you understand the problems that need to be solved, which is completely false. What would Barry Segal [founder of the Segal Family Foundation] know about smallholder farmers in Malawi and how to solve their problems? He made money through real estate, and then he's figuring out how to add value. He doesn't pretend, but instead finds the people who know how to do this. The paradox in the philanthropic sector is that you see these larger organizations trying to think about something like agriculture, but they've never been farmers themselves and have zero experience or connection to farming."

He muses, "I like to say this to funders: 'You have the resources, but I don't think you have the ideas. So your responsibility is to find the people that have the ideas and are doing this.' "

This was something the Segal Family Foundation itself had to learn before being able to help other funders adopt these strategies. As Dedo describes it, "Before 2015, 75 to 80 percent of Segal's portfolio was made up of entrepreneurs from the US and Europe working in Africa, but now we have changed that trajectory. It was just the lens through which we were looking for talent and leadership." The foundation started applying the vision that proximate entrepreneurs and leaders know better how to solve the problems in their community and broker relationships, and thus changed their approach to grant-making. It became more about change-making over the long term, and Segal's portfolio has reversed dramatically.

"Who are the people who are trying to broker change in ways we don't always appreciate or that are not always at the forefront, [who are working] in ways that are often unsexy, as in not a vaccine or a technology? Who's actually innovating?"

Dedo sought to create local hubs, first in Malawi and now across the African continent, to better source and support local visionaries, adopting a much-needed new process to look beyond the typical US or European organization. "We were one of the early funders in the racial justice and equity space; we realized there was no money going to entrepreneurs of color. How do you do that in the long term, being flexible and giving multiyear funding? We're not looking for entrepreneurs with a million dollars. In order to get to a million, you have to start somewhere."

In a January 2021 article in *The Guardian* cowritten with Katie Bunten-Wamuru, Dedo points out, "Worldwide, more than 99 percent of humanitarian and philanthropic funding goes to predominantly white-led international NGOs. Despite Africa's growing and dynamic social sector, only 5.2 percent of US foundation giving to Africa goes to African-led organisations."

For those who want to start out in the social impact space, Dedo has some advice when confronting your own shortcomings: "One thing that is really, really important is to have the sort of patience to learn, because oftentimes we get so much into ourselves, into the glory of being an entrepreneur, a founder, and then we forget that it takes time to learn and to build networks and trust. Oftentimes the entrepreneurs and young people are doing this donor/investor dance and forget why they started their ventures in the first place."

Unpack Your Shortcomings and Personal Kryptonite

As you wrestle with the Impact Paradox (or even with the *multiple* contradictions) in the social impact space, you also have to wrestle with your own paradoxes, recognizing that none of us are perfect.

We all live with real shortcomings, biases, privilege, and even cognitive dissonance.

Before the pandemic, I might have been on a plane every one or two weeks. I enjoy a good steak once in a while. I definitely end up with plastic bottles in my hand sometimes, and there are countless other ways my carbon footprint likely puts me in the top 5 percent in the world, if not the top 1 percent. (I don't even know, actually, though I am sure there is an app for that.) Yet I care deeply about climate change. At Solve, we host many open innovation challenges around environmental sustainability. I know many of the steps I can take, but I don't take them consistently. And believe me, this is but a small part of a longer list of my shortcomings.

When confronting your shortcomings and examining your privilege, it's important to just start, even if it's uncomfortable.

Once you start doing that, there are three things you can do that are critical in this space, and I would argue in life in general:

1. You can approach the work with humility. You do not have all the answers, and you might not be best placed to do this, so you need to listen and develop relationships.

2. You can find co-travelers and partners who will complement your shortcomings.

3. You can invest in yourself, learn to understand yourself better, round out some of the rough edges, and gain new skills, insights, and experience over months and years.

QUESTIONING YOUR SHORTCOMINGS

So how do you start unpacking your shortcomings? This is a tough question... but believe me, it's helpful and necessary.

Let's start:

1. What do you know that you're *not* good at doing?

2. What don't you enjoy?

3. What stresses you out to no end?

4. What is your story, your lived experience? What are the wounds and trauma you carry with you that have shaped your journey, and thus both your superpowers and your shortcomings?

Yes, these questions mirror the ones I asked you to think about in Chapter One. Some of your shortcomings are mirror images of your superpowers. And you won't be able to let go of your shortcomings completely because they make you who you are. But I believe we can each learn to modulate and tone down our adverse aspects, as well as learn to recognize when we need help balancing them.

So, what are the mirror aspects of your superpowers? What is your personal kryptonite?

One of my superpowers (probably the top one, in fact) is that I am really good at getting things done—understanding the vision, breaking it down into actionable steps, corralling the people and resources needed to help accomplish the plan, getting everyone moving in the right direction and on time for deadlines, and achieving what I set out to do. I often am able to do this in record time compared to others.

The mirror of that is that I put a lot of pressure on myself to be productive and to achieve. In fact, I often measure my self-worth based on productivity and achievement. I try to contain the pressure so it's just on myself, but sometimes I fail, especially if I am feeling stressed. Then I might also put pressure on the people with whom I am working.

Some people handle pressure really well, and in fact thrive in that environment; they need someone to give them a target and deadlines, which really motivate them to get going. But other people, like me, have already piled on the pressure within themselves. So they understand where I am coming from, but my pressure probably just adds to their stress. And then there are people who do not like pressure at all (and some prefer no deadlines, either). What can I do about this?

First, I try to delve into the issue more deeply. Why is my self-worth so attached to productivity and achievement? Is this driven by fear, trauma, and/or unhealthy behavior patterns? Where is it helping me, and where is it failing me? How could I better regulate this internal aspect to tone down my kryptonite elements?

Second, who can I surround myself with to complement these shortcomings? The temptation is to surround yourself with people who "get it"—who are exactly like you. Yes, this can work for a time. But then again, we feed off each other—and we risk making each of our own shadow aspects worse.

Getting a diverse mix of people who in fact complement and balance your personal kryptonite(s) in the long term is a better strategy. For my particular shortcoming, I try to find both people who in fact thrive with some pressure added and others who don't like it all. I try to learn from and listen to others' viewpoints because they often have the ability to see other ways to go about things. Do we really need to do this before the end of the year? If the team is working too hard and risks burnout, what can we do to alleviate some of the pressure?

Third, I try to adopt tools and techniques that help modulate the pressure I put on myself (as well as others). These include both large and small things: not checking emails too late at night; writing down the next day's tasks before going to bed so that they stop swirling in my head when I can't get to sleep; doing some painting as a form of meditation; and questioning whether something needs to get done this week versus next week—if it were to slip, would anyone but me actually care? Will they even notice?

Iman's Growth: Learning about His Own Shortcomings to Have More Impact

"It was a struggling moment, the moment when I [wondered]: Am I a good leader? During that process of reflection, I didn't want to talk in public." For all of his success, Iman Usman is one of the humblest people you will meet, with a lack of ego born out of a learner's mindset.

Back in 2014, Iman had the idea for Ruangguru, the Indonesian edtech company I introduced in Chapter Five. Iman was a few months away from leaving Indonesia for the United States to attend graduate school at Columbia University when the idea took hold. "So we basically launched this idea while I was at school, and while my cofounder was also at school."

For once the myth of the dorm-room start-up holds true! In 2020, Ruangguru raised over $150 million dollars and now has over four thousand employees and over twenty million users. The company is now the largest education company in Southeast Asia, but the initial idea came from reckoning with an early failure: "The reason I started the company was actually quite accidental. After graduating from college, I was thinking about becoming a teacher. I wanted to do something about the policies, and I thought, I don't want to be that policy maker who creates policy about education but has never had experience in a classroom."

Despite having graduated from one of the best universities in Indonesia—one of only a few people from his province to do so—Iman's teaching dreams were stopped in their tracks. "I was rejected by all the schools that I applied to [for a teaching position]. And then I applied to a couple of nonprofits, and I didn't get in there either. So, it was actually quite frustrating at the time." From this early failure, however, came creativity. "I realized that if I couldn't be a teacher in the normal definition of what a teacher is supposed to be, then let me define what kind of teacher I want to be using technology and digital platforms. This is essentially what made me start Ruangguru."

Iman admits he knew almost nothing about business when he began. "I never had any idea that I would need to fundraise hundreds of millions of dollars or talk to investors or deal with legal and all of this stuff. When I started, I didn't know about start-ups at all. It was really because I wanted to solve a problem and wanted to define my contribution in society. And that's basically what triggered me to start."

He credits graduate school with having provided a good place to be able to take risks. Although he and his cofounder, who was at Stanford at the time, were working long hours and navigating different time zones between New York, Palo Alto, and Jakarta, there was space for experimentation and failure. If it did not work, Iman could apply for a job; and while at university, he had access to many professors and other resources to support him.

Iman also acknowledges that there was a fair bit of luck involved in his success. "I think we definitely came in at the right time, and we had the first mover advantage as well. There were a few players who had been around [before us], but they ran a typical and traditional company, not a digital company. Of course, there were a lot of challenges. This is technically my first job. I have never actually worked for someone before. I was never prepared to have this responsibility. No one trained me to lead thousands of people, no one taught me how to operate in multiple countries or how to launch products. With every milestone that I've achieved, I've definitely encountered different challenges."

In 2015, seemingly out of nowhere, half of his leadership team resigned more or less at the same time. That was what he calls his "struggling moment." At first, Iman reasoned that maybe they all just wanted to pursue better opportunities. But then he realized there must have been something wrong. After a cooling-off period of a few months, several of the departing staff (friends he'd known well before he started the company) told him that they didn't like his leadership style. "They said they liked me as a friend but felt I was not a good leader."

Iman realized he'd been singularly focused on achieving results and meeting the company's targets. "I didn't really pay attention to the well-being of the team and building meaningful relationships. Every time I met with them, I never actually talked about anything personal. And for them, that was troubling, because they didn't want to lose the friendship."

This was particularly difficult for someone who'd been defined all his life as a "youth leader," an activist from the age of ten, when he launched a library to teach younger kids. For a young entrepreneur who preached a lot about leadership, losing so many executives at one time "was actually quite terrifying," he recalls. After some reflection, he vowed first to talk less about leadership in public, but more important-ly to invest more in relationships, "not just because I want my company to thrive and survive and to have good people, but also because I think I started to genuinely care about the people that I worked with." Iman describes it as "quite a turning point in my leadership journey. Looking back, I think I wouldn't be where I am today if it hadn't happened."

Understanding and Acknowledging Your Own Privilege Is Paramount

Let's dive deeper into uncomfortable territory—let's talk about privilege.

This subject might even be triggering for some, but it is critical to discuss in the social impact space, which by and large is controlled at the top—holding the purse strings gives the most privileged the lion's share of influence. Since this topic is hard, I will inevitably be imperfect in my approach, but I will do my best to navigate it in these pages.

In previous chapters, we talked a bit about power as a positive; this includes your superpowers and any other powers you can use as levers for good. But power—your ability to influence someone else's behavior through access to valuable resources you can trade, as per Julie Battalina's definition—does not exist in a vacuum or anything like a just or fair playing field. To state the obvious, we are not born with equal amounts of power.

The American political philosopher John Rawls, still one of my favorites, rests his theory of justice and how we could create a social contract on the concept of a "veil of ignorance." His idea is that in creating fair and just rules for how a society should operate, we should all imagine that we sit behind a veil of ignorance that keeps us from knowing who we would be in this society or what role would be ours—whether we would be the president, a farmer, or someone born with a physical disability (or all of the above). He believed that with this lack of knowing where we each might end up, we could devise a more just system. But unfortunately, this veil of ignorance does not exist in real life, nor has it ever. In fact, the lottery of birth—the zip code in which we're born, the color of our skin, our gender, and other factors—unfortunately determines our power to an excessive extent, at least the power that we start with, whether that is through our family's money or our access to education, health, networks, and other resources.

Although not the best movie ever made, *In Time*, starring Justin Timberlake and Amanda Seyfried, illustrates this well. In the film, the currency of the world they live in is time/life energy. Everyone has a clock imprinted on their wrist, and if your clock runs out, you die. People born in certain zones have very little time. They have to work really hard to get just a bit more time, enough to get a bus ticket or some food so they can survive another day before their clocks run out. People born into other zones can spend eight months of their time/life energy on a plate of spaghetti, because they have a thousand years on their clocks.

Although this is meant to be a futuristic cinematic dystopia, is it drastically different from the world we live in today? This is why science fiction can be so good: it presents us with an extreme form of the present and thereby helps us imagine what could be possible. Then, perhaps we can make decisions that may help course-correct our future path. To me, this time/life energy notion also illustrates that if you are born with more privilege, you need to spend more time/life energy and money doing good in the world and redistributing your privilege. As my Solve colleague Hala Hanna says, "Turn your privilege into your superpower, that is how you really give back!"

But of course, we also need to change the system so that it's fairer to begin with, because we should not accept a system where we rely on those with privilege to be so generous in giving back; as we know, that does not work.

Let's start with the numerous aspects of my own privilege, some of which I covered in the Introduction. My lottery of birth was hugely positive: I was born in one of the richest countries in the world, with well-educated parents who were keen on me becoming bilingual; they had sizeable ambitions for me and invested heavily in my education and development. It didn't hurt that the French government heavily subsidizes schools, day cares, and even sports and after-school activities.

Although my parents would not have been able to afford a bilingual education of that quality for me in a place like New York City, where tuition can run $40,000 a year for a private kindergarten, the good news was that they could afford a lot of the best things in Paris, as it was much, much cheaper thanks to the role of the government in education there. (My school fees never went over $1,000 a year, and that included free books provided by the state.)

I am white and European, something that undeniably affords me incredible privilege in many settings. I remember having to spend three hours on a stage in Cambodia at a Save the Children event with my boss and a dozen Cambodian Ministry of Education representatives while "We Are the World, We Are the Children" played on repeat in as many versions as likely exist: the English version, the Cambodian version, the rock version, the hip-hop version, the jazz version—believe me, it was really hard to get the song out of my head after that! The event celebrated the opening of the newly merged Country Office of Save the Children, but I had no idea why I was on stage. I whispered the question to my boss, who calmly replied, "Because you are white."

And although my immediate family on both sides escaped wars in their home countries of Algeria and Russia, as well as Communism, anti-Semitism, and Nazism, very few people would know this from looking at me. Some people do recognize my surname as Jewish, and in France, a few people might know it's more specifically Pied Noir, literally "black foot"—a very racist expression meaning from North Africa. But most people would miss this nuance.

Admittedly, in both the UK and France, people have a hard time placing my accent in either language. They know it's not quite from London, Paris, or the countryside. Often enough, I get the question, "But where are you *really* from?" It's a question that many people are subjected to when they do not quite fit people's expectations of what a French or British person should be or sound like. Furthermore, I have still felt excluded at various times when I had to fight to get into rooms where no one looked like me, often in terms of my gender or my age. You would think in the social impact space that would be less the case, but misogyny rears its nasty head everywhere.

So how do you think about your own privilege in general, and specifically in relation to social impact?

Rebecca Obounou, Assistant Dean of Social Innovation at MIT's PKG Public Service Center, points out that notions of privilege and identity are often defined in Western terms that can be misleading. It's all about context: "For example, at least in the US, my skin color may not be celebrated. But I can go to other parts of the world, and as a Black woman, that identity is celebrated."

As Rebecca observes, there is more than one kind of privilege. She stresses the inherent power and humanity of the people you want to help. "I feel that sometimes, even with the marginalized, their privileges aren't acknowledged. And no one ever wants to be portrayed as just that single story. If someone is simply labeled as 'poor,' agency is implicitly stripped from the narrative of that individual; but everyone *does* have power. If you recognize their power, then I think you're better able to collaborate with them. I've learned that firsthand. For me, I learned that when I was able to leverage that, specifically in one of the last projects I did, we passed along ownership to that group, so they became the owners of the project we were helping them with."

To better understand various facets of privilege, take a look at some of the self-assessment tools available. Some give you a list of identity markers to consider—some visible, others invisible, including race, gender, sexual orientation, disability status, and more. Some are more situational, and I think those are more interesting.

As an example, the California Partnership to End Violence adapted another self-assessment from Diane Goodman and Paul Kivel that includes statements like these:

- I worry that people may not hire me because of the color of my skin, my name, the way I look, or my gender.

- I tend to see people of my racial or ethnic group portrayed negatively in newspapers, television, movies, and advertisements.

- I need to hide, change, or minimize parts of my identity to reduce the chances of mistreatment.

- I face physical barriers accessing public buildings and using the transportation systems.

I like this type of assessment better in the sense that through taking it, you start to see how people who might face systemic oppression of all kinds may experience the world differently than you on a daily basis. If you are not a wheelchair user, you will never think twice about that two-inch step you walk over every day or how it stops a wheelchair user like Solver Yuriko Oda from entering a building without help.

The way I see it, a good place to start is to ask these questions: Where in my life do I feel safe when I know others may feel unsafe in these same situations? Where in my life have I felt unsafe in general, or in particular situations? For me, at its most basic level, privilege is the expectation and presumption of safety. Without safety, all else—your joy, peace of mind, and access to opportunity—is curtailed. As Hala Hanna says upon reflecting on her childhood in Lebanon, "The biggest privilege of all, one that I think many Americans are not as aware of, is peace."

Not feeling safe is what is reflected when Black and Brown parents in the US have to teach their teenagers to stay extraordinarily calm if pulled over, and when people of color of all ages must live with very real fear of getting shot by vigilantes or even by the police. Not feeling safe is part and parcel of most women's experience, when they have to look over their shoulders constantly when walking down an empty street late at night. Not feeling safe is also when a single mother does not know where her children's next meal will come from.

Most people in the world feel unsafe, sometimes on a daily basis. They rightly fear for their lives, their bodies, and their livelihoods, often because of their gender, sexual orientation, skin color, or other factors. What would it mean if everyone could feel safe? How can we create a world where everyone has the right and opportunity to feel safe? We want a world where everyone is freed from living in fear and feels safe from war, poverty, human trafficking, police brutality, bullying, discrimination, hunger, and other injustices.

When Miranda Recognized She Had Opportunities Others Would Never Have

As MIT's Rebecca Obounou states, privilege is often something relative to where you are and your situation, but it is always critical to understand. Miranda Wang of Novoloop grew up in a suburb of Vancouver. While she was not well-off, as a child, she came to recognize that she still had privilege when her parents sent her to live with her paternal grandparents in the north of China for a year. She attended sixth grade at a local public school; the classes were all in Chinese and the school did not have flushable toilets, so it was quite a change. But after a couple of months, Miranda started making friends.

One of the friends she'd walk home with was a girl who was a top student in the class. Her parents owned a grocery store; they sold vegetables at the local market every day. One day, Miranda asked her what she wanted to be when she grew up. For her part, Miranda says she was thinking, "My parents will pick me up in May and I will go back to Canada, and then I'll do whatever I want. At the time, I was really into astronomy."

She imagined her smart friend would envision something like a future legal career. But her friend said, "I want to grow up and get out of this tiny little town. I just want to go somewhere bigger."

Miranda recalls, "That hit me really hard as I realized how privileged I was just because my dad was able to leave this place and emigrate. Probably what this girl was able to do in her lifetime wasn't even close: we weren't even on the same level, just because of the families we'd been born into. That was a really emotional moment—the instant when I realized that everything I had was not really based on who I was—it had been given to me. And in that moment, I really wanted to do something purposeful and meaningful in my life because I'd started with so much more."

Deconstructing Privilege Is Key to Changing the System

Why is privilege of particular importance with regard to social impact? The answer can be put in just a couple of words: the Impact Paradox. The whole social impact industry stems from a colonial/neo-colonial savior mentality, and these dynamics are still very much present today. The language of "aid," "capacity building," and "beneficiaries," along with many associated top-down practices, is rooted in the power dynamics of privilege.

In his book *Decolonizing Wealth*, Edgar Villanueva, a member of the Lumbee Tribe, argues that the philanthropic industry has evolved to mirror colonial structures and reproduce hierarchy. Therefore, it more often than not ends up doing more harm than good: "The field of philanthropy is a living anachronism. Colonialism in the empire's newest clothes. Racism In institutional form.

"Almost without exceptions, funders reinforce the colonial division of Us vs. Them, Haves vs. Have nots, and mostly white saviors and white experts vs. poor, needy, urban, disadvantaged, marginalized, at-risk people (take your pick of euphemisms for people of color). The basis of traditional philanthropy is to preserve wealth; and all too often, that wealth is fundamentally money that's been twice stolen, once through the colonial-style exploitation of natural resources and cheap labor, and the second time through tax evasion. Mostly white saviors and experts use this hoarded wealth to dominate and control—obviously or subtly—the seekers and recipients of those funds."

When funders reflect and perpetuate the same underlying dynamics that caused the problems in the first place, nothing really changes, except at the margins. It's thus critical to understand your own privilege, where you are coming from in relationship to the systems you are trying to change, and how to work on solutions that are not rooted in maintaining this top-down/neo-colonial approach to social impact.

And let me be clear: If you are born with a hugely positive privilege balance sheet, this is not to say you cannot help because you are not proximate. On the contrary, do all that you can to redistribute the fruits of privilege, but in the right way—by listening, learning, codesigning, giving, and elevating others. If you do not come from the same community as the people you seek to serve, take the time to understand other people's lived experience, your power and privilege versus theirs. Build real relationships with them where you acknowledge and make space for their power—relationships in which they are not subservient to you. In some cases, the people you are serving may come from the same community you do, and you can claim real proximity to them—great! But this does not mean you have the ability to accurately represent their needs and experiences, either.

These are difficult conversations to have with yourself, your team, and your key stakeholders: the people you serve, donors, fellow volunteers, and others. Such discussions can be uncomfortable for everyone, no matter their background, and people will approach these issues with various levels of sensitivity (and often ignorance as well). That is not a good reason *not* to have these conversations. As societies and individuals, we don't move forward by adopting ostrich policies such as, "I don't see color."

It is important to learn to be sensitive and to avoid triggering, retraumatizing, or tokenizing others, but I do believe we only move forward when we acknowledge and see power, and when we use our own power as best we can to help transform systems so that they will be fairer and more just.

PART III
SOLUTIONS AND GRIT

AMANDA'S JUSTICE

In the fall of 2016, Amanda Nguyen was at Camp David, the one you hear about in the news when a US president is trying to negotiate a peace treaty or some other diplomatic endeavor. Sometimes it's also used for slightly more mundane purposes, and in this case, Amanda was there for her day job as deputy White House liaison at the State Department, training other presidential appointees. At Camp David, phones and all other devices are taken away.

At day's end, Amanda was in the bar at Camp David, the Shangri La. The bar's TV, the only portal available to the outside world, was tuned in to C-SPAN. Amanda watched the Senate prepare to vote on a bill. It wasn't the Survivors' Bill of Rights, the bill she had spent months working on with colleagues and allies, but she figured it might be on the floor any moment. It would very soon be do-or-die.

Eager to contact the outside world, Amanda remembered that the Camp David chaplain had a phone and a computer. She ran out of the Shangri La and saw Golf Cart One glistening in the fall sunlight. (Yes, that is the President's golf cart. I have to say, Americans have a real skill when it comes to naming things.) Desperate to get to the chapel, she decided to commandeer Golf Cart One, pressed the pedal, and promptly went backward. It turns out Amanda doesn't know how to drive.

The naval officers who staff Camp David might have been amused by the scene of a young Asian woman screaming her head off while going backward—very slowly—on Golf Cart One. Eventually Amanda managed to drive the cart to the chapel, where she promptly crashed into a tree (a small crash!). She found the chaplain inside and told him, "Sir, you don't know me, but I'm Christian, and I need your phone."

He replied, "What?"

She persisted, "Turn on C-SPAN! There's a bill—twenty-five million rape survivors' lives are on the line!"

He believed her (and one hopes her Christianity was irrelevant to the decision). Once he handed her the phone, she made another round of phone calls, doing her part to ensure the final passage of the bill.

Later, in the car traveling from Camp David back to the capital, Amanda watched the speech made by Senator Grassley and the final vote on her phone. The bill passed unanimously. Her team called. They were celebrating at The Hamilton, a bar just steps from the White House. After telling her team she'd meet them later, Amanda made her way to the Lincoln Memorial, where she was thankfully on her own: "If anyone saw me there, they might have thought I was a lunatic, because I just literally *let it out,* sobbing and laughing at the same time. It was justice."

In October of 2016, President Barack Obama signed the Survivors' Bill of Rights Act into law. It established statutory rights for survivors of sexual assault and rape for the first time, impacting nearly twenty-five million estimated rape survivors in the United States. The law overhauls the way rape kits are processed in the US and how assaults are reported. The overall goal is to lessen the burden on survivors of assault, who are so often discouraged by the hurdles they face. Under the statute, survivors are given the right to have a rape kit preserved for the length of their case's statute of limitations, the right to be notified of an evidence kit's destruction, and the right to be informed about results of forensic exams.

For Amanda, it was "the biggest moment of justice I've ever felt."

CHAPTER SEVEN

Stay Optimistic and Look for Simple Solutions

Optimism: A Crucial Ingredient

At the end of the day, pessimists don't change the world—they don't even get started. While I spent the whole of Chapter Six discussing the many contradictions of the social impact world and asking you to look at your own shortcomings and privilege, now it's time to circle back to optimism. Yay!

To improve and repair the world, you first need to have a vision for a better world, as well as the belief, whether that belief is realistic, bold, or really ambitious, that it can be changed. In and of itself, this vision is fundamentally about optimism—imagining that something better is possible. You also need to believe in the human spirit and its overall goodness (even if we all have demons, some of us more than others), not to mention the equal value of all human life. Again, that's still about optimism: the belief that despite wars, conflict, and genocide, we can all aspire to be better.

The good news is that overall, being an optimist will make you happier. On average, you'll be healthier and better able to cope with setbacks, as

Arthur Brooks often discusses in his courses and writings. Of course, blind faith optimism can lead to an overestimation of one own's abilities, an underestimation of risk, and a failure to see the realities of the world. Hope is key, and optimism is a force multiplier—something that will allow you to bring others along in your efforts to help achieve your purpose.

Optimism in and of itself can be a force for good. In looking at social trends affecting inequality, Carol Graham from the Brookings Institution discusses how optimism itself (or even a sense of hope) can lead to improved economic outcomes and life expectancy, especially for low-income and vulnerable populations, and how the optimism gap that exists between rich and poor in the US is creating a more divided society.

To me, optimism is the first step in adopting what I call the problem-solving mindset, which we will discuss further in Chapter Nine. With optimism, you are more open-minded, creative, and collaborative, as well as more focused on the solution and the bigger picture, rather than only the problem and the many barriers preventing it from being solved. If you can be optimistic and surround yourself with people who share that optimistic outlook, you'll be shocked at how much you can get done, even if you are born a refugee from one of the poorest and most misogynistic countries in the world.

Roya Mahboob's Story: Optimism and Coding vs. the Taliban and Patriarchy

Afghanistan is not the first country you might think of when it comes to optimism. But in a sense, an attitude of hope is needed there more than ever. It's certainly the first thing you need to get started.

So how does an all-girl robotics team from Afghanistan inspire a nation and the world? With hope, resilience, and the perseverance to keep going, qualities that Roya Mahboob has always had in spades.

Roya was born in 1987 in Iran, where her family had fled during the Soviet-Afghan War, a war that paved the way for the Taliban's first takeover of Afghanistan a few years later. In 2003, she returned to her family's hometown in Afghanistan, the city of Herat. She was inspired both by her mother, who worked as a government employee—something that was at the time rare for a woman—and by her father, who encouraged her to pursue her education, career, and dreams. She became the first female tech CEO in Afghanistan, and in 2013, she created Digital Citizen Fund. Digital Citizen Fund was founded to help young women in Afghanistan and other developing countries access global markets through technology and education. Key to Roya's vision is the chance to change how conservative societies see and treat women.

In her pitch at the Solve Challenge Finals in 2017, Roya talked about going to the only internet café in her hometown at the invitation of a friend, though women were rarely seen in those spaces. Growing up in Herat, she recalled, "There was only one library, where we had to go to get books—all old books. We had nowhere else to do research or get information. And we had only one reality your father, the mullahs, or the teachers would tell you about." When she heard about the "magic box" that supplied all the information you might want, she knew she had to see it for herself. "For the first time, I realized there was more out there than what was around me. Right then, I made up my mind to somehow make technology the center of my career." She went on to college and graduated in computer science.

In starting Digital Citizen Fund, Roya wanted to share her optimistic vision of the internet as a means to access the world. She wanted others to have "the opportunity I had when I was very young to access technologies on the computer. That's why and how I decided to give back to our community. I found out that there are millions of girls out there just like me, with curiosity and a vision of exploring the world."

Lest you think that lack of access to technology is confined to developing nations, consider the fact that in the richest country in the world, the United States, over nine million kids aged three to eighteen still don't have online access at home. Many low-income students rely on public libraries across the country to get access to books and the internet. During the pandemic, with public buildings closed, some American families even parked their cars outside libraries to allow their children to attend Zoom classes and do their homework. In many states, school buses became Wi-Fi hot spots for kids to use to complete their coursework.

While many of us are constantly connected through numerous devices (even our refrigerators and light bulbs are hooked up to the internet), nearly four billion people in the world today still do not have internet access, and many more have only a slow and very limited connection. This is what people in the social impact world mean when they talk about "the digital divide." This divide, which exacerbates inequities between rich and poor, has been reinforced through the pandemic, during which the value of access to information from home has become even more crucial to all areas of our lives including work, education, health, finances, and more.

In Afghanistan, just as in many other parts of the world, computers and internet connection give young women like Roya a voice, as well as access to information. To date, up to the point when the Taliban retook Afghanistan in August of 2021, Digital Citizen Fund had built thirteen centers across Afghanistan and enrolled over 10,000 women in digital training. In order to reduce the yawning inequality of Afghan society, her organization was also building IT centers inside public schools to provide training for young girls aged twelve to eighteen in social media, technology, and coding, as well as robotics and blockchain technologies.

The women who work with Roya were encouraged to take payment of their wages in bitcoin or other cryptocurrencies. This was helpful given that even before the 2021 takeover, the value of Afghanistan's currency was not always stable, and given that many girls and women do not have a bank account or may have difficulty accessing their own funds if the accounts require a man's authorization. With many Afghans now trying to flee their country, these cryptocurrency wallets are providing a lifeline for some as access to funds in bank accounts is more difficult than ever.

Roya has to stay optimistic when confronted with challenges. Initially, she struggled to get people to work for her. As she explains, "Even if you're the CEO, they don't see you as a leader of a company. Sometimes people don't want to pay you because you are a woman, or they want to pay you less than the price they normally pay in the market. Some of these challenges are faced by most women when they start businesses, but we have to deal with the Taliban. Some conservative men in the same industry followed us and spied. They were always creating challenges to make it more difficult for me and also for my family. For example, they shot my sister's car when she went to one of the IT centers in Kabul.

"So, there's all kinds of things that make everything more difficult for you to continue. You wake up every day knowing there will be some kind of problem. You have to be prepared, because sometimes you don't know when, where, or by whom you're going to get attacked or have to deal with some kind of new challenge. Every minute and every second of every day, you have to be prepared for something unexpected to happen. One thing I do right now: I always have a Plan B and a Plan C, if Plan A doesn't work out for me. I'm going to put 100 percent of my focus on Plan A happening, but if it doesn't, I've prepared myself with Plans B and C as well."

Despite all of this, Roya has been undeterred in her mission to give women a voice through access to technology, and back in 2017, another opportunity presented itself: a robotics competition. FIRST Robotics was created in 1992 based on a famous MIT course designed by Woodie Flowers, a longtime professor at MIT's school of engineering who passed away in 2019. Taught for nearly five decades, Course 2.007 is still taken by MIT undergraduates every year. It relies on hands-on methods to teach the basics of mechanical engineering, culminating in an exciting robot battle competition.

FIRST Robotics went on to globally expand the concept to younger students—think of it as the Olympics of robotics. Teams of high school students from all over the world work with a mentor in their country over the course of several months to build a robot that can complete a specified set of tasks (for example, picking up and moving blocks from one side of the arena to the other). Their robots are then shipped by FedEx free of charge to the city where the contest is being held. Then the teams travel to compete against all the other teams in several rounds over a few days.

In addition to mechanical engineering and programming skills, the kids learn to raise funds for their projects and to create a brand that will help build support and respect for STEM (Science, Technology, Engineering and Mathematics) programs in their respective communities. Through this process, the teams get to practice skills such as leadership, team building, communication, and strategy to complement their new technical expertise. Hopefully, the robots also ignite a passion for engineering and technology that will fuel students' dreams and ambitions to go on to higher education.

In 2017, Roya was asked to put together the first-ever robotics team for Afghanistan to enter FIRST's Global Challenge robotics competition in Washington, DC. She fielded an all-girl team, but initially, their visas were denied. It was a fraught time to attempt to enter the US; in January of 2017, with little notice, President Trump signed an executive order banning entry from seven predominantly Muslim countries for ninety days and prohibiting any other refugees from coming into the country for 120 days.

Roya and her team used social media to reach out to members of the US Congress, and fifty-three representatives signed a letter to the State Department asking the administration to change its mind. News of the all-female Afghan team's visas being denied made headlines around the world, and the six team members, ranging in age from fourteen to seventeen, were thrust into the spotlight.

After an international outcry, the United States reversed its decision. At the last minute, President Trump approved the visas, allowing the Afghan girls to enter the country through a "parole" process that authorizes otherwise ineligible visitors on humanitarian grounds or because it benefits the public. The girls arrived in Washington, DC, in July of 2017 to extensive press coverage. Ivanka Trump attended the competition and even invited the team to the White House.

The team had only two weeks to build their robot for the event because a shipment of parts was delayed, but they won a silver medal for courageous achievement. For Roya, this event captured what she calls "the message of hope and determination" that the Afghan girls conveyed to the public. But what happened next mattered even more: "We also saw the delight in our own country, because powerful people, policymakers in the government and the community, started to change their views on women's participation in science and many other industries. This was the victory for us."

As the Taliban retook Afghanistan in August, 2021, the robotics team, which had also been developing a low-cost ventilator to treat COVID-19 under the guidance of MIT, was quickly identified as a potential target for reprisals. Given the bloodshed and crackdown of the 1990s, Roya was afraid that the students at her Afghan Dreamers Institute, the STEM high school she created, could be a target. When Herat collapsed, Roya asked the girls' parents for permission for them to travel. Some of the girls were very young, and while she couldn't get permission to take some of them, she was able to bring nine of the "Afghan Dreamers" with her to Kabul. The girls had previously been invited to Qatar in 2019, so Roya and her team then reached out to the Qatari government, which agreed to expedite their visas.

Roya recounted the moment for a September 2021 article in *Vogue* called "Stories of Triumph and Heartbreak from Nine Women Involved in the Evacuation of Afghanistan," as told by Marley Marius. For the girls, "Many of them saw the Taliban in the streets for the first time." Thankfully, the girls were able to get out and continue their education safely in Doha, but there are still many students left in Afghanistan, and Roya worries about their future. "I don't know when we'll be able to get them out, but I promise that they're not going to be forgotten."

Still, despite the news, Roya told me she still believes that the robotics team "was the first step in the journey for equality," showing Afghan's leaders the potential of Afghan youth, especially young women, in development and technology.

"One thing is I'm very persistent person. I like the challenge. And I believe like technology really can change things. And I just want to make sure that we have to prepare our younger generations, especially in developing countries. I'm in the US and I don't want to take for granted. But I'm Afghan, and I've been there. I know that there are 27 million in younger generations under twenty-five, and I want to do all that is possible in my own ability to make sure that I pass this on for these younger generations."

What Makes a Good Solution?

By this point in your journey, you should have a better sense of how to think about your superpowers and your shortcomings, and how to identify a real problem affecting the most underserved that could become your purpose. Do not worry if all of this is still very much in draft form, whether in your mind or on paper. Reading a book will not immediately give you all the answers for a lifetime's quest. This journey will truly be a constant growth process, so even a messy draft is already a good place to start.

It's time to celebrate: you are ready to think about finding solutions. I know it takes time, but true problem-solving is about asking the right questions in the first place.

So how do you find a solution in which you can invest your resources?

It's important to say "find" rather than "invent," because you should never start from scratch, as if no one has come before you. While you may still need to innovate and bring a brand-new piece to the puzzle, there is almost always a solution out there (with people already working on it) from which you can start. Since the talent and ingenuity of others is already in play, you should definitely do your homework and avoid reinventing the wheel.

At Solve, we have spent a lot of time thinking about what makes a good solution. When we open up a Challenge, we announce very clear criteria for selection, which are what the judges use to score applications and whittle them down first to a shortlist of finalists, then to the selected Solver teams. These criteria are thus of prime importance, and we have learned a lot from feedback over the years.

As you think of your own solution, and as you meet organizations and people who might have solutions you would like to support as a volunteer, investor, philanthropist, or employee, I think it's useful to keep the following criteria in mind:

1.   **Alignment:** If the solution you have in mind worked and could be scaled, would it actually solve the problem you care

about? Would it at least solve a good portion of the problem, if not all of it? This is not by any means a trivial concern. Many applications submitted to Solve get a low score here because they do not demonstrate that their solution is actually a good potential answer to the problem at hand. For example, in 2016, we launched a Challenge around chronic diseases: diabetes, cancer, chronic respiratory disease, and others. One solution that was good overall, but not aligned, related to dentistry. If the dentistry solution had been targeting mouth cancer, and if mouth cancer was a significant proportion of cancers and something that was not being addressed, then perhaps that solution would have aligned well; but the application did not make these arguments. It does not mean the solution lacked promise, but it answered a different question from the one Solve posed at the time.

Once you identify the problem you want to solve, the one that can become your purpose, you need to make sure your solution is aligned with it. Are you jumping into a solution that does not actually solve the problem you care about? Or does your plan solve it only at the margins, and will not actually move the needle if scaled? Don't let yourself get distracted by shiny glitzy technologies or solutions that answer a different problem if you are committed to your purpose. Coming up with the next ill-considered "Uber for X" app is not what this is about.

2. **Potential for Impact:** Does your proposed solution have the potential to impact lives in a positive and meaningful way? Does this strategy solve the problem better than the current solutions out there, both in terms of breadth (number of people) and depth (the amount of positive change per person)? At the end of the day, it's about the best

outcomes for the most underserved people. Measuring your impact is not easy. I'll come back to this in Chapter Eight.

3. **Inclusive Design:** Who are you solving for? Are you looking at solving a problem for the top 1 percent (or 30 percent) or for the bottom 10 percent? Does your solution change things for historically marginalized or otherwise underserved communities? As mentioned before, I do not believe in trickle-down economics or trickle-down technology. On the contrary, we should start by solving for the most underserved among us first, because this is where the greatest potential benefit for our society is found. If you solve a problem for them, it will work for everyone.

    How proximate are you to the population for whom you seek to find solutions? Are you part of the community? Have you (or has someone close to you) experienced this problem? If not, have you spent significant time listening, learning from, and partnering with this community? Are you consulting them, or even better, codesigning with them rather than designing something top-down? It won't work if it's all handed down from the top by "helpers" who just parachuted in.

4. **Feasibility:** Based on available data, is your solution feasible? Does it have a plan for financial sustainability? If your solution already has a pilot somewhere, does the early data indicate that it works? Has your solution worked elsewhere, and do you have reason to believe it would work in the community where you seek to implement it? Of particular concern is, if the solution is based on a technology: does this technology work, and has it been proven? And if not, why should it work based on what you know? How will you show that it works? What data will you collect throughout to demonstrate that it is working? How

are you going to pay for your solution? Will it be funded through grants, investments, recurring revenue from customers, the government, or other sources?

5. **Innovative Approach:** What is different about your solution both as opposed to the status quo and as compared to other solutions out there? What about the current solutions doesn't work, and what makes you think your solution *will* work? What is innovative about it? It could be a new technology, but as discussed earlier, it's not all about technology. A new application of technology to a particular population or geography, a new business model, or a new policy, law, or process might fit the bill. I like Peter Drucker's seven sources of innovative opportunity from his book *Innovation and Entrepreneurship:* the unexpected, incongruity, process need, structural changes in industry and markets, changes in perception, meaning and mood, and new knowledge.

6. **Scalability:** How will you scale your solution, and what do you need to do so effectively? Will your solution scale through the growth of your organization? If so, does the financial sustainability plan for that work? Or will it scale through replication and dissemination of the model? What is your plan to encourage others—government(s) as well as other companies and organizations—to adopt your solution? Is your model for scaling more about breadth (meaning the number of people who may be positively impacted) or depth (outcomes improving further for a small number of people)? The social impact world tends to think of scale more in terms of breadth and number of people, which can also be a conceptual fallacy deriving from a colonial hangover, as Rebecca Obounou of MIT points out.

Sometimes, she says, she even has issues with the word

"scale": "In the places where deep lasting impact is happening and important work is being done, it's not always touching millions; does that mean it's not worth undertaking? I think the notion that it must be [scaled up has to be] balanced. Colonialism was a form of scaling, right? Different countries decided to go and spread their religion, a form of domination. We have to acknowledge language and the unintended harm that it can do sometimes. We need to understand that the way we approach our work is informed by the way we talk about the work." You should still think of scale in terms of being able to move the needle on the problem you care about, but the scale itself can vary. And keep in mind that you do not need to do it all yourself: it could be the globe, or it could be your community, town, or country. It can be more about depth than breadth, but you should be able to show how the needle can truly be moved through your solution.

7. **Partnership Potential:** Who are the partners you need to make this solution work? How will you get them to partner with you, and how will you access the resources you need? No one is an island, and in this game, we cannot do it alone.

As you go about working on a solution, start small and lean, get to a prototype quickly, be sure to listen to users, get feedback often, and be ready to fail and try again, as Rajesh Anandan of Ultranauts did.

Back to Rajesh's Story: Starting Small to Support Jobs for the Neurodivergent

Rajesh started Ultranauts as an experiment to help people with disabilities find work, initially with just three recruits. "I had been doing some work with UNICEF. Every year, UNICEF picks a topic, an issue area relevant to kids. This one year, the topic was disabilities. A lot of the data around disabilities pointed to some obvious gaps in needs. One of them was around work, Because even in a best-case scenario where you had a family with means and an inclusive education system, when kids aged out and had any kind of perceived disability, they were highly unlikely to be able to find work."

Wanting to find a solution, he enlisted a friend who helped him look "for any attributes or traits or strengths that could map to skills and traits that were in demand with the modern workforce. That led to autism and some of the more common strengths likely to be found in an autistic population relative to the general population, like visual pattern recognition ability, creative problem-solving, heightened focus, and so on. That's not to say that everyone on the spectrum has these strengths, or that someone not on the spectrum doesn't. It's simply over-indexing. If you're looking for those strengths, you should look where you're more likely to find them.

"When I explained what strengths are common among autistic adults to my former roommate and eventual cofounder, Art Shectman, who had been a serial entrepreneur in the software space, he said, 'You know, I can never find what you are describing. This is exactly the kind of profile I would look for in a quality engineer. I can never find good quality engineers. And whenever I hire folks from outside service providers, it's hit-or-miss. If you can find me three people who fit that profile, we'll literally put them to work next week.' "

Rajesh had his work cut out for him! He went with Art to a couple of nonprofit advocacy groups that work with adults on the spectrum and put together a job description. "We had a hundred and fifty applicants in three days. A third had graduate degrees; no one had any meaningful work experience. We fumbled our way through picking three folks and very quickly had them do some work for my cofounder's other company. Within a couple months, we could see that two of the three ended up really enjoying the work—things worked out for them. With those two folks, we could see that the results they were delivering were so much better than the work that other people who'd been doing this for years were producing. That was kind of the evidence we were hoping to find, and as a result we launched Ultranauts, then called Ultra Testing, as its own company in the summer of 2013."

Lean and Inclusive Design

A good way to think about starting lean and small is to utilize Eric Ries's *Lean Start Up* methodology, adapted by Ann Mei Chang for social impact in her book *Lean Impact*. Rajesh's story illustrates this well—he started lean, with just a few recruits, and then took the time to build in processes with real user feedback as he went.

Lean design is about starting with a minimal viable product that you can constantly evaluate in cycles of testing with the users you seek to serve, growing and adding complexity only as you find is needed. This is a good process for impact innovators whether they are entrepreneurs, intrapreneurs working inside larger organizations, academics, or activists. And you, too, can apply lean principles even if you are not starting your own solution but joining someone else's.

Starting simple and lean helps you avoid wasting resources, which is important, especially if you are relying on donor money (or your own). It helps you to avoid doing too much harm if things are not working, because if you start small, it's low risk. It means your solution can stay cost-effective and thus affordable for the people you seek to serve and/ or the government that has to pay for it.

Finally, it allows you to start doing good right now instead of waiting around three or four years doing nothing in hopes of coming up with a "perfect" solution. Don't let perfection be the enemy of the "let's try this!" I still see too many overengineered solutions and well-meaning programs designed top-down in the labs and workspaces of those who are too far away from the people they serve, and too close to a coalition of funders who take four years to meet and decide what they are even working on.

At the same time, simple and lean solutions are not about short-term fixes or thinking. You still want to build solutions that can change the system overall. The particular perils of short-term thinking have been tragically highlighted by the coronavirus pandemic. LifeBank's Temie Giwa-Tubosun points out the critical need to build an affordable primary health system that is durable, not just one that responds to a new epidemic each time one shows up: "I would rather the world health community stop solving single problems and instead solve the problem of the basic system, which can then be either dialed down or dialed up to respond not just to pandemics, but also to epidemics and diseases."

Avoid the Graveyard of Good Intentions

In thinking about solutions, beware of the Graveyard of Good Intentions!

The important question is: how are solutions designed by, with, and for the people that they seek to serve? And in evaluating a technology, product, or service, the corollary questions are: how is it deployed, made affordable, and actually used consistently? Many promising solutions—especially technological "magic bullets" designed in the garages of well-meaning Americans—soon wind up in the graveyard of good intentions. There are unfortunately so many examples of this that it could be worth making a museum out of them. Brace yourself; here are some of my unfortunate "favorites."

PlayPump was a technology designed in 1989 in South Africa by Ronnie Stuiver, a borehole driller and engineer. Trevor Field, an agricultural executive, saw the device at an agricultural fair and licensed it. Field installed the first two systems in South Africa in 1994 and began receiving media attention in 1999, when Nelson Mandela attended the opening of a school with a PlayPump. In 2000, PlayPump received the World Bank Development Marketplace Award. The concept was attractive to many well-meaning foundations and charities, including the Clinton Global Initiative: bring water to thousands of African communities by harnessing the power of children at play. As kids pushed on a merry-go-round and then went for a ride, they would pump water into a storage tank. Ingenious! But things didn't go as planned.

PBS's *Frontline* documentary unit first reported on the pump in 2005 as a silver bullet solution. But by the time they went back in 2015, dozens of PlayPumps in Mozambique sat idle. In many villages, PlayPumps had been removed and replaced by hand pumps; images of exhausted women turning the PlayPumps to get water out of the ground are seared into my memory as a part of this particular graveyard of good intentions. What went wrong with a project that excited backers ranging from former First Lady Laura Bush to Steve Case of AOL and his wife Jean, who poured millions into the idea through the Case Foundation?

Water experts speculated that the PlayPump was the wrong solution to begin with, because it only works in specific situations where there is sufficient high-quality ground water close to the surface, for one thing. As with many other well-meaning projects, maintenance was also a big issue. What happens when the pump breaks down? How do you get spare parts? But more importantly, when you think of it, the whole concept starts resembling child labor if children *have* to keep playing to turn the pump.

Ultimately, PlayPumps caught on as something that pleased donors rather than a fix that solved the real problems of the community. Was the issue that pumps were too hard to operate in the first place, and if so, why would children playing help that? Or rather, was the issue that there was not enough water access in any case and that women had to walk miles every day to get water for cooking and cleaning? If so, how would PlayPumps help? If more pumps across more sites was the issue, why not install the tried and tested, not to mention far cheaper, hand pumps?

Or could pumps that run on energy from diesel generators be a more workable solution, or even better, solar pumps, though each of these would need maintenance? If the aim was to really fix the problem, why not help communities invest in proper water systems that would bring taps inside or at least closer to homes? Then there is one more big problem: it's not just about access to water, it's also about making sure the water is clean and purified, given that according to the World Health Organization, 3.4 million people still die from water borne diseases every year.

Have we learned from this failure? While PlayPumps have been retired from techno-utopia, the organization called charity: water still raises millions of dollars every year from small donors on social media and from tech titans like Uber. These funds are used to parachute in and dig wells in remote villages without taking into account maintenance, water cleanliness, and most importantly, community design. charity: water founder Scott Harrison loves to bring donors to see the pump they have funded and the plaque with their name inscribed on it in a remote village of Ethiopia, as though this should matter one bit.

MIT had its own techno-utopian failure: the One Laptop per Child initiative. This was the brainchild of Nicholas Negroponte, founder and first director of MIT's Media Lab, who was determined to get hundred-dollar laptops to children all over what he termed "the developing world." The intent was good—as was the case with Roya and the Afghan girls she works with, access to computers and the internet is paramount for access to information, finance, and jobs in the twenty-first century.

Nick started the One Laptop per Child (OLPC) organization to transform his vision into reality. Backed by the United Nations Development Programme, OLPC generated a lot of enthusiasm and acceptance from both world leaders and the media. But as the time to ship out the devices drew near, problems arose. By 2009, only a few hundred thousand laptops had been shipped to developing nations. When the hundreds of millions of orders envisioned by Negroponte never materialized, the project seemed to fade from view.

What happened? For one thing, the machines themselves proved disappointing in many cases. They were slow, built with older technology that was quickly obsolete. And while the price tag was initially attractive compared to computers back in 2005, the cost of laptops went down very quickly, meaning it no longer made sense to buy these slower machines. There was also very little IT support for the laptops, and as with PlayPumps, maintenance had not been thought through. Nor had the issue of charging them: what happened if you did not have electricity in your house or your school, which was the reality for a majority of the children for whom these computers were intended?

But even if the laptops had been sturdier and worked flawlessly, the initiative might still have proved disappointing given the inherent problems with solutions that rely solely on technology. Even with the best online courses (and back in 2005, they were definitely not the best), an educator—be it a teacher or parent—is still essential to help answer young people's questions, ignite their curiosity, and spur peer-to-peer collaboration.

Back to Temie's Story:
Starting Simple Before Scaling

In contrast to the graveyard of good intentions, real-world community-based solutions begin with deep understanding of a real problem, and then take the next steps with a simple idea, similar to how Rajesh started Ultranauts. This idea could be a new technology, but it need not be—it could be some other kind of idea that is innovative in terms of its application to a new context. This is how Temie Giwa-Tubosun of LifeBank started.

Temie found inspiration in a story set in Viganella, a small village in the Italian Alps that went without sunshine for eighty-four consecutive days every winter. For more than three months each year, residents lived in extreme cold and darkness. Then in 2016, someone came up with the idea of strategically placing mirrors to reflect light into the village. Could the solution to this centuries-old problem be that simple? Mirrors have after all been around in their modern form since the nineteenth century, and in more primitive forms for over eight thousand years.

Given that the sun's position changes throughout the day, the mirror solution had to go one step further—and this is where modern technology came in. Sponsors invested to produce a mirror controlled by heliostat technology, which uses geolocation data and automated motors to change the mirror's orientation. The system tracks the sun's movement and aligns the mirror with it, reflecting the best possible light into the village.

As Temie points out, "Simple solutions like the wheel, the printing press, and the phone have made modern life possible. While recent technological advances continue to usher us into an exciting future, numerous problems remain unsolved for the world's most vulnerable people, leaving them behind. These problems require simple, tech-enabled solutions that meet customers where they are economically, socially, and technologically."

When she and her colleagues began building LifeBank, they launched an app inspired by Uber so that hospitals could order blood on demand. But it didn't work! Hospitals still made phone calls to order blood. So she and her team took a step back and set up a call center that was open 24/7; orders rose by over 300 percent. Then, after building rapport and trust with their clients, they encouraged them to order via the app.

When it came to delivery, they chose motorcycles to navigate the congested, traffic-laden streets of Lagos and boats to reach rural islands off the coast. Calls centers and motorbikes—nothing about them was new or innovative per se, but their application to local needs was. Only later, and in response to real demand, did LifeBank add drones for delivery and blockchain technology to trace each blood packet and ensure its safety, even though it could have been easy to jump to glitzy technologies immediately in order to attract investors. All of these simple, tech-powered solutions have enabled Temie's team to move over 17,000 blood products, as well as oxygen and vaccines, to over 450 hospitals, saving over 6,000 lives.

Temie observes, "As humans, we are naturally drawn toward new and exciting ideas. [But] to drive true impact, human advancement will require pragmatic, tenacious innovations that meet people where they are, work around their current limitations, and prepare them for the future. We must make a conscious effort to scale these simple solutions lest they be starved of resources and support."

One of the judges who selected Temie as a Solver in 2018 as part of the "Frontlines of Health" Challenge was Dr. Mary-Ann Etiebet of Merck for Mothers, a corporate philanthropic initiative that focuses on improving maternal health globally. Her enthusiasm for LifeBank's simple but highly effective solution resulted in a number of follow-up meetings and introductions. In 2020, the MOMs Initiative, a partnership between Merck for Mothers, USAID, DFC, and Credit Suisse, made a five-million-dollar commitment to Temie's organization, LifeBank—a mix of both grant and investment funding to supply an expected one million additional units of blood and other lifesaving medical products to help save mothers' lives.

Busting the Techno-Utopia Myth

Now let's dispel another pervasive myth. Though I head up Solve, and even though MIT is probably the greatest engine of technological innovation in the world, I don't necessarily see technology as the silver bullet cure for the ills of the world. Yes, many of the stories here are about tech-based entrepreneurs, but none of these stories are *really* about the technology itself (in case you haven't noticed!). They're about people taking action to solve problems using tech or policy change or other means as tools for change.

Akshay Saxena from Avanti says it well: "One of the big learnings from failure for us, and I myself have a massive bias [toward this way of thinking], is that most engineers grew up in an ecosystem where we're told tech and smartness can solve everything. It can't. It's really, really important to focus tech on things that it *can* solve. We're learning more and more of that every day, especially when you apply tech to people. People are pretty weird, and they act in weird ways. They don't behave like robots."

As Akshay jokes, "that often gets in the way" of tech solutions working out as planned. As a side note, this is also my pet peeve with a lot of economists and economic models. Many assume that we humans act rationally (do we ever?) and somehow justify the failure of their models when we do not.

When thinking about the uses and limits of technology, I like to employ the analogy of enjoying a delicious meal. When you are feasting, you aren't thinking that the knife, the saucepans, and the stove were involved in producing the meal, or even that they are what make the meal truly delicious. You'll think about the chef and the quality of the ingredients first, and then likely the service or your company for the meal, and then maybe, possibly, if you are an obsessive budding professional chef, you might care enough to ask the waiter how that perfectly charred vegetable was cut and grilled.

That isn't to say that you can make a meal without a knife, a saucepan, and a stove—these are necessary in almost any kitchen. But we can all agree that they are not sufficient in and of themselves, or even usually the most important pieces of the puzzle. In fact, we can sometimes do without them altogether. I will say one of my favorite meals ever was cooking meat, potatoes, and asparagus on a star-gazing camping trip, and all we did was dowse everything in barbeque sauce, wrap it in aluminum foil, and throw it in the open fire pit. Admittedly, as you get more into cooking, an open fire pit is probably not enough, and having the right blender, the right knife, and the right steamer becomes important. It seems that every day, someone comes up with a new gadget to poach eggs in a better way; but again, these are means to an end.

I also define technology very broadly. On one of our Solver teams, Kristin Kagetsu from Saathi, along with her fellow MIT alum and colleague Amrita Saigal, designed a biodegradable banana fiber sanitary pad for use by women in India. Indigenous and ancestral technology, including historic building techniques like Roman concrete or the use of raw bitumen by the Indigenous Cree and Dene peoples to waterproof canoes, are also now being recognized as more sustainable technologies than some of the advances of the last centuries. So let's take a deeper dive into Indigenous excellence and ancestral technology.

The Answer Is You

Gloria Lane's Story: Indigenous Solutions and Knowledge

In October of 2019, I had the opportunity to go to the Pine Ridge Reservation in South Dakota for a weekend spent in the homeland of the Oglala Lakota Nation. Our summit there, Solve at Pine Ridge, brought together the MIT Solve community, educators, students, and tribe members to celebrate sustainable tech innovators across Indian Country. This was my first visit to Pine Ridge, although not my first visit to a tribal reservation, having made several trips in 2018 to the Standing Rock reservation in neighboring North Dakota. Standing Rock was made famous worldwide thanks to the Dakota Access Pipeline protests of 2016–2017, which were very much youth-led.

With few resources besides the power of social media, young people from Standing Rock organized a huge protest against the pipeline that was set to go from oil fields in North Dakota to southern Illinois, crossing beneath the Mississippi and Missouri Rivers, as well as Lake Oahe near the Standing Rock Reservation. Routing the pipeline so near all these waterways meant risking oil spills, as well as the destruction of natural habitats, sacred burial grounds, and local water supplies. In surprisingly little time, the movement spread, and over 10,000 people from all over the US and the globe began coming to Standing Rock and hastily setting up camps. Many came from other Native American tribes, as well as Indigenous communities from around the world. The resistance to the pipeline united Indigenous people globally and shone a spotlight on the massive importance of Indigenous people's rights around environmental issues: 80 percent of the world's species biodiversity is in 20 percent of the land in Indigenous hands.

But purposeful disobedience and activism is not the only way Indigenous leaders of all ages are using their superpowers to have an impact in their community—and going back to ancestral innovation and traditional knowledge systems is something we could all learn from when it comes to sustainability.

Gloria Lane is a Solve Indigenous Communities Fellow who took part in the Solve in Pine Ridge summit. Her family runs the Navajo Ethno-Agriculture Project, an educational farm along the San Juan River in northwest New Mexico which passes along knowledge of preserved Navajo heritage crops and farming techniques. Gloria and her daughter Nonabah's family have been farming fourteen acres for generations. As Nona, Gloria's daughter, explains, "We've just never stopped. It's been my grandma, my mom's grandparents, my grandparents, my mother, and my generation. All of this is around traditional foods. It's all around the culture."

Their Navajo Ethno-Agriculture Project started after a major environmental catastrophe, the Gold Key Mine Spill, dumped hundreds of thousands of gallons of contaminants into the water, a toxic disaster caused by EPA personnel trying to drain toxins from a mine in Silverton, Colorado. The spill affected the whole agriculture industry in adjoining states as well, and Navajo farmers were unable to sell their produce due to the contamination. Nona's and Gloria's farm was a site where water scientists were testing the local soil and water after the spill. Soon enough, the water and soil were no longer contaminated, and further downstream, farmers were starting to sell their produce again.

But in the Navajo Nation, Nona and her family felt that the tribal government was more concerned with holding the EPA accountable for lost tax revenue and environmental damage via lawsuits than it was in supporting Navajo farmers who had lost their income in restarting farming and selling their produce. Nona elaborates: "We were just left out of that equation. After the Gold Key Mine Spill, I just felt that the community was really broken and the agriculture part of it was lost. It was going to be gone if we didn't do something."

Nona and Gloria brainstormed ways to revitalize farming on Diné lands using both science and Indigenous methods. They worked with a Navajo hydrologist who could translate their findings into layman's terms. They also encouraged farmers to resume their work, setting up a de facto cooperative to help farmers sell their produce. It was also crucial to the project to encourage tribe members to both buy fresh local produce and to learn more about traditional foods and farming. Another crucial element is that the farming methods being presented are Indigenous. As Nonabah observes, this is the core of the food sovereignty movement: "We really tried to elevate other organizations and other farmers, trying to rework their land with their families. Maybe we had an influence because we've done it for such a long time."

Local students, notably including participants from the Navajo Preparatory School, are invited to come to work on the farm as part of the coursework, learning not only about water, soil, and farming methods honed over generations, but also about a heritage Nonabah calls "something that is already like blood memory. It's in them, whether they've done it before or not." At the same time, the family is integrating hydrology, physics, and chemistry into their project, which is particularly important to Nonabah's father, a retired educator whose own father spoke only Navajo. Blending Western science with Indigenous knowledge and technology allows students to learn and work with both.

What we call "sustainability" is inherent in the ways Indigenous cultures have lived for generations. Learning or returning to these practices to create a future that works is key for all of us.

Coincidentally, when I visited Pine Ridge in 2019 and caught up with Gloria, Greta Thunberg was there, too, at a community event organized by the Oglala Sioux Tribe, the Lakota People's Law Project, and Red Cloud Indian School. Greta was in conversation with another perhaps even more impressive sixteen-year climate activist, Tokatawin Iron Eyes. At thirteen, Tokatawin had cut her teeth in climate activism as one of the young people who began the Standing Rock #NoDAPL movement to protest the Dakota Access Pipeline.

Over 250 mostly local Oglala Lakota community members filled the Red Cloud Indian School's gymnasium. I was one of perhaps ten non-Indigenous people there, and except for Greta and her father, I was almost certainly the only foreigner. It felt like a real privilege to be part of such a community gathering in the first place, let alone one of such momentous importance. Greta had recently made national and international news when she took a boat across the Atlantic, with hordes of reporters meeting her as she arrived on shore. She then went on to meet with President Obama, address the US Congress, and speak to world leaders at the United Nations during the UN's General Assembly Week.

It was in fact at an Amnesty International meeting in Washington, DC, that Greta and Tokatawin met as they were both honored with awards. After the two struck up a friendship, Tokatawin invited Greta to visit Pine Ridge and Standing Rock. Western South Dakota is home to three counties which have the highest poverty rate in the nation. Life expectancy on the Pine Ridge Reservation is the lowest anywhere in the western hemisphere except for Haiti. For men, it's forty-eight years; for women, fifty-two years. It also has the highest infant mortality rate in the United States.

It was wonderful that Greta had come to these Indigenous lands, including some of the poorest counties in the United States, and some of the most famous because of the #NoDAPL movement. It certainly wasn't the usual route for someone who had just been crowned *TIME Magazine*'s "Person of the Year." Here was Greta in a completely different environment from the ones where she'd been seen in the media. When we arrived, there were already lots of people claiming seats in the school gymnasium, even though the event was not due to start for another hour. It began with a meal, as well as prayers, songs, and speeches from community leaders. I'd been to a few of these types of events before in Standing Rock and was aware that that all these steps were important and significant: feeding the community with large vats of delicious chili, and spiritually nourishing the community by acknowledging the land, the ancestors, the elders, the youth, and more.

When Greta finally appeared, she looked much smaller and quieter in person than expected. She stood with her father on the side of the gymnasium in her typical oversized blue hoodie. Greta and Tokatawin then began their conversation with Tokatawin's father, Chase Iron Eyes, acting as a moderator, although he quickly became superfluous. Greta was humble and deferential, inviting Tokatawin to start and comment often. You could see a shared sense of purpose between these two teenagers whose upbringings and circumstances could not have been more different. Despite Greta's tiny stature and her deference, she drew you in immediately. Everyone, including me, seemed to be leaning in to catch her every word. In a sense, it was a demonstration of the principle that sometimes speaking quietly rather than screaming loudly gets people to listen more intently.

Greta complemented Tokatawin to a tee as they exchanged reflections on the climate crisis, their work as youth activists, and the importance of Indigenous peoples' rights as a key part of the solution.

"We need to see the planet and nature as something which has a value of its own that we cannot own and exploit as we want," Greta told the gathering.

Tokatawin added, "If you are not including Indigenous people in conversations and actions about solutions, the solutions that you create are not sustainable."

CHAPTER EIGHT

Measure. Fail. Try Again!

How Do You Know if You Are Having an Impact?

Measuring impact is hard, but essential. To be honest, one of the biggest dirty secrets of the whole social impact world is that very few institutions and programs measure well whether they are having an impact, and some don't even bother with measuring at all. David Wilkinson, who was the Head of Social Innovation and Civic Participation under President Obama, used to love quoting this fact: Out of an estimated $800 billion spent in the United States on social services delivery annually (the figure is from 2015), there is evidence of impact for less than 1 percent of the total discretionary federal spending.

Yes, you heard that correctly. A good example he uses to demonstrate his point as quoted in *The New York Times* for a 2018 article by Tina Rosenberg: "Take workforce training. We tend to pay for how many people receive training. We're less likely to pay for—or even look at—how many people get good jobs."

The number of people who have received trainings would be an output metric, whereas whether people get jobs—good, well-paying ones, at that—is an outcome metric, which is fundamentally what you should care about. Then there should be more questions to measure longer-term impact: whether people kept those jobs over the long term, earn more year over year, are more financially secure, and are better able to buy a house, invest in their family's education and health, and weather shocks.

And really, you would need to compare your metrics to a control group or another program: Is your workforce development training program better than other programs? Say your program costs more for each participant who receives the training (i.e., when you look at outputs). Some people might say, "We can use another provider who can do it cheaper." But what if your program has better outcomes (i.e., more people do get jobs at the end of the program, and those jobs pay better)? The cheaper provider may train more people, but what if you looked at the outcomes and saw it was no better at helping people get jobs than if they did not attend a training at all? If this is the case, your program is more affordable when taking the desired outcome into account, while the other program should be discontinued altogether.

Worse, of course, would be if neither workforce training program could demonstrate they were helping people get jobs, when compared to not taking a training program at all. Then both programs would be a waste of money. Or maybe the issue is not workforce training, but something else   for example, ensuring that people know what types of jobs exist, and then helping them with the relevant interview process. Who knows?

For the US government, a lot of the social services budget is allocated based on where it has gone in the past, and is presumably based on various lobbying efforts. This does not mean that all of this money is wasted and is not doing any good whatsoever; but if you are not measuring the impact, you do not know. Until you start measuring the outcomes of the programs (not just the outputs), you just don't have the right data—and unfortunately, far too many programs are run without proper results measurement! That is a problem, especially when you spend $800 billion annually.

Caveat: You Can't (and Shouldn't) Measure Everything, Either

Enter the effective altruist saviors!

In reaction to the general lack of good results measurement in the social impact world, a number of people have sought to attack the problem head-on by quantifying everything through a series of tools and indicators. In particular, the effective altruism movement led by Peter Singer, who is "widely regarded as the world's most influential living philosopher" (at least according to his organization's own website, but I have to say that is quite the claim), has sought to develop a more data-driven and quantifiable approach to social impact. Like crypto experts, effective altruists are often found in the techno-utopian enclaves of Silicon Valley, and they share the same zealous passion. Without having ventured that far outside a twenty-five-mile radius, they posit that measuring everything will solve everything, and that you should not do anything you cannot measure precisely.

The issues with this extreme approach are manifold. It costs a lot of money to measure everything, sometimes more than the program itself, which will drive up the overhead costs (and then the overhead police will not be happy!). And it obviously does mean less money going to the program itself. There are also some things that are easier to measure than others.

For example, let's take education: you can measure a number of things related to whether children receive a good education and are well prepared for the future. There are a number of fairly commonly recognized metrics for math, reading, and other subjects both at the national level and internationally; for example the OECD has the most well-known and used tool called PISA, which stands for the Programme for International Student Assessment. And while having these metrics is a good thing, they do not tell the whole story.

Relying solely on the metrics that you can measure may mean making decisions that are not equitable or fair. For example, one school may do worse in reading and math than another; if you look just at those numbers, you might say, "Let's defund and close down that school because it's not effective." But if you realize that the teacher absenteeism rate at that school is sky-high, and often there is no coverage for absent teachers, you might instead say, "Oh, we need to give that school more money so that they can ensure better coverage when a teacher is not showing up."

You may also realize that most of the kids from the other school are from higher-income families and getting private lessons and after-school classes, so their higher reading and math scores may have nothing to do with the schools themselves. Or half the kids from the lower-income school may live below the poverty line and experience hunger, which has been shown time and time again to limit students' ability to learn—can you think as well when you are hungry? If that is the case, you might need to invest more to ensure healthy and hearty school meals are served.

When I was at Save the Children, the organization had a program called Rewrite the Future. They noticed that primary school education enrollment around the world was improving; the social impact world was celebrating this. It sounded like great news, except that if you disaggregated the data, in conflict-affected countries, education rates were stagnating or in decline, which was not surprising given that war tends to be a big barrier to accessing education safely.

Save the Children decided to invest millions focusing specifically on conflict-affected countries such as Angola. However, they did an evaluation after the first five years, and the results were not great. Though students in the program were coming to class and enrollment was up, they were not necessarily learning. In Angola, it was because the teachers often spoke different languages and dialects than the students. Because they were focused on enrollment as the key metric, they had missed lots of other issues. Save the Children obviously decided to recalibrate the program to include broader metrics, including criteria relating to the quality of learning environments and learning outcomes.

When you dive deep into education, you quickly realize that there are lot of factors that affect educational outcomes and that it might cost a lot more money in some places than in others to raise reading and math scores. If you were to take a purely data-driven approach, you would say, "Let's focus on a country where English is widely spoken, or on urban children, who are easier to reach than rural kids; our money will go farther that way than trying to provide education to refugee children, those with disabilities, or children living in remote locations." But is that equitable? Instead, shouldn't we provide education to those who are most underserved, even if it may cost a lot more per child?

Further, metrics can be reductionist. Reading and math scores at grade levels are good metrics to know if kids can...read and do math. But they are not good metrics to tell you if children will be ready for a job in the twenty-first century, if they are ready for higher education, or if they will become productive and ethical citizens. Such data might be a good proxy (i.e., if the school is effective at teaching reading and math, maybe they are good at teaching these other things), but who knows?

This is especially true when test scores become so important for funding allocations, leading to an optimization of those metrics and in fact deprioritization of other goals and objectives. Then you get perverse outcomes (for example, kids who are good at taking tests but lack core skills like sustained reasoning and logical thinking, not to mention writing and creative ability). Then there's the issue of tests always favoring higher-income students, whose parents have money to pay for private tutors. In some countries such as South Korea, which excels in the PISA metrics, there is grave concern about the mental health of kids, given the pressures on each of them to ace their standardized tests. In fact, 34 percent of South Korean adolescents have considered suicide due to academic pressure.

The extreme use of metrics also often means that funders spend months or even years crafting well-intentioned strategies detailing how they might give away their money in the most optimized way. Program officers or consultants sitting in plush offices in Manhattan or Geneva come up with a Theory of Change, a framework which spells out the objectives of the program and its activities following a fairly simple equation to be validated:

$$\text{Input} + \text{Activities} = \text{Outputs} \rightarrow \text{Intermediate}$$
$$\text{Outcomes} \rightarrow \text{Longer-Term Impact}$$

But as Dedo Baranshamaje from the Segal Family Foundation points out, the issue arises with "the idea that you can engineer change on a Theory of Change diagram as if things are very static. People follow their strategy very rigidly, but without understanding that changes happen in an ecosystem; they're affected by time, by situations, by anything. Yes, it's good to have a Theory of Change, and it's good to have a sort of roadmap or compass, but oftentimes life is between the plans. So, I see a lot of people spending way more money on a Theory of Change than on actually monitoring and evaluating. Who looks into the outcome?"

Not measuring any outcomes is bad, but only doing stuff you can measure fully and making all decisions based purely on quantitative data and cost-effectiveness, is also not ideal. The middle of the road option is to do the best you can measuring the outcomes that really matter. Combine quantitative data with qualitative input to get as full a picture as possible about whether or not you are having an impact, taking into account input from the people you are actually serving. Best yet, you can involve your customers or users in the design of measurement tools and have them take part in evaluating outcomes. This is what Ko Chijota from Malawi, an African visionary who Dedo supports and funds, does with his smallholder farmer cooperative program, GGEM Farming. Farmers themselves are the ones collecting data, with support from staff and the GGEM app, which works both offline and online.

Approach Results Measurement as You Would a Hypothesis

When thinking about which solution(s) might work best—one that already exists, or one you are building yourself—and how to measure things as you go to learn and try things out, *I always think it's worth going back to the scientific method.* (After all, I am originally a biochemist and now work at MIT, so you were going to get some science thrown in here at some point.)

The key here is to remember that initially, you are testing a hypothesis; as you work with your solution over weeks, months, or even years, you measure what makes the most sense and gather qualitative evidence as you repeat the process, learning and improving outcomes as you go. You should remain clear throughout that one metric or one single result is never enough to give you the full picture.

THE SCIENTIFIC METHOD, ADAPTED FOR SOCIAL IMPACT

1. **Make an observation.** Listen, do research, and learn about the problem you want to solve. Do so not with a top-down approach, but in consultation with the population with whom and for whom you are working for positive change.

2. **Ask a question about the problem you want to solve.** Make sure the question is human-centered and does not predefine the solution. For example, "How might we use blockchain to price carbon?" is not a good question. It presupposes that blockchain is the answer and that pricing carbon is the problem. Pricing carbon might be a good solution, but it's best not to jump too many steps ahead. The problem in this example is about climate change and working to remove or lower carbon emissions, yet there is no human being mentioned in the question. A better question in this area might be, "How can individuals and corporations manage and reduce their carbon contributions?"

3. **Form a hypothesis.** Based on your many observations and your question, now is the time to make an educated guess or prediction that can be tested through an experiment. (In a sense, your minimal viable product is your experiment.) In this scenario, your hypothesis could be:

   • The reason individuals and companies do not reduce their carbon emissions is that they are not incentivized to do so.
   • If we could price carbon fairly, governments, companies, and individuals would respond to this incentive and reduce their emissions.
   • Prior attempts to price carbon have failed because there has not been a good tool to do so, but a secure blockchain ledger would do the trick nicely, like the one our fictional company (let's call it CarbonPrice) has just designed. Or

perhaps you decide to create CarbonPrice because having looked at what is out there, you couldn't find an existing tool to do this.

As you can see, there are quite a few assumptions in this hypothesis, but that is okay because this is an educated guess, and that's how you move the field forward to innovate.

4. **Test your hypothesis through the experiment you design.** Say you go on to help CarbonPrice; can you get ten companies to download the app and use it? Over a period of ninety days, what happens?

5. **Observe and analyze the results as objectively as possible.** During the ninety days, have the companies reduced their carbon emissions? If so, by how much? Does that beat the other competitive app that isn't based on blockchain? Going back to the original question, are there other solutions (e.g., regulation) that have been shown to reduce people's carbon contributions more? Measuring whether your solution is having an impact is no trivial feat. However, at the hypothesis stage, it's fine if your measures of success are proxies and not necessarily full proof, as long as you are clear on this fact.

6. **Draw conclusions.** Is your solution better than the status quo? Is it worse? (That does happen, unfortunately!) Did it work well for five companies, but not so well for five other companies? What might be going on there?

7. **Provide feedback to the parties involved.** Even if it's a failure, sharing failures is valuable and important, and whoever took part in the pilot and helped you deserves to know what happened. They might also be able to help.

8. **Iterate.** What is the next hypothesis you should test? If it worked well with all ten companies, can it work with a hundred? Can you do the test for a year? If it worked well with half the companies, why might it have succeeded only with that half? How do you need to change the solution to make it work for all companies, or at least for a large majority? If it failed completely, what is another hypothesis you could test via experimentation?

The 2020 Nobel Prize in Economics went to Esther Duflo and Abhijit Banerjee, two MIT professors who study how to measure the impact of development programs and seek to do so in a more scientific manner through what is called Randomized Control Trials (RCTs). Their book on impact measurement and development economics in general, *Poor Economics*, is definitely worth a read.

These RCTs have found good footing over the last few years thanks in no small part to the Poverty Action Lab, or J-PAL, that Esther and Abhijit run at MIT, as well as a number of innovative financing tools. For example, social impact bonds are a form of pay for success financing, where a government will only pay if an outcome is achieved, and investors provide the funds up front for a particular program. If the project succeeds, the government pays back the investor with interest, but the government can afford to do so because of the savings or extra tax income created by the program. If the project fails, the government does not have to pay for the program, since it's the investors who have taken the risk and who do not get their money back. For this type of project to work, good measurement tools to validate results are key.

However, RCTs can be expensive and time-consuming to run (on average five years), so they are not always well adapted to all social impact programs. If your solution is at an early stage, I would suggest not starting with an RCT; but thankfully, other tools geared toward early-stage pilot projects have also been developed, such as those from Innovations for Poverty Action and 60 Decibels.

What about your individual impact? You obviously won't be running a RCT on your volunteer side project or your giving, but you can have influence on the organizations with which or for which you work to help improve their results measurement and ultimately their outcomes. It's also always worth going back to yourImpact Balance Sheet every year or even every few months and asking: How am I doing in each of my core categories and with my levers of power? Where am I doing better or worse? Where can I improve my impact?

Back to Akshay's Story: Measuring and Pivoting Along the Way

According to Akshay Saxena from Avanti, "You need to see some evidence of the model working and to be able to at least articulate a clear thesis."

Between 2010 and 2013, he and his colleagues were able to "find really smart kids and help them." That's not a very sharp Theory of Change. For Avanti to be an organization worth scaling, the thesis needed to be stronger. But they moved on to saying, "We actually believe that classrooms are broken, and that some alternative, either technological or pedagogical, is going to change how classrooms run." They decided they had a pretty good shot at figuring out what that was for the poor. As Akshay explains, "[We needed] the articulation and confidence that our answer would not just be going classroom by classroom and strengthening what I believe is a completely broken system—that we would actually be disruptors in the ecosystem and be able to track it."

Even with evidence of success, Akshay and Avanti's journey was not smooth by any means. As he and his cofounder learned and failed along the way, they pivoted and refined their model. Avanti started as a volunteer-based organization. Akshay only committed to being full-time with Avanti when he "felt we could go in to start teaching and learning," which they did for a year or so as a nonprofit. Then they tried a for-profit social enterprise model, but over time, Akshay realized that did not quite work, either. "We were constantly moving upstream, moving away from the kids we really wanted to work with. Also, the for-profit structure was actually constraining innovation because it was pushing us down paths where we could monetize, not paths that could solve the problem. Another reason why we had made such little progress solving for education is that the government model pushes you down one path that doesn't lead to any innovation. But innovation in the commercial context is like healthcare—a pretty constrained system that tends to push you down another pathway, away from impact and toward making money. So we're currently in the middle of pivoting away from that. Avanti has been three different start-ups, in different ways."

Failure in Social Impact Is Inevitable, and It's Important to Learn From It

To really change the world, you need to have the courage to fail.

We all need new solutions and innovations, and thus need to experiment and take risks. Some of these will pay off, and some (likely the majority) will fail; but provided that we are in fact measuring whether we are failing or succeeding, we can learn from these failures by observing and analyzing results, correcting the effort's course, trying again, and ultimately going on to succeed—an essential process for many of the problem-solvers in this book, including Akshay.

This goes for social impact solutions you work on, as well as for your own life. I realize this is difficult and that not everyone has the same ability to take risks. Failure is quite taboo in the social impact space, especially because in some cases, "solutions" end up doing more harm than good. But if we don't face the reality of the results of our actions, we don't learn and grow. One way to look at it is to recast failure as research and development (R&D), and in many industries, this is big money. Pharmaceutical companies spend on average 17 percent of new revenue on R&D. The average R&D to marketplace cost for a new drug is nearly four billion dollars, and at times, the total price of developing one new drug can exceed ten billion. Most of the cost is due to the failure rate of drugs: nineteen out of twenty promising experimental medicines fail before ever being brought to market.

It's not always easy to show over the short term or even the long term whether your solution has failed or succeeded, especially when you're trying to change behaviors and systems. The right mix of quantitative and qualitative data is crucial; otherwise, a failing project can go on for years without course correction. The incentives to acknowledge failure are also not there; donors are more likely to give money to organizations that have succeeded. And whether you are a government, a corporation, or a philanthropist, you don't want to find out that your money has been wasted, especially when it's geared toward saving lives. Thus, the tendency is to avoid looking for bad news.

The problem with this kind of reasoning is that it inherently causes the social impact community to have a tendency to not look for or measure failure, and therefore to take less risk and, ultimately, innovate less. With that bias, we're all less likely to invest in the ideas that will lead to game-changing breakthroughs. A lot of donor checks only go to proven organizations with proven solutions; even if we do not want to waste money, this economy often comes at the expense of innovation and new ideas. And as Dedo Baranshamaje described so well in Chapter Six, it often serves to box out proximate and local social innovators who cannot even get in the room, let alone go on to apply for funding, because they do not have the track record of larger "status quo" organizations.

On paper, providing mobile services to sub-Saharan Africans in the early 1990s was never going to work. Mobile phones were just starting to appear in mass market numbers in the United States and Europe, but they were expensive to buy and worked on monthly subscriptions. You also needed a lot of capital to get cell towers up and running. So traditional investors and foundations shunned Sudanese-born Mo Ibrahim's venture Celtel, which sought to provide mobile services to sub-Saharan Africa. Fortunately, the CDC Group (a development finance institution owned by the UK government) and the IFC (an investment arm of the World Bank) were willing to take the risk and invest.

The investment in Celtel proved very profitable, but more importantly for this book, it has undeniably contributed to economic development for the millions of Africans who now own SIM cards, allowing them to leapfrog the need for landlines to access information. There is a good argument to be made that the mobile phone—along with the risk that Mo Ibrahim took—singlehandedly helped support access to education, health, information, and finance for the whole continent and beyond, more than anything else has in the past few decades.

And interestingly, there were relatively small innovations that were key to Celtel's success. First, they did away with monthly contracts, instead replacing them with pay-as-you-go SIM cards, enabling users to add very little money each time (e.g., they could purchase one dollar's worth of credit). Second, they created diesel-powered cell towers that were inexpensive to set up and easy to maintain. In addition to this, the banking service M-PESA, a mobile payment system initially started in 2007 by Vodafone, bypassed the need for people to have a bank account, at a time when only about 30 percent of Africans had them.

Failing more, taking more risks, and innovating are necessities if we are truly going to tackle the biggest challenges. Even if you're not Bill Gates, who likes to talk about "big bets," and you can't take risks at the same level as he can (let's face it, none of us can), thinking about whether you are failing enough to really push the boundaries of your work toward greater impact is essential.

One of Solve's partners is Carrie Morgridge, who runs the Morgridge Family Foundation with her husband. Their foundation focuses on climate action, education, and workforce development, primarily in the United States. Carrie is a self-identified "Chief Disruptor," and she talks a lot about democratizing philanthropy, which is why she supports a number of the giving circles we talked about in Chapter Five. She sees her philanthropy as "courage money." I like this idea very much: Are you making the first bet? Do you have the courage to move the space forward even if you might fail?

Thanks to Carrie, Solve has been able to start a number of projects we could not otherwise have gotten off the ground so quickly, if at all. This notably includes Solv[ED], a new program to support young people aged twenty-four and under to become problem-solvers in their community and the world. She wrote the first check to get that project started, and that is still too rare. Typically, many donors wait until a project like this has external validation from other donors before jumping in.

Kevin's "Failures" and Iterations

It took Kevin Adler six years from his original GoPro experiment to come to the point of feeling that his nonprofit, Miracle Messages, was finally going somewhere. There had been numerous challenges and some failures along the way. After the first well-publicized family reunion for his unhoused client Jeffrey, Kevin didn't move to do more at first. "I didn't think I was the right person for the job." He figured that Jeffrey's "Christmas miracle" reunion with his family was an exception, "a lucky needle in a haystack." And Kevin admits, "I prayed that this would not be my work. It was hard; I didn't think I was up for it." Three months later, he went to a shelter and "kind of begrudgingly," as he describes it, offered his services. "If anyone's interested, great; if no one takes me up on it, then it was a one-off and we're done."

He made an announcement to this effect at lunchtime in the shelter's soup kitchen. No one took him up on it. But then, as Kevin got ready to walk out the door, a man approached him and said, "Excuse me, I heard you mention reconnecting to your family. I haven't seen my family in over thirty years." His name was Johnny. Within three weeks, members of Johnny's family had recorded video messages, flown from around the country on their own dollar, and reunited with him in person for the first time in decades.

Now Kevin knew that his involvement with this community was not a one-off, and equally important, he understood that he "could be part of what would bring this to fruition." In contrast to secretive founders who are protective of their stealth start-up ideas, Kevin says, "I was like, steal this idea! Go do it! Literally, take it and run."

For the first couple of years, he tried a number of things, some of which worked and some of which failed. He stresses the importance of listening to your real customers, "the power of just listening and being in relationship with the people you're wanting to serve."

Miracle Messages had set up an advisory board full of well-intentioned tech start-up folks who donated money and time. They were excited about the idea of technology solving the problem, so Miracle Messages started a pilot project in which iPads were installed in the lobbies of homeless shelters so that residents could record their videos whenever they had a chance and reach out on their own to friends and family.

But there didn't seem to be much action in the new digital kiosks. For one thing, very few shelters have good Wi-Fi, so Kevin and his team created big banners advertising the service with a Miracle Messages number to call for help with using the iPads if needed. All of a sudden, they were getting a lot of calls asking how to reach out to loved ones, but still no use of the iPads. They dropped the iPads, but kept the idea of a number to call and set up a toll-free hotline, 1-800-MISS-YOU.

It was a painful failure for Kevin and his team, but a valuable lesson in listening. Whose advice are you taking? It probably should not be the people who have scaled billion-dollar products and apps but have never set foot in a shelter in their lives.

Even as Kevin was starting to arrive at answers, he was still barely getting by. At one point, he was down to six hundred dollars left in his bank account, though he stresses he had family who could have helped: "Rock bottom was never going to be so rocky." In 2016, he decided that if he hadn't raised a certain amount of money by a designated date, he would have failed in his responsibility to the organization. If that happened, he felt he would be better off getting a job elsewhere and using that money to pay the part-time team member that he himself was funding.

Shortly thereafter, still with no funding coming in, Kevin got a job working for the 2016 Hillary Clinton election campaign in Wisconsin. He was learning a lot, but he realized he was immediately applying each thing he learned to Miracle Messages in his head: "Oh, great messaging tactic, we could really use that. Let me take a note. Oh excellent, I should give a talk on this, or this would be a great partnership."

After a week, he realized his heart was still with Miracle Messages. He sent the campaign an email saying that he had to step away to keep going on his journey, even if he wasn't yet sure where it would take him. He signed off by saying, "I'm so sorry." He turned off his phone to avoid any angry or disappointed return messages, because as he puts it, "I hate letting people down."

When Kevin turned his phone on again, he found two messages in his inbox. One was from NowThis, a media company that wanted to make a video about Kevin's work. Their video wound up getting twenty-six million views, putting Miracle Messages on the map.

The second one was from the TED organization, offering Kevin Adler a residency in New York. It was then that Kevin made a realization. "I had to be willing to fail in order to truly succeed. I had to be really willing to give it up, to hit rock bottom, to feel embarrassed and ashamed, all those ego things. I had to squelch them all."

When you accept the need to fail, then you should seek to fail as fast as you can. After all, you want to waste as few resources as possible in trying your idea out, and then go on to succeed as fast as possible. Of course, it will inevitably take some time to see whether your project is having real and lasting impact; after all, you're trying to change people's lives, and that's never instantaneous.

Once you have a better sense of your superpowers and the problem, there's no reason not to get started if you start simple and lean and are ready to work with your community, learning from your failures in order to drive innovation. So what are you waiting for?

CHAPTER NINE

Invest in Yourself and the Problem-Solving Mindset

My Story: Why It's Hard for All of Us Some Days

On the Saturday of Solve Challenge Finals in New York in 2019, I decided to sit in on the "Healthy Cities" finalist interviews along with the judges. Little did I know that I'd once again find myself in tears at work. The finalists had been selected from hundreds of applicants who had answered the call to present a solution to this challenge: How can urban residents design and live in environments that promote physical and mental health? Everytown for Gun Safety, an initiative of Michael Bloomberg's that was one of our many prize-funding partners, provided a $100,000 prize pool for any solution in this challenge that specifically looked at how to make communities safer and reduce gun violence.

According to the CDC, nearly 40,000 Americans die each year from gun-related causes. American children are almost forty times more likely to be killed by a gun than children in other high-income countries. As Vivek Murthy, Surgeon General of the United States under both

President Obama and President Biden, said: "Gun violence is a public health issue."

Tim Makris is one of the many fathers who lost a child during the Sandy Hook massacre on December 14, 2012, when a gunman walked into an elementary school in Newtown, CT, and indiscriminately killed twenty children aged six and seven and six teachers before taking his own life. Everyone deals with grief in very different ways. Tim decided to try and do something about the issue of gun violence in schools to stem this epidemic. In 2016, Tim created the advocacy group Sandy Hook Promise with his cofounder Nicole Hockley, also a parent of a child killed in the massacre. The foundation's goal is to prevent gun violence (as well as other forms of violence and victimization) *before* it happens by educating and mobilizing both youth and adults to identify, intervene, and get help for anyone at risk.

At Solve Challenge Finals that day, Tim was pitching a digital platform called Say Something, an anonymous reporting system which enables users to submit safety concerns about someone considering violence to others or themselves. The reports are then assessed by a 24/7 crisis center, which in turn alerts local schools or police teams to intervene to prevent tragedy. Since Sandy Hook Promise launched Say Something in 2018, it's been used by over a million students in over five thousand schools in twenty-four states, and Tim reported that its reach continues to grow. The platform is designed for both first-person and third-party reporting and has helped prevent multiple school shooting plots, suicides, bullying, and more. Sandy Hook Promise's goal is to scale it nationwide, revolutionizing school safety and violence prevention.

During the Q&A period, Tim shared that most calls the crisis line receives are not about school shootings, but rather about suicide. Suicide rates for young teenagers in particular are the highest since tracking began in 1960, and the most common method of suicide for teens is firearms. As Tim talked about his incredible organization and the work they do, and as the judges peppered him with questions to dig deeper into his impact,

I had to excuse myself. I didn't think having the executive director cry during a finalist's pitch was quite appropriate. Say Something hit home hard for me because one Sunday—on May 3, 2004, to be precise—my brother Louis killed himself.

I was twenty-one, he was seventeen. We were not close.

I missed the signs, just like everyone else. And there were some signs.

I was in China teaching English at the time. We used to communicate sporadically via MSN messenger—which, back in the day, was as cool as TikTok. He had written on his status, "Becoming a psychopath." When I asked him why he had written that, he told me it was how he felt. I told him it was silly and suggested he remove it before people got the wrong idea. I told my father that he should encourage my brother to remove the posting.

What if I had known then what I know now—about depression, about suicide prevention, about listening more to people's feelings in general? Could I have engaged him in a real conversation and realized he needed help?

But there were other signs, too, that other people missed. As it turned out, over the course of several months, he had confided in a few friends at school that he was suicidal, notably to a friend who'd been heartbroken after breaking up with her boyfriend. It seemed as if they'd found comfort in sharing their depression. But Louis did not confide in my parents, our brother Antoine, nor myself, nor did he disclose his feelings to anyone who might have realized he was serious and then could have gotten him some help—or so we thought. Later, we discovered that the Friday afternoon before that fateful Sunday, a classmate of Louis's had gone to the principal's office. Though the principal wasn't there, Louis's classmate told her assistant that he was worried Louis might harm himself.

The Answer Is You

For whatever inexcusable reason—the assistant was not trained properly, and it was Friday afternoon, which in France means the day is basically over—she didn't pass the message on to the principal. If the principal had received it, I'd like to think she would have had the common sense to call my parents. Who knows what would have happened if my parents had been alerted and had had a conversation with Louis? He had been bullied years earlier at school had likely suffered from undiagnosed depression for many years. But as far as we know today, this was his first suicide attempt, one he had planned for months, telling at least a handful of his classmates, giving them multiple opportunities to alert the school authorities and my parents. In fact, one of them had sounded the alarm and gone to the principal's office.

As Tim explained his work to the Solve judges, it was impossible for me not to speculate: What if this platform had existed in France back in May 2004 and someone had called about Louis? Could his suicide, like so many others around the world, have been averted with a timely intervention?

We all deal with trauma and have our own lived experience, whether we grew up in the slums of Karachi or in a lovely leafy neighborhood in Paris. And even if we and our loved ones have somehow magically escaped trials, tribulations, and tragedy, we can relate to the human condition and say, "What If?" What if it was me? What if it was my daughter, my mother, my brother?

In the end, Tim's solution was not selected as a Solver. The judges decided another eight solutions out of the hundreds of submissions were better poised for Solve's support; but like many others who do not get selected, this takes nothing away from Tim's amazing work. I have no doubt he will continue on his journey to take his own tragedy and transmute it into doing his best to improve the world.

Always Remember to Put on Your Own Oxygen Mask First

Regardless of the problem you choose to focus on, it will always be very personal.

This is either because the problem has affected you, your family, or your community, or because it resonates deeply with your Story of Self, even if indirectly. Like Rajesh Anandan from Ultranauts, who works on autism rather than, say, the Sri Lankan post-civil war reconstruction, I do not work on suicide prevention. Nor do I think I ever will, as it's probably still too traumatic for me, even years later. It took me almost a decade before I could really talk about it with a therapist, let alone with friends, and it's still not something we talk about in my family. But in a sense, my mission, equality of opportunity, is both universal and deeply personal. There is a link to my brother, who did not get to realize his full potential. So I would like to see that everyone, no matter who they are, can realize theirs.

Like so many of the people in this book, I have the immense joy of knowing and living my purpose. Over the long term, this is most rewarding, and according to studies, it appears I may live longer thanks to it! But that does not mean it's an easy path. It's also immensely exhausting, confusing, pressure-filled, and sometimes lonely, at least for me.

While Luis Garza says of Kinedu, "It's a business that lets me sleep well at night," I would disagree. I often still have insomnia-filled nights thinking about Solve, where my brain is filled with all the to-dos I have not yet done and all the new ideas I have yet to implement. Fundamentally, my mission of equality of opportunity is one that will never be done, not at least in my lifetime—and for me, that is still a constant source of pressure.

It's taken me years to understand the importance of investing in myself, of healing, of taking care of myself first.

And I would say I am still at the start of that particular journey. I can't say I have found the recipe that works for me, but I think I am starting to find a few ingredients.

My friends were all surprised when I decided to spend December 31, 2019 at a mostly silent meditation retreat somewhere in the middle of nowhere in Pennsylvania. They would much more have expected me to attend three different parties in a sequined dress, celebrating the new year and its hope and optimism. But 2019, just like the previous three years, had been as harrowing as it was fulfilling. Behind all the Solver teams, the millions of dollars we were disbursing, and the impact we were having were a litany of meetings, conference calls, pitch presentations, and conferences in glamorous and less-than-glamorous places. Our work had involved an army of trains and planes, and a suitcase that was never quite unpacked, Not to mention budgets, HR, bureaucracy, politics, disappointments, and many, many a "no" for each "yes."

Leading Solve was without a doubt the best job for me—the opportunity of a lifetime. I was meant to be living my best life. Often enough I was and still very much am, but the analogy I like to use is that at the beginning, it felt (and sometimes still feels) like drinking hot chocolate out of a fire hose. Even if this is your all-time favorite hot chocolate, there is only so much you can take at once, and you end up drowning in the stuff.

We were a start-up supporting start-ups, and we were growing fast. There were a lot of stakeholders—Solver teams, donors, and MIT senior administration who were supportive, but who also expected success and immediate results. Certainly, I was also putting a lot of pressure on myself: I wanted to make things happen fast, because the problems of this world cannot wait.

So at the end of 2019, having tried yoga, Pilates, acupuncture, therapy, coaching, melatonin, and a few other things that worked only mostly at the margins, I could think of nothing better to do than to celebrate the new year in silence—to try and set an intention for 2020 to be the Year of

Balance. But my whole concept of balance, just like the rest of the world's, would of course be thrown into question a mere two months later.

I put my phone and laptop in the safe at the retreat and surrendered to the process. I was in bed by nine-thirty, something that had probably not happened in a decade (except when I had jet-lag), and especially not on New Year's Eve. Every morning, we (fifty or so people of all ages) would get up, meditate several times a day, eat all our meals, walk around, and practice yoga (though I did not), all in silence. I can't say I love the act of sitting uncomfortably on a cushion for forty-five minutes several times a day. It's not my favorite activity, and it likely never will be. I am a better meditator when I am walking or even painting. But I had told my family, friends, and work colleagues that I would not be available and had given the emergency number only to my mother and assistant, with strict instructions to not call unless it was really, truly an emergency. And that peace—being disconnected with no responsibilities or expectations—was immensely liberating. It was a luxury I had not experienced in years, not since getting a BlackBerry that allowed work emails to ping me whenever, wherever.

I still remember the days at Save the Children when they gave me a Nokia smartphone; it tried to behave like a BlackBerry but did a pretty poor job at it. Because of that, I always left it in my desk at work and only used it when I traveled. When I left the office, usually at six o'clock, I was done for the day. The distant memory of that freedom felt like such a luxury!

At the retreat, the only time we were allowed to speak was during one or two sessions a day where we would discuss a key topic (e.g., equanimity, tolerance, or our meditation practice itself). During these rare times, we were still not allowed to speak with each other, only to one of the teachers. One day, we practiced a blessing meditation. You would bless yourself first before blessing others and the world. The teachers advised that given that this was the first time we were doing this meditation, we should spend the time only blessing ourselves. They told us that the next day, we could add in our family and community, and then the world. "May I feel peace, may

I feel love, may I feel safe, may I feel joy," was the instruction to repeat in silence for forty-five minutes.

I loved it. This was the most eye-opening moment of the retreat for me. I realized that most of the time, I forget that step of blessing myself—of taking care of myself before taking care of others. And in the business of social impact, I do not think I am the only one who forgets that step.

The blessing came back up during one of the group discussions, the one time a day when we were allowed to pose questions to the teachers. A man, white, perhaps in his early fifties, was confused and asked the teacher, "I understand peace, love, and joy, but I do not understand 'safe.' Why do I need to bless myself to feel safe?"

The teacher paused, then diplomatically replied, "If it does not speak to you, you can use another blessing or drop that one."

On my side, I wanted to scream—*in silence*—"You have never felt unsafe?! You cannot relate to people wanting to feel safe and blessing themselves to feel that way?! You cannot relate to wanting to bless other people and wish them safety?!" Going back to our earlier discussion about privilege in Chapter Six, what a privilege to always feel safe and to think those around us feel safe, too. Peace, love, joy: I wish these for everyone all around the world. But the prerequisite for all of these is safety.

Coming out of the meditation retreat, I can't say my life was transformed instantaneously, or that I suddenly started sitting on cushions and meditating twice a day, or that I slept through the night, or even that I found the peace and balance I had set out to find in 2020. I mostly dove right back into work, which got busier when the pandemic hit as we launched a Challenge on Health Security and had to move all of our in-person events to virtual ones with very little notice. However, the blessing did stay with me, and I have been able to remind myself of it when I need to. While the pandemic has been tough on everyone, I do have immense gratitude for the safety of family and friends and recognize the immense privilege I have in being able to continue to live my purpose and to earn a good living from the comfort of a warm home. I share the above with you not to say you should all go meditate in silence for five days, but rather that before anything else, do remember to take care of yourself first.

Doing good in the world will be fulfilling, rewarding, and also really, really, hard, so always put on your own mask before helping others. (The airplane oxygen mask analogy is particularly on the nose with COVID-19.)

For one, witnessing the unfairness of this world on a daily basis can be trying. Secondly, you almost never have quite enough of the resources you need—you always need to stretch your budget, your time, and more. In some cases, you might be working really long hours in tough conditions, for example, right after an emergency or disaster has struck, whether you are on the ground or seeking to raise money for the cause. Thirdly, wrestling with the Impact Paradox can often be upsetting. You will face real barriers: entrenched interests, slow-moving bureaucracies, the morass of the status quo, the graveyard of good intentions, and outright rejection. You need to develop grit to keep going in the face of all of these.

There is a lifetime's worth of religions you can study, books you can read, new-age practitioners you can go see, and retreats of all kinds you can attend on how to find balance and develop resilience. Since I haven't found any cure-all recipe for myself, I cannot tell you I have the "magic bullet" energy healer that will give you the answer. But as with your superpowers, I am pretty sure everyone is unique in terms of how they can best take care of themselves—and that the journey of self-discovery is one worth pursuing.

Some people like to exercise, while others focus on meditation, sound healing, apps that count sheep, or other self-care modalities. The only advice I can give here is to first test out any number of things that sound appealing to you until you find what works. Second, surround yourself with people who care about you and who can support you throughout your journey, even and especially when you face hardship. Third, remember to learn to take care of yourself without always relying on others; no one can do all of it for you. Fourth, just as there are professionals for your physical health, there are professionals for your mental health, and you should at some point in your life consult one (or several) of them. If you are one of these people who thinks they do not need a therapist, then I am afraid I must say that you probably *do* need a therapist; but please feel free to call them a life coach if that makes it more palatable.

Finally, the 10 percent analogy also holds true here; take one step to try and move the self-care needle 10 percent in a positive direction. Dan Harris even has a whole website and meditation series based on his book, *10% Percent Happier*, which may be of use as you work out that step.

As you invest in yourself, you will learn, grow, and be better able to take care of your purpose.

Coming Back to Kevin's Story: Learning to Balance Service with Self-Care

When he started out, Kevin F. Adler of Miracle Messages was running himself into the ground trying to support his unhoused neighbors and make San Francisco a better place. He recalls, "I was working nights, weekends, seventy to eighty hours a week." At the time, it was even considered cool in the Bay Area to brag about how hard you worked. Kevin realized he was making himself "the first casualty of my work," overloading himself with effort and stress while trying to improve the world. He was not taking care of himself, he was not eating well, and he was miserable.

Kevin traces his lack of self-care back to the loss of his mother to breast cancer at age fifty-nine, when he was twenty-three. "She was my best friend and my foundation and the pure embodiment of who I am and my values." After she died, he returned to his childhood home and spent eight months getting it ready to rent out. "I was boxing things up and going through family heirlooms, [spending nights] sleeping on a mattress in the living room. I had keys to two or three neighbors' houses to have dinners and sleep on their couches, just so I wasn't lonely. It was a very dark period of my life." He realized that he'd lost the person who had really taken care of him. For the first time in his life, he had to consider "what it would look like to feel healthy as an adult—and I didn't have an answer to that."

After starting his own nonprofit in the education field, he went to Mexico for a year on a Rotary scholarship that involved working with Indigenous women entrepreneurs in small villages and getting to know them and their stories. Encountering people very different from himself for the first time, he saw their commonalities in their shared "values and aspirations as human beings." He didn't realize the value of his insights from this period right away. He simply felt he had to make up for lost time and started pushing hard when he came back to the US, first working in edtech and then starting Miracle Messages.

Kevin didn't get back on a healthier track until he took an opportunity to spend a summer at Singularity University, a program that supports would-be entrepreneurs. While the classes and network were helpful, it was the simple things that were most transformative for Kevin: getting back into healthy food and meditation, and forming new relationships. He was on a new and more productive path to getting back to work, but this time with a far better sense of how to balance self-care and commitment. Now, he stresses the importance of getting a "PhD in yourself."

We Can All Cultivate the Problem-Solving Mindset

Kevin has something in common with the other problem-solvers profiled here: what makes him, Carlos, Amanda, Luis, Iman, Roya, and Temie special is not that they are superheroes, but rather how they respond to challenging situations. When confronted with a real problem, they do not look away, but rather seek to apply their unique skills to find a solution.

While everyone has unique superpowers, you can cultivate some of the magic that the people in this book possess within yourself. Cultivate the *problem-solving mindset*—the qualities that make you able to really see a problem, devise solutions that are workable for you to carry out, and do your part to repair the world. *Problem-solving is a discipline that can be learned and practiced*, just like what Peter Drucker says about innovation. Though there are innovations that spring from a flash of genius, most of the successful ones result from "a conscious, purposeful search for innovation opportunities."

The problem-solving mindset is perhaps what best ties together the impact innovators you have met throughout this book. And we need all of you to adopt this mindset and become problem-solvers, at least for 10 percent of your time; we need you to build a just and equitable problem-solving table everyone can access.

Emma Yang's Story: It's Never Too Early (or Too Late!) to Start

You can start with the problem-solving mindset at any time; in fact, you can start at any age. At thirteen, Emma Yang became the youngest Solver ever when she was selected to join Solve's "Brain Health" class of 2017. As she puts it, "Everyone may not have a skill, but they have a unique perspective about a problem they see in the world, in their community, or even in their family. The perspective that technology can help the elderly population was derived from the fact that I spent so much time with my grandmother growing up. I came to understand how technology could assist in communicating with elders because we spent lots of time trying communicate, which illuminated some of the challenges. When the motivation and purpose are there, they'll carry you through the process of developing something that can help someone. Just diving into it is a really important first step."

Emma's age should not keep you from recognizing the value of her advice. Her mobile app Timeless empowers Alzheimer's patients to live a better daily life. Powered by an artificial intelligence-based facial recognition technology, the app helps Alzheimer's patients to remember events, stay connected and engaged with friends and family, easily contact loved ones, and recognize people by their name and their relationship to the user.

Emma was inspired by her bond with her grandmother, who was diagnosed with Alzheimer's disease when Emma was seven. "Initially, when my parents went looking for an app to help us communicate with my grandmother, we found a gap in the market where the elderly population wasn't being addressed. There's this stereotype that old people can't use technology, but in fact, I think innovation should be universal so that everyone can benefit from technology in some way. I wanted to leverage the fact that I was really passionate about computer science and use it to create something for good."

Timeless evolved not just from her love of her grandmother, but also from her from love of coding. Emma started learning how to write computer programs at age six when she discovered Scratch, a free program and on-line learning community developed by the Lifelong Kindergarten Group at the MIT Media Lab. It enables kids to create their own stories, animations, and games they can share with others all over the world. Scratch was Emma's "gateway" to programming and its range of possibilities. Emma also used MIT App Inventor to create Android apps. From there, she went further into various programming languages and formal coding. Between age ten and eleven, Emma started participating in things like Technovation Girls, which runs coding challenges, and which as Emma says, "pushed not only coding for girls, but also using STEM and computer science to create something to do good."

Now sixteen, she says coding is a part of her life. "I love working on what goes into creating an app. I saw it as an opportunity to create something and to figure out how an app works. The byproduct was, how can I help my grandmother?"

Once the first version of Timeless got some attention in the media, Emma started to see the possibilities for a broader audience of other families around the world. "Timeless grew into something more impactful than I thought it was going to be initially." After at first being rejected by funders and then going on to win challenge competitions such as MIT Solve, Emma developed Timeless into an app downloaded not only in the US, but also in Asia and in the Spanish-speaking world.

By channeling her love of coding to fill a need in her immediate family, Emma has demonstrated with impressive clarity that what begins as an impulse to solve a problem close to home, her "Story of Self," can become something to share for the greater good, a "Story of Us."

Like other problem-solvers in this book, what makes Emma special is that when confronted with a real problem, she didn't look away. As she put it to her audience at the end of her TEDx talk, "What will *you* do?"

What are the Traits of a Problem-Solving Mindset?

Whether you are just starting out or well along in your impact journey, cultivating the problem-solving mindset is critical. While I generally despise listicles (since life is not something you can hack in ten easy steps, after all) and have sought to steer clear of them in this book in favor of stories and frameworks, let me give you one here that covers the five key traits of the problem-solving mindset. Many of these will feel familiar since they have all shown up throughout the stories of the problem-solvers highlighted in this book. *Disclaimer:* Not all problem-solvers exhibit all of these traits all the time. No one is perfect, and this is a model to strive for rather than an expectation with which one should constantly comply. The good news is that the problem-solving mindset is not something unattainable—it is within your reach.

THE FIVE TRAITS OF THE PROBLEM-SOLVING MINDSET

1. **Start and stay with optimism.** You have to believe in the good of humanity, and that solving complex challenges is possible.

2. **Listen in order to broaden your perspective.** You do not have all the answers, and you need to spend a lot of time understanding the problem and the systems that perpetuate it, which is why Kevin Adler talks about the critical need to "widen your aperture." Stay curious throughout. This will ultimately serve you well in connecting the dots and driving creativity.

3. **Build relationships with real proximity and empathy.** Whether you are already proximate to the problem or not, spend time building real relationships with the population you seek to serve rather than exacerbating the power dynamics of privilege.

4. **Seek out co-travelers and partners to complement you.** No one can do this alone, and even with lots of self-reflection, you will still have shortcomings and biases. As Rebecca Obounou of MIT says, "The superhero is really the collective. A team that comes together and makes things happen, that's what social innovation really is, and should be."

5.   **Build your own problem-solving table, one that is just and equitable.** Staying inside the box and abiding by the system will always constrain you, and in fact will likely make you unable to solve the problem.

I hate when people talk about needing to think outside the box to innovate. You need to abandon the idea that there is even a box to think outside of, like the kid in *The Matrix* who reminds Keanu Reeves, "There is no spoon," as he bends it with his mind.

Yes, you need to understand the problem deeply, as well as the barriers that have historically prevented the problem from being solved, and the reasons why institutions that were meant to solve the problem have failed up to this point or not gone far enough. But you must not get so familiar with the conceptual box that you become bogged down by the status quo. In fact, I would argue that the metaphorical box is the very system that keeps the status quo in place; it is ultimately the system that you will need to change, reform, or even completely tear down. Instead, you need to build your own table—one that is fair and that lets everyone have a seat next to you and others.

Without the box bogging you down, you have the opportunity to innovate much more freely. I first learned this from Miranda Wang, who was raised in a Chinese immigrant community in Vancouver, Canada. "I didn't just think outside the box," she says, "I didn't know the box existed." Miranda's key insight came early, at a bus stop one day in eleventh grade. She credits much of her creativity and originality to a sense of ease with being different, in that she doesn't feel pressured to agree with other people's viewpoints and doesn't waste a lot of energy trying to fit in.

She calls her longtime partner Jeanny Yao "the better part of my brain." She adds, "From what I've seen, it seems that the smarter you get, the less likely that you're able to build constructive relationships that stick. And that is one of the biggest barriers for humans with different perspectives who have high levels of intelligence: the lack of an ability to do something together that translates to results. If you want to move fast, you can go by yourself. But it's clear that if you want to go far and make a lasting impact, you have to work with people who think differently but have certain shared values. I think that this type of collaborative spirit and the process of collaborating are not actually taught enough."

Many impact innovators profiled in this book talk about the ingenuity that comes with starting from the perspective of an outsider; although I want to be clear, that should only apply to the thinking leading to solutions, not to developing an understanding of the problem—to understand the problem, proximity matters a great deal.

One of the US's most famous and inventive refugees, Albert Einstein, was concerned with the need for a new ethical perspective following the rush of nations moving to arm themselves with nuclear weapons. A quote that is often attributed to him states: "We cannot solve our problems with the same thinking we used when we created them."

In his book *Decolonizing Wealth,* Edgar Villanueva points out, "Those most excluded and exploited by today's broken economy possess exactly the perspective and wisdom needed to fix it. Evolution and innovation arise from difference and variation, not from sameness."

This mindset is also how Rajesh Anandan, who grew up half Sinhalese and half Tamil in Sri Lanka, came to envision a fairer future for the workplace. As with most entrepreneurs, he and his partner found that "naivete was our friend" when they started Ultranauts, even though he had spent years listening and forming an understanding of the problem and the potential solution before starting.

The experts in the field told them they couldn't build a remote company for autistic talent because they would have to provide close, on-site supervision. As Rajesh recalls: "These were of course neurotypical experts. Nobody on the spectrum told us that! We just didn't know any better. It didn't really make sense—why can't you? And so we just did."

"Our informal tag line at Ultranauts is 'different better,' which is short for a belief we all share at the company that our differences as individuals make us better together. In our context, the differences we mean are specifically the cognitive differences that our neurodiverse team brings to the table so that we can attack problems with unique points of view and generate unique insights.

"Because of my childhood experience, I default to appreciating the differences we bring to the table. It's not a superpower at all; it's simply pausing to consider the alternative, the contrary opinion, the excluded point of view, the marginalized voice. And given that what we're trying to do has no precedent, it's really important that we're open to the answers coming from anywhere, and to the answer we currently have being completely wrong."

Innovative thinking that leads to solutions comes from a deep understanding of the problem and the community you seek to serve. It also comes from not letting the constraints derail you, no matter who you are or where you've come from. Changemakers reimagine the world, seeing it through fresh eyes. The big challenges of this world are systemic and enduring, and they will not be solved overnight. It's important to remember that none of the problem-solvers profiled here succeeded in creating their solutions in a single moment of inspiration. An insight they may have had years earlier likely took equally long to become an actual solution or organization. Sometimes they spent years thinking about the problem before even getting started, gathering information and gaining insight as they moved forward little by little. Further, by definition, if you set an ambitious purpose, it might take years to see the needle move.

Iman Finally Realized His Work Mattered

"There was a time where I thought of giving up. It was very difficult. Every month there was a day where I thought, I'm going to give up. But then, every time that crossed my mind, I would think, *If I was not doing this, what would I possibly work on?*"

Iman Usman's success with Ruangguru, although now enviable, was far from instantaneous. "We sometimes try to make plans perfectly, and we try to put things in order, but life is not always in order, so don't overthink too much. In the process of doing, you're definitely going to face a lot of rejections and failures. See that rejection not as a permanent condition, not as something that defines you. See it as just as another phase in life that you can move on from."

In fact, Iman only realized that what he was working on was something special three or four years ago. "I took a public train, and a mother in her forties approached me and told me, 'Hey, I think I saw you on social media. Are you the founder of Ruangguru?' She told me her kid was using it and how it had changed their lives; not just because they could save a lot of money, they were struggling. She told me how it had changed her child's perspective about learning, how her child had been inspired by me, and how it made the kid also want to dream big. That's the moment when I realized I actually work on something that matters—and it actually helps people."

Iman had already won many accolades by then; he had raised millions of dollars, and Ruangguru was already used by millions. But an unexpected conversation with a stranger on a train meant a lot more to him than these abstract facts. When that chance meeting happened, Iman knew that he had "potentially reached a certain scale. This made my job become a lot more rewarding, but also much more nerve-wracking as well. My anchor in life is my purpose. It's very simple: I want to leave this world better than when I came."

AMANDA'S REFLECTION

Amanda Nguyen of Rise Justice Labs believes in working within the system to make change. As a result, she's often been told that she's not radical enough. For instance, in the campaign to pass the Survivors' Bill of Rights, a section about emergency contraception for rape survivors was in the draft, but key Republicans wanted the section removed given their stance on contraception and abortion. She was presented with a choice: "We're not going to do this entire suite of civil rights legislation if you keep this, but if you take it out, we will pass it."

In order to pass the bill, she accepted the compromise. And in the thirty-plus laws she and her colleagues at Rise Justice Labs have helped pass since then, emergency contraception has been put back in. Incremental change can be hard to swallow, but sometimes it's the only way, because, as Amanda observes, "What is fair and what can happen are often not the same things."

What's key is to know the contours of your battleground and to keep pushing for justice, even if it's only an inch at a time. She doubts that an initiative like hers would even have succeeded if it had come from the White House, given the wall of opposition President Obama faced in the Republican Congress. In this instance, by exercising her rights as a US citizen, Amanda was perhaps in a better position to effect legislative change than the President himself.

One of Amanda's core beliefs is that successful campaigns are not centered on politicians. Rather, successful campaigns are centered on people. "That's how we were able to cut through." She and other survivors would fly into DC and sit in front of senators like Charles Grassley of the Judiciary Committee to say, "Look, we're not here to talk about any other agenda. And even if this issue is usually slotted into more liberal progressive spaces, we're here to talk to you because you represent us." Amanda and her allies were able to find a common space by sitting with politicians and ignoring every single thing they said on other issues, focusing instead on the one piece of change they sought.

Radical empathy is absolutely essential. Even if Amanda didn't feel that some senators acknowledged her humanity as she sat in front of them, she still had to acknowledge theirs: "It's really, really difficult. And it's not for everyone."

After her time working with the Obama administration, Amanda took a big leap to become a full-time activist. She was convinced that by dedicating herself full-time to gaining rights for survivors, she could pass more laws, so after passing the Survivors' Bill of Rights, Amanda and her team persisted at the state level as well, since most rape cases are adjudicated in state courts. She also heard from over a million people who reached out to say, "I'm a survivor, I need this, too. Thank you so much for passing this. I'm going through this in my own community."

The overwhelming number of letters Amanda received from survivors and allies made it clear she had a window of opportunity to do more. She had learned so much in seeking justice both for herself and for fellow rape survivors that now she had a clear recipe for how to advocate successfully for legislative change. There was still so much to be done for civil rights and an ever "more perfect union."

She started Rise Justice Labs to give people a chance to learn how to change laws in their own communities on issues beyond sexual assault. The first pilot Rise did helped the Parkland survivors with their legislative advocacy on gun violence prevention. Some of the other recent grant recipients have focused on environmental justice, stopping bullying, and working to end food insecurity. The only criterion is that the project needs to be community-driven and that these emerging activists commit to doing difficult things like sitting in front of people, practicing radical empathy, and strategizing to get those civil rights laws passed.

In 2020, Amanda applied to one of the Challenges Solve runs for one of our partners, the Elevate Prize Foundation. Through the Elevate Prize, the foundation distributes up to five million dollars annually. Out of over 1,300 applicants, Amanda ultimately became one of the ten Global Heroes selected to share the prize, which includes a two-year year coaching and support program. Along with the additional mentoring, the money will allow Amanda to grow Rise Justice Labs further so that it can support more causes and more emerging activists like herself.

Amanda stresses that it's key to remain laser focused on the end game of changing laws and the system. For those considering activism, she advises, "The most powerful thing you have is your voice." Grit, which she sees as her superpower, is essential as well. "It's getting knocked down and getting up again, and it's the ability to withstand a lot of pain." She isn't talking about her own trauma, not even "the secondary retraumatization from working within this field." Even after all these years, she still faces off with the injustice of the system and the prejudice of those who think she does not belong in the commanding rooms of imposing US government buildings.

The first time she testified before the US Senate, she was the only person of color present, not to mention that she was decades younger than the other witnesses. But she had every right to be there as a "consensus witness" invited to the hearing by both Democrats and Republicans. Even so, she was determined not to be a pawn of either party, but rather to stay focused on the issue at hand, the Violence Against Women Reauthorization Act of 2018.

Each witness received a formal invitation letter and had been asked to meet with the senators in an antechamber before the hearing started. Amanda walked into the reception room of the Senate Judiciary Committee and introduced herself, but initially received an untoward sort of welcome: "The receptionist refused to believe that I was a witness, even if I had my letter! It was humiliating." As she sat, the white witnesses were escorted to the hearing room while Amanda was left waiting.

"It was only when one of the council members recognized me that they said, 'Oh, my God. We're so sorry! We're taking you in right away.' "

From Amanda's perspective, making progress is all about realizing that no matter how long this takes or how unfair the system still is, the fight is worth it. Often, it's about doing the work and taking none of the credit. "What's important is what's wrong with the system and how we're going to fix it. It's the ability to think big picture and just get back up."

Amanda has achieved more than most in her short life as an activist. And she's sharing her superpowers—her knowledge of how to get laws changed to protect civil rights—with others to create a new generation of solution activists able to work with those in power to help change the laws.

Facing the Lincoln Memorial's reflecting pool on the day in 2016 when the Senate passed the Survivors' Bill of Rights, Amanda reflected on her journey, from feeling entirely alone as she left the hospital after her assault to having moved the nation to change this law. "How hilarious it felt. How absurd, yet how appropriate for a child of boat refugees to pull this off."

If Not You, Then Who?
Just Start Now

"If not us, then who? If not now, then when?"

—Attributed to Rabbi Hillel (110 BC–10 AD)

Make a Ten-Year Plan to Leave Room
for Miracles (and Catastrophes)

This is the final rallying cry, the final leg of this invitation to do the hard work to better this messy, crazy, unfair world.

Let's go back to yourImpact Vision, Mission, and Values exercise I introduced earlier and start putting together a ten-year plan.

Why ten years and not one, three, or five? Solve Advisor Noubar Afeyan was born in Beirut to Armenian parents; he emigrated first to Canada and then to the US. He feels that being an immigrant made him adept at learning, experimenting, and adapting to many different circumstances.

A graduate of MIT, Noubar went on to devote much of his career at Flagship Pioneering to supporting entrepreneurially minded scientists "who invent seemingly unreasonable solutions to challenges facing human health and sustainability." You've likely heard of one of the firms Flagship Pioneering started: Moderna Therapeutics, one of the companies that developed one of the mRNA COVID-19 vaccines. Noubar is their cofounder and chairman.

I'd like to share some advice Noubar once gave me (that I am paraphrasing here): Five years is too short a time range to make a good plan. You will wind up focusing on implementation right away and then forcing yourself to think small to fit that timeline. This insight was developed over years of scientific experiments that started out free of preconceived ideas. On the other hand, Noubar advised that ten years leaves room for miracles, so you can be ambitious; and you need to be ambitious if you are going to change the game.

I have updated Noubar's advice in the face of the recent crises: Ten years leaves room for miracles but also catastrophes; that way, there is still space for you to be as ambitious as you need to be, even if a particular year (like 2020) is a wash.

In those ten years, I am confident you will find that you are not alone—that millions will join you. If we learn lessons from this pandemic, and if we really listen to and support Black, Indigenous, and People of Color around the world fighting for justice as well as young people protesting in favor of climate action, we can create a real groundswell movement that can change the game for good.

First things first: for this ten-year plan, do not forget that the journey matters as much as the destination, and that your impact (both positive and negative) starts now. Finding and then living your values and your purpose is crucial.

Of course, it takes time to chart your journey and to change the game. Along that journey, you may have to make hard choices—you may have to abandon the idea that success is defined by the brand names you work for or wear, the dollars in your bank account, or your number of social media followers.

QUESTIONS TO ASK YOURSELF FOR YOUR TEN-YEAR PLAN

- What's the one step you can take today? And the next one tomorrow? Can you maybe make a donation to a charity you have always admired, no matter how small the amount?
- Go back to your Impact Balance Sheet that we discussed in Chapter Four. Where in your life are you, and how can you be most impactful? Where are you most falling short? How can you make positive changes, starting with 10 percent of your activities?
- Where would you like to be in ten years? What impact would you like to have? Who can you bring with you? What could you mobilize? Think big, be ambitious, and for now, forget the constraints.
- Accept now that you will never get 100 percent of your time and money fully devoted to positive impact and that is okay; but what would it take to get much closer? What is an "affordable loss" that will in fact liberate you? Stated another way, what do you have to let go of to move closer to 100 percent impact?
- Finally, never forget that the game—including the systems we have set up, and even the social impact world—is rigged and unjust. This world does not work for the majority of the nearly eight billion people who inhabit it. Don't ever get too

comfortable, and keep these questions in mind: What should the system be? What big and small things can I do over the next ten years to change it?

This work takes courage. Some of the people you have met throughout this book have put their lives on the line and endured real pain to keep going. But Temie Giwa-Tubosun of LifeBank stresses the importance of just starting. "I know a ton of people I went to college and grad school with who had all sorts of big plans, and a lot of them didn't do what they said they were going to do. I think many of them were constantly doing research to try and figure out what they were supposed to do and to learn to feel ready. For women especially, there is never an ideal time to get started. Many times, women wait for approval—for friends, family, or mentors to offer encouragement. They wait for a request so they can say 'yes.' But you owe it to yourself to stay the course no matter what people say. Learn on the job, from the ground up."

Temie sums it up in this way: focus on what you can accomplish in your own back yard, citing a famous Nigerian saying: "If we sweep our yards, then the country will be clean."

My Final Thoughts

Amanda, Hala, Nona and Gloria, Temie, Roya, Miranda, Julia, Yuriko, Rebecca, Emma, Sara, Angela, Isis, Iman, Luis, Akshay, Carlos and Clara, Rajesh, Kevin, and Dedo—Remember them, but not because they are superheroes; they are not. You do not need to be a superhero to have superpowers and use them to change the world.

On the contrary, we can and will change the world when we all come together and choose impact as the metric of success for our lives. Let's make it the coolest and most fashionable thing we can do, so that when you go to a dinner party, you don't get asked "What do you do?"

but rather, "What are you doing to make the world a better place?" or still my favorite, *"Who are you?"* with the implication that who you are can be a myriad of interesting things encompassing your career, relationships, family, volunteering, and giving, but that they are all bending toward positive social impact.

In writing this book, I wanted to showcase great stories of people who could be you or me—individuals who are just doing their part and devoting their skills and life energy to improving the world. Their diversity makes it evident that everyone, no matter who or where they are, has a role to play. Whether they are refugees, survivors of sexual assault, or Indigenous people still living on their land for generations, they all decided to get in the game to try and change the system.

Out of the twenty-one people I interviewed for this book, two thirds are female. I have included voices from Afghanistan, Nigeria, Lebanon, Sri Lanka, Japan, Indonesia, Mexico, India, Brazil, and Burundi. There are also a lot of US-focused voices, including several who are now based in the US, even if they grew up elsewhere as I did. This over-indexation on US-based voices is partly my own bias, since this is where I live now, and you should always first look in your own backyard. The large majority of US-based changemakers are Black, Indigenous, or People of Color, and often they are also immigrants or first-generation Americans. In fact, out of the US-based voices, only one, Kevin Adler of Miracle Messages, is white.

I give you these statistics to make it clear that people who are solving world challenges hail from all geographies, all genders, all ethnicities, and all walks of life, not just the ivory towers of academia and the enclaves of venture capital. There is incredible talent and potential everywhere, including your own, and we need to harness it all to change the world for the better.

There is still much work to be done. We need you and your energy, enthusiasm, skills, experience, and resources to continue this fight and solve the big challenges of our time.

You don't have to be perfect or do it all at once, but no more excuses: the good work starts now.

With much appreciation and gratitude,

Alex Amouyel

HELPFUL RESOURCES TO CREATE A LIFE
FULL OF IMPACT

The list below is by no means complete, but I thought it best to provide a manageable list of resources you might actually find useful. If you are looking for something specific, get in touch through my website, yourimpactlife.com. I look forward to hearing about your own stories of impact!

First, here are some helpful resources connected to the people interviewed in this book, in order of appearance. It goes without saying that donating to any of these projects will go a long way toward making a difference.

Me: See my personal website to read more about impact at yourimpactlife.com, and Solve's website if you are interested in becoming a Solver team or supporting Solve: solve.mit.edu.

Amanda Nguyen and Rise Justice Labs: To apply to their accelerator, visit risenow.us.

Julia Kumari Drapkin and ISeeChange: To join their climate monitoring efforts as a citizen climate journalist and contribute your hyper-local data, visit iseechange.org.

Isis Bous and Lex Mundi Pro Bono Foundation: To find out if your organization is eligible for their pro bono legal services, visit lexmundiprobono.org.

Yuriko Oda and WheeLog!: Use the web version of their app or download it at en.wheelog.com.

Miranda Wang and Novoloop: Check out her company to recycle previously unrecycled plastics at novoloop.com.

Rajesh Anandan and Ultranauts: To hire their neurodivergent talent to provide data and software quality engineering services, visit ultranauts.co.

Carlos and Clara Pereira and Livox: To utilize their technology to support communication and learning for people with nonverbal disabilities, visit livox.com.br/en.

Kevin F. Adler and Miracle Messages: To volunteer and become a Miracle Friend, visit miraclemessages.org.

Temie Giwa-Tubosun and LifeBank: To learn more about delivery of blood and other medical resources to women and others in Nigeria, visit lifebankcares.com.

Dedo Baranshamaje and the Segal Family Foundation: To apply to become an African Visionary, visit segalfamilyfoundation.org.

Luis Garza and Kinedu: To download the app to support your child's development from infancy to four years old, visit kinedu.com.

Akshay Saxena and Avanti: To sign up for live classes and find out more about how Avanti supports student achievement in India, visit avanti.in.

Dr. Angela Jackson and New Profit: Are you a proximate entrepreneur based in the US involved in reimagining the future of work? If so, you can apply for a grant or investment for your organization at newprofit.org.

Hala Hanna, Managing Director, Community at Solve: To apply to Solve Challenges, read more about our incredible innovators, comment, or vote, visit solve.mit.edu.

Iman Usman and Ruangguru: To utilize their growing education platform, currently available in Indonesia, Vietnam, Thailand, and soon in more countries, visit ruangguru.com.

Roya Mahboob and Digital Citizen Fund: If you want to further their work helping Afghan girls to learn STEM skills and concepts, visit digitalcitizenfund.format.com.

Nonabah and Gloria Lane and Navajo Ethno-Agriculture: To learn more about traditional Navajo farming and buy local produce, visit navajofarming.org.

Emma Yang and Timeless: Download her app, which empowers Alzheimer's patients to live a better day-to-day life, at timeless.care.

ADDITIONAL REFERENCES BY CHAPTER

Chapter One: Reveal Your Superpowers

Commencement Address given by Steve Jobs at Stanford University in 2005: news.stanford.edu/2005/06/14/jobs-061505

Power for All: How It Really Works and Why It's Everyone's Business, by Julie Battilana and Tiziana Casciaro, Simon and Schuster, 2021: simonandschuster.com/books/Power-for-All/Julie-Battilana/9781982141639

"Should You Agitate, Innovate, or Orchestrate?" by Julie Battilana and Marissa Kimsey, *Stanford Social Innovation Review,* September 18, 2017: ssir.org/articles/entry/should_you_agitate_innovate_or_orchestrate

Chapter Two: Solve Problems that Actually Matter

Public Narrative Participant Guide, originally adapted from the work of Marshall Ganz of Harvard University and modified by Serena Zhang and Voop de Vulpillieres. Here is material from Professor Ganz's exercise if you want to work on your Stories of Self, Us, and Now: ndi.org/sites/default/files/Public%20Narrative%20Participant%20Guide.pdf

LEAPFROG: The New Revolution for Women Entrepreneurs, by Nathalie Molina Niño, Penguin Random House, 2018: leapfroghacks.com

"Effective Change Requires Proximate Leaders," by Angela Jackson, John Kania, and Tulaine Montgomery, *Stanford Social Innovation Review,* October 2, 2020: ssir.org/articles/entry/effective_change_requires_proximate_leaders#

Chapter Four: Choose Impact As Your Metric for Success

Your Money or Your Life: 9 Steps to Transforming Your Relationship with Money and Achieving Financial Independence, by Vicki Robin and Joe Dominguez, Penguin, revised and updated 2018: yourmoneyoryourlife.com

Financial Samurai, Sam Dogen's blog for all things personal finance; while it's not focused on impact, I think it's great on stocks, bonds, real estate, and retirement: financialsamurai.com

Chapter Five: Start with 10 Percent of Your Time and Money

The 10% Entrepreneur: Live Your Startup Dream Without Quitting Your Day Job, Patrick J. McGinnis, (Penguin), 2016: patrickmcginnis.com/the-10-entrepreneur

Philanthropy Together, a nonprofit dedicated to democratizing giving through circles. If you want to start or join a giving circle, take classes, watch videos, and find helpful resources, look no further than Philanthropy Together. I took their five-week course online via Zoom during the pandemic, and it was great! Visit their website at: philanthropytogether.org

The Life Changing Magic of Tidying Up: The Japanese Art of Decluttering and Organizing by Marie Kondo, Ten Speed Press, 2014. konmari.com

Drawdown: The Most Comprehensive Plan Ever Proposed to Reverse Global Warming by Paul Hawken, Penguin, 2017. Find the Project Drawdown nonprofit website here: drawdown.org

Carbon Calories—To look at carbon statements, budgets, and daily carbon quotas: carboncalories.com

Chapter Six: Wrestle with Your Personal Kryptonite and the Impact Paradox

Winners Take All: The Elite Charade of Changing the World, by Anand Giridharadas, Penguin Random House, 2018. anand.ly/winners-take-all

A Theory of Justice, by John Rawls, Harvard University Press, 1971. This is likely the most important book I read while studying for my master's degree: hup.harvard.edu/catalog. php?isbn=9780674000780

Oppression and Privilege Self-Assessment Tool, developed by the California Partnership to End Domestic Violence; adapted from Diane Goodman and Paul Kivel. cpedv.org/sites/main/files/ oppression_and_privilege_self_assessment.pdf

The Danger of a Single Story, by Chimamanda Ngozi Adichie, TED talk, 2009. Adichie is probably my favorite author ever; please also read *Half a Yellow Sun* and *Americanah* if you can: ted.com/talks/ chimamanda_ngozi_adichie_the_danger_of_a_single_story/ transcript?language=en

Decolonizing Wealth: Indigenous Wisdom to Heal Divides and Restore Balance, by Edgar Villanueva, Penguin Random House, 2018. If you can only read just one more book, I would say this is probably the one: penguinrandomhouse.com/books/588996/ decolonizing-wealth-by-edgar-villanueva

Amanda's Justice

The Survivors' Bill of Rights Act, United States Congress, 2016: congress.gov/bill/114th-congress/house-bill/5578

Chapter Seven: Stay Optimistic and Look for Simple Solutions

How to Build a Life, Arthur C. Brooks's column in *The Atlantic.*
theatlantic.com/projects/how-build-life

Happiness for All?: Unequal Hopes and Lives in Pursuit of the
American Dream, by Carol Graham, Princeton University Press,
2017. press.princeton.edu/books/hardcover/9780691169460/
happiness-for-all

An inspiring speech by Greta Thunberg at the UN where she asks, "How
Dare You?": youtube.com/watch?v=KAJsdgTPJpU

Troubled Water, reported by Amy Costello, PBS FRONTLINE/World,
2015; a documentary on the PlayPump, the hopes it raised,
and ultimate disappointment: pbs.org/frontlineworld/stories/
southernafrica904/video_index.html

The Lean Startup: How Today's Entrepreneurs Use Continuous
Innovation to Create Radically Successful Businesses, by Eric
Ries, Crown Business, 2011. theleanstartup.com

Lean Impact: How to Innovate for Radically Greater Social Good, by
Ann Mei Chang, Wiley, 2018. annmei.com

Chapter Eight: Measure. Fail. Try Again!

Poor Economics: A Radical Rethinking of the Way to Fight Global
Poverty, by Abhijit V. Banerjee and Esther Duflo, Public Affairs,
2011. economics.mit.edu/faculty/eduflo/pooreconomics

MIT's J-PAL Poverty Action Lab: povertyactionlab.org

ACKNOWLEDGEMENTS

I have to admit, when I read books, I love reading the acknowledgements section. To many, it might appear similar to the boring list of thank-yous people recite when they get an Oscar or an Emmy, but I love finding out about the people who are part of someone's inner circle or tribe, who invariably make it into this section.

Now that I have written my first book, I have a much better appreciation of how much it takes a village to actually birth a book, and that so much of one's time is not actually spent interviewing people and writing, but proposing, discussing, editing, and then proofreading ten times over.

So without further ado, my sincere and heartfelt thank-yous to:

- All the incredible problem solvers I have interviewed for this book. You took time out of your busy schedules to sit down with me and recount not only your life stories, successes, and achievements, but also your trials, tribulations, doubts, and questions about purpose and the social impact world. I hope I have been able to capture some of your magic in these pages; please keep doing what you are doing.

- Patricia Mulcahy, writer and editor extraordinaire, who has helped and supported me throughout this endeavor from our initial discussion on a phone call while I was on a rooftop in Stone Town, Zanzibar, to working on what has felt like the hundredth version of the manuscript. I could not and would not have done this without you.

- Jennifer Weiss, my agent, supported by Howard Yoon and Sarah French. You got what I was trying to do and shepherded me masterfully through many drafts and many a no until there was a yes, and then stayed by my side with sound advice and encouragement throughout. And a special shout-out to my former intern, social entrepreneur extraordinaire Abbey

Wemimo, who first introduced me to Jen when I discussed the idea of writing a book with him.

- My publisher and editor Brenda Knight, and all of the team at Mango: Robin Miller, L. Artemisia Noble, Shelby Bradford, Briana Cool, Morgane Leoni, Megan Werner, Veronica Diaz, and Geena El-Haj.

- My family, especially my mother Carol, an extraordinary editor who has read and edited many of my writings throughout my life (including all those college essays and my final master's dissertation that I was up writing until three in the morning) and who was kind enough to do this once again for this book, even when I dared call her an "intellectual hoarder" in Chapter Five.

- My Solve colleagues Hala Hanna and Sara Monteabaro, who were interviewed for this book; Gabi Bianchi, who transcribed a number of the interviews; Andrea Snyder and her mother Lorraine Shanley, who provided support and encouragement throughout; and the entire Solve team. I am so deeply proud of all the work you have done over the last few years to build Solve into what it is today.

- Rafael Reif, Sanjay Sarma, Marty Schmidt, Suzanne Glassburn, Alfred Ironside, and many others at MIT: your advice and support in building Solve has been invaluable.

- Jason Pontin, Greg Morgan, and Israel Ruiz, who initially recruited me to MIT to lead Solve, and whose counsel and encouragement were paramount in getting started.

- My former bosses and mentors: Bob Harrison, Ed Hughes, Elsa Palanza, Tomas Hatem, Pam Innes, Mark Edington, and Karalee Close, for guiding me on this impact journey.

- My friends Margie, Q, Liz, Terry, Cecile, Sophie, Shabrina, Dedo, Akshay, Zach, Jess, Lauren, Prune, Rob, Fahad, Matt, John, Kav, Tom, Paula, Lanah, Tony, David, Timmy, Ariane, Will, Aash, Laura, and many others who have discussed this project with me, fed my belly and my soul, read early drafts, provided moral support, and been by my side throughout thick and thin. You are my chosen family, whatever happens and wherever we end up in the world.

Whoever you are, go forth, be fierce, dismantle injustice, and change the world.

P.S.

Thank you so much for reading the book and getting to the end!

I sincerely hope you have enjoyed this book and its stories and found it helpful in creating and living a life full of impact, wherever you are on this journey. I would love to connect with you and find out what you think of the book, what you found helpful, and what questions you might have.

Notably, I'd be super interested in hearing about the one next step you will take after reading this book, and if you get to it, your ten-year plan for creating a life full of impact. I encourage you to write to me about your impact plan, and if you consent, I'd be happy to feature them on my website: yourimpactlife.com. You can also contact me and read more about my musings there, as well as sign up for my newsletter. You'll also get to see some of my art and the official yourImpact mascot, a mini-Schnauzer mix named Sweet Pea. Please feel free to reach out to me on social media via Twitter @alexamouyel and share #yourImpactLife.

I welcome all reader feedback. If you like the book, do let me know at alex@yourimpactlife.com, and post a review on Amazon or Goodreads, as these are very important.

ABOUT THE AUTHOR

Photo credit: Tony Luong

Hi! I am Alex Amouyel. I have spent over fifteen years working in the social impact space, first for one of the largest children's nonprofits, Save the Children, then for the Clinton Foundation, and now leading Solve, an initiative of the Massachusetts Institute of Technology (MIT). I am French, British and American, grew up in Paris, and have worked across the world. I now live in Cambridge, Massachusetts, with frequent trips to New York and Europe.

As the founding Executive Director of Solve, I have built and now oversee a fast-growing team of more than thirty full-time employees whose mission is to drive innovation to solve global challenges. To do that, we find, fund, and support the most promising social innovators and entrepreneurs all around the world. We call them Solver teams. To date, we have brokered funding commitments of over fifty million dollars to our Solver teams and entrepreneurs worldwide.

Previously, I was the Director of Programs for the Clinton Global Initiative, on whose behalf I curated content for meetings (including the flagship Annual Meeting) and oversaw speaker and government relations. At the Clinton Global Initiative, I worked with a variety of cross-sector leaders with whom I met in the greenroom to discuss and prepare their speeches and panel; they included Nobel Prize winners, presidents, CEOs, celebrities, astronauts based at the International Space Station, and dozens of social entrepreneurs and activists.

Prior to the Clinton Global Initiative, I worked for Save the Children International in London and across Asia, the Middle East, and Haiti. I started my career in strategy consultancy at the Boston Consulting Group in London and have a double master's degree in International Affairs from Sciences Po, Paris, and the London School of Economics, as well as a bachelor's in Biochemistry from Trinity College, Cambridge, UK.

Mango Publishing, established in 2014, publishes an eclectic list of books by diverse authors—both new and established voices—on topics ranging from business, personal growth, women's empowerment, LGBTQ studies, health, and spirituality to history, popular culture, time management, decluttering, lifestyle, mental wellness, aging, and sustainable living. We were recently named 2019 *and* 2020's #1 fastest-growing independent publisher by *Publishers Weekly*. Our success is driven by our main goal, which is to publish high-quality books that will entertain readers as well as make a positive difference in their lives.

Our readers are our most important resource; we value your input, suggestions, and ideas. We'd love to hear from you—after all, we are publishing books for you!

Please stay in touch with us and follow us at:
Facebook: Mango Publishing
Twitter: @MangoPublishing
Instagram: @MangoPublishing
LinkedIn: Mango Publishing
Pinterest: Mango Publishing
Newsletter: mangopublishinggroup.com/newsletter

Join us on Mango's journey to reinvent publishing, one book at a time.